CW00765227

ONE THOUSAND WAYS TO MAKE $1000

BY

PAGE FOX.

COMPRISING

The Rounds and Bounds of Money-Making; The Arts of
Getting a Living; Old and New Opportunities for
Fortune; A Storehouse of Facts, Hints, Helps
and Practical Ideas, in all Kinds of Business,
and Hundreds of Trade Secrets
Never Before Given Away.

All rights reserved. No part of this publication may be
reproduced, stored in a retrieval system, or transmitted in any form or by any means, electronic, mechanical, photocopying
or otherwise, without the prior permission of the copyright owner.
The views and ideas expressed in this book are the personal opinions of the author, and do not necessarily represent the
views of the Publisher.

© Copyright 2019 by Stanford Pubublishing

stanfordpub.com

TO THE READER.

FRIEND—Are you looking for a place? We tell you how to find it. Are you poorly paid for your work? We tell you how to get better wages. Have you goods you want to sell? We suggest new plans.

Are the profits of shop, store, office, or farm unsatisfactory? We tell you how to increase your income.

Do you want to change your business? We suggest a vast number of new ways to make money.

Have you a boy whom you wish to put to a trade? We tell you what occupations pay the best.

Do you wish to make money in your own home? We give you a list of 100 paying articles which you can make and sell.

Have you a little plot of ground around your house? We tell you how to make it yield you a yearly revenue.

Do you want to know how our rich men made their money? We give the secrets away by the hundred.

Do you want to know what to do with your savings? We give you a list of the best-paying investments.

Have you practical ideas? Are you skilled in the use of tools? Would you like to take out a patent? We present to you a list of over 300 inventions needed, and in some cases even suggest how the article should be made.

Have you literary ability? or reportorial talent? or advertising genius? We mention 100 ways by which you may be able to make a living by the pen.

In short the 1,000 ways of money-making in this book are 1,000 nails to hang your fortune on. Others have profited by these suggestions. Why may not you?

CONTENTS

The Tumbler of Peas. The Hanging Turnip. Bleached Leaves. The Artificial Plant.

Section 2—Tea Dishes.

Delicious Ham. Choice Tongue. Artificial Honey.

Section 3—Pastry.

Angel Cake. Dominos. Soft Gingerbread. Doughnuts.

Section 4—Sweetmeats and Confectionery.

Walnut Candy. Chocolate Caramels. Peppermint Creams. Molasses Candy. Blanched Almonds. Fig Paste. Fig Layer Candy.

Section 5—Preserves, Pickles, and Jellies.

Orange Marmalade. Brandied Peach. Ox-Heart Cherry. Pound Pear. Grape Jelly. Sweet Pickles. Chow-Chow. Pickled Walnuts.

Section 6—Toilet Articles.

Rose Oil. Cologne Water. French Face Powder. Night-Blooming Cereus.

Section 7—Varnishes and Polishes.

Stove Blacking. Shoe Blacking. Furniture Cream. Leather Polish.

Section 8—Soaps and Starches.

Poland Starch. Glue Starch. Gum-Arabic Starch. Starch Luster. Hard Soap. Savon D'Amande.

Section 9—Soft Drinks.

Root Beer. Ginger Pop. Lemonade and Orangeade.

Section 10—Dairy and Other Farm Produce.

Golden Butter. Fresh Eggs. Sweet Milk. Sparkling Honey. New Cheese. Clean Lard. White Pork. Poultry to Order.

Section 11—Garden Vegetables.

Cut-to-Order Asparagus. Quick Market Strawberries. Round Tomatoes. Pint Peas. String Beans. Green Corn.

Section 12—School Supplies.

Book Covers. Artificial Slates. Cheap Ink. School Bag. Pen Wiper. Children's Luncheon.

Section 13—Christmas Presents.

Sofa Pillow. Jewel Tray. American Flag. Hair-Pin Case. Chair Cushion. Lamp Shade. Bookmark. Handy Work-Box. Pincushion. Catch-Bag. Court-Plaster Case. Postage-Stamp Holder. Photograph Frame. Match Safe. Wall-Pocket. Glove Box.

Section 14—Miscellaneous Articles.

Hot Gems. Sliced Watermelon. Toothsome Pies. Ice Cream. Pork and Beans. Tomato Ketchup. Mince Meat. Dried Apples. Peanuts. Cigarettes. Tallow Candles. Lung Preserver. Poison Killer. Mucilage. Pop Corn.

Money in Pears. Greenbacks in Greenings. Plums of Gold. The Raspberry Acre. Profits in Big Peaches. Easy Tomatoes. Assorted Strawberries. Livings in Lettuce. Sovereigns in Spinach. Thousand-Dollar Celery. Fortunes in Water-Cress. The Dollar Blackberry. Nickels in Pickles. The Beet Lot. The Roasting Ear. Paying Peas. Grated Horseradish.

The School Store. The Hand Album. The Novelty Bakery. The Front Yard Snap. The Pet Dog. The Box Lunch. The Hairdresser. Typo and Steno. The Sewing School. Flat Hunting. A Tea Room. Dress Mending. Lace Handling. Intelligence Office. Professional Mending. The College Cram. Shoe and Wrap Room. General Convenience Room. Sick-Room Delicacies. Shopping Commission. School Luncheon. Hatching Birds. Butter-and-Egg Store. Saratoga Chips. Fancy Lamp Shades. Bee-Keeping. Cleansing and Bleaching. Fancy Soaps. Home Architecture. Home Ornaments. Doubtful Debts. Dressing Dolls. Fruit Preservers. Mushroom Cellar. Poultry Raising. Home Hothouse. Art Needlework. News Agency. Women's Wants. Home Printing Press. Short Service Bureau. Delicatessen Room. Miscellaneous Exchange. Cap and Apron Plan. Kitchen Utensils. Wedding Manager. Foreign Homes. Lady Barber. Mineral Collections for Schools. Turkish Bath. Trained Nurses. Traveling Companion. Paper Flowers. French Perfumer and Complexion Expert. A Woman's Hotel. Guide for Shoppers. Bicycle Instruction. Cooking School. Boarding House. Pen Engraving. Ladies' Restaurant. A Woman's Newspaper. Advertising Agent. The Civil Service. Post-Prandial Classes. Women Druggists. Almanac Makers. Women Lecturers. Magazine Contributors. Women Physicians. Paper Box Making. Horticulture. Vocalists. Packing Trunks. Women Costumers. Express Office. Fancy Bakery. Women Grocers. Food and Medicine Samples. Samples in Stores. Samples from House to House. The Woman Beautifier. The Manicure Parlor. The Massage Treatment. Ice Cream Parlor. Flower Packets. Lady Caterer. Delicacies for Invalids. Insect Powder. Rice Cultivator. Yeast Cakes. Physical Culture. House Cleaning. Selling Oysters. Pie Cart. Men's Neckties. Dancing Teacher. Haberdasher. Lady Architect. Lost and Found Agency.

Section 1—How a Boy Can Get a Place.

Free Service. Special Department. Show Superiority of Goods. Advertising. Influence. A Trial Week. Commission.

Section 2—What Boys Can Do.

The Boy Magician. The Glass-Blower. The Dime Lunch. Cancelled Stamps. The Boys' Press. Saw and Scroll. The Magic Lantern. Candy-Making. Odd Jobs. General Employment Agency. Collect Magazines. Vacant Lot. Bicycle Teaching. First-Cost Sales.

Book Agency. Patent Agency. Commission Merchants. Insurance Agency. Traveling Salesmen. Supply Companies. Agencies for Teachers. Clerical Agency. Matrimonial Agencies. Agency for Servants. Agency for Farm Hands.

Healing Ointment. Spasm Killer. Anti-Malaria. Hostetter's Bitters. Toothache Ease. Candy Digest. Cough Lozenges. Lovers' Hair-Oil. Purgative Powder. Consumption Wafers. Beef, Iron and Wine. Spring Tonic. Dr. Pierce's Golden Medical Discovery. Bed-Bug Exterminator. Catarrh Cure. Lip Pomatum. Ointment for Chapped Hands. Cod-Liver Oil Emulsion. Beauty Water. Cough Mixture. Dr. Sage's Catarrh Remedy. Diarrhea Mixture. Blood Purifier.

City Property. Pleasure Resorts. New Town Sites. Western Lands. The Apartment House. The Sky Scraper. The Jersey Flats. Abandoned Farms.

Crayon Work. Drawing. Photograph Coloring. Oil Painting. Water Colors. Wood Engraving.

Book Decoration. Dyeing. Designs. Engraving on Glass. Embroidery. Lace Making. Drawing in Charcoal. Painting on China. Portrait Painting.

Bicycle Factories. Double Profit Furs. Mica Sheets. Artificial Marble. Artificial Whalebone. Artificial India Rubber. Artificial Camphor. Car Building. The Transverse Wooden Pavement.

Nevada Silver. Aluminum, the New Mineral. North Carolina Mica. Kansas Zinc. Missouri Cottas. Nickel Mines. Mexican Iron. Tennessee Limestone. Fortunes in Copper. German Amber. African Diamonds. Tasmania Tin. Georgia Sapphires. Rock Salt. Asbestos Pockets. Prospects in Platinum. Petroleum Wells. Gold Discoveries. Prospecting for Mines.

Section 1.—Money in Bicycles. A Non-Puncturable Bicycle Tire. Bicycle Holder Attachment. The Bicycle Umbrella Holder. A Bicycle Cyclometer Clock. The Double Power Bicycle. The Folding Wheel. A Bicycle Support. The Cushion Saddle. A Bicycle Guard. A Combination Bicycle Lock. A Bicycle Trunk. The Unicycle. A Bicycle Cover. A Package Holder. Handle Bar Cyclometer. The All-Selling Wheel. Toe-and-Heel Clip. The Extension Bicycle. A Bicycle Shoe. The Stirrup Pedal. The Home Bicycle.

Section 2.—Money in Building Contrivances.

The Ornamental Floor. The Secure Window-Blind. The Self-Locking Window. The Adjustable Blind. The Dollar Door Closer. Sectional Window. Adjustable Storm Door. A Hinge Lock. Double Window. Hot-Blast Furnace. The Weightless Window Sash. A Floor Cover. Sash Balance. Painting Machines. The Pneumatic Water Tank. The Wood-Pulp Floor.

Section 3.—Money in the Kitchen.

The Cheap Washer. A Meat Chopper. Automatic Stove Damper. Potato Extractor. Knife Sharpener. Cold Handle. The Electric Stove. Fruit Jar Holder. Can Opener. Odorless Cooking Vessels. Coal Filled Flat-Iron. Automatic Soaper. Dish-Washing Machine. A Stove Alarm. The Elastic Clothes Line. Combination Line and Pin. A Fruit Press. The Can-Slide.

Section 4.—Money in the Parlor.

The Chair Fan. The Rocking-Chair Fan. Christmas-Tree Holder. Picture-Frame Fastener. Adjustable Head Rest. Imitation Coal Fire. Music Turner. Roll-Front Fire-Screen. Removable Rockers.

Section 5.—Money in the Bedroom.

A Noiseless Clock. A Narcotic Pillow. Electric Fire Igniter. Bedclothes Fastener. Easy-Working Bureau. Extensible Bedstead. Movable Partition and Folding Bed. An Attachable Crib. Pulse Indicator. Dress-Suit Hanger. The Anti-Snorer. The Ventilated Mattress.

Section 6.—Money in the Cellar.

Furnace Feeder. Ice Machine. Stove Ash-Sifter. Jointed Coal Chute. Combined Pan, Can, Sifter and Roller. Ash-Barrel.

Section 7.—Money in the Library and the Schoolroom.

A Paper Binder. The Correspondent's Desk. Book-Duster. The Portable Library. Pocket Lunch Basket. The Multiple-Leaved Blackboard.

Section 8.—Money in Meals.

Butter and Cheese Cutter. Paper Tablecloth. Scroll-Edge Meat Knife. Carving-Knife Holder. Lamp Cooker. Wine Tablets. Extension Table.

Section 9.—Money in the Business Office.

The Keyboard Lock. Automatic Safe Opener. Paper Binder and Bill Holder. Book Lock. The Perpetual Calendar. The Lightning Adder. Copyholder. Envelope Moistener and Sealer. Multiple Lock. Office Door Indicator. Automatic Ticket Seller. Perforated Stamp.

Section 10.—Money in the Packing-Room.

Nonrefillable Bottle. Collapsible Box. Bottle Stopper. Combination Cork and Corkscrew. Collapsible Barrel. Self-Standing Bag. Barrel Filler and Funnel Cut-Off. Folding Crate. Paper Barrel.

Section 11.—Money in Articles of Trade.

The Tradesman's Signal. Barrel Gauge. Elastic Chimney. Air Moistener. Automatic Lubricator. Short-Time Negative. Drying Apparatus. Rotable Hotel Register. Glass Dome. Round Cutting Scissors. Casket Clamp. Self-Winding Clock. Dose Stopper. Faucet Measure. Automatic Feeder. Coupon Cash Book. Gas Detective. Paper Towels. Water Filter. Pneumatic Freight Tube. Storm Warning. Heat Governor. Automatic Oil Feeder. Paint Brush Feeder. Inside Faucet. House Patterns. Extension Handle. Wire Stretcher. Price Tag. Handy Vise. Folding Ladder. Smokeless Fuel. Finger-Ring Gauge. Laundry Bag. Sole Cement. Goods Exhibitor. Shoe Stretcher. Cork Ejector. Lemon Squeezer. Spring Wheel. Plural Capsule. Dose Bottle. Fisherman's Claw. Pocket Scale. Toy Bank and Register. Paper Match. Illuminated Type. Paper Bottles. Paper Sail.

Section 12.—Money in the Street.

Street Sweeper. Phosphorescent Street Numbers. Buggy Top Adjuster. Shoulder Pack. Adjustable Cart Bottom. Nailless Horseshoe. Elastic Ring. Heel Cyclometer. Whip-Lock. Rein-Holder. Automobile. Low Truck. Automatic Horse Fastener. Foot-Cycle.

Section 13.—Money in Farming Contrivances.

Corn Cutter. Frost Protector. Farm Fertilizer. Postless Fence. Automatic Gate Opener. Corn Planter. All-Seed Planter. Fertilizer Distributor. Bone Cutter. Bucket Tipper. Post Hole Digger. Well Refrigerator. Multiple Dasher Churn. Fruit Picker. Portable Fence. Poultry Drinking Fountain. Poultry Perch. Mole Trap. Seed Sower. Milker and Strainer. Paper Milk Can. Plant Preserver.

Section 14.—Money in the Mails and in Writing Materials.

The Reversible Package. Copying Paper. Word Printing Typewriter. Transparent Ink Bottle. Double Postal Card. Safety Envelope. Combination Cover and Letter. Always Ready Letter Paper. Ink Regulator. Pen Finger Pen Rest. Perpetual Pen Supply. Letter Annunciator. Envelope Opener. Mail Stamper. Rotary Stamper. Invisible Ink.

Section 15.—Money in Dress.

Bachelor's Buttons. Shoe Fastener. Trousers' Guard. Twentieth Century Shoe. Combination Tie and Collar. Spring Hat. Rear-Opening Shoe. Detachable Rubber Sole. Instantaneous Cement. Elastic Hat Pin. Starch-Proof Collar Band. Dress Shield. Sleeve Holder. Convertible Button. Paper Clothing.

Section 16.—Money in Personal Conveniences.

The Pocket Umbrella. The Million Match. Finger-Nail Parer. The Watch Pad. Pocket Bill Holder. Extension Umbrella. Portable Desk. Flower Holder. Hat Lock. Spring Shoe Heel. Self-Igniting

CHAPTER   **XVI.**
MONEY IN THE SOIL.

FOREWORD

"I like numbers, it started before I can remember," Buffett tells a group of Omaha Central High School students in the film. A voracious reader his entire life, at age seven he read a book he borrowed from the library, One Thousand Ways to Make $1000, and, inspired by its lessons, began selling Coca-Cola, gum and newspapers. His father, a salesman who survived the Depression, was elected to Congress when Buffett was 12, moving the family to Washington. Displaced and unhappy, Buffett lost interest in academics, attending the University of Nebraska at his father's insistence; he was turned down for admission by the Harvard Business School. This rejection was propitious: Buffett discovered that two of his financial idols, Ben Graham and David Dodd, taught at the Columbia Business School; he wrote them a letter and was accepted there. From Graham he learned what he calls the "two rules of investing": "Rule #1: Never lose money. Rule #2: Never forget Rule #1." First published in 1936, One Thousand Ways to Make $1000 is the long out-of-print book that Warren Buffett's biographers credit with shaping the legendary investor's business acumen and giving him his trademark appreciation of compound interest. After pulling a copy of One Thousand Ways off a library shelf at age eleven and devouring F.C. Minaker's plucky and practical business advice, Buffett declared that he would be a millionaire by the time he was 35. Written in the immediate, conversational style of Dale Carnegie's How to Win Friends and Influence People, this book is full of inventive ideas on how to make money through excellent salesmanship, hard work, and resourcefulness. While some of the ideas may seem quaint today-goat dairying, manufacturing motor-driven chairs, and renting out billiard tables to local establishments are among the money-making ideas presented- the underlying fundamentals of business explained in these pages remain as solid as they were over seventy years ago. Covering a wide spectrum of topics including investing, marketing, merchandising, sales, customer relations, and raising money for charity, One Thousand Ways to Make $1000 is both a durable, classic business book and a fascinating portrait of determined entrepreneurship in Depression-era America. Every effort has been made to reproduce the content exactly as it was originally presented.

The Publisher

INTRODUCTION.

THE object of this work is to help people who are out of employment to secure a situation; to enable persons of small means to engage in business and become their own employers; to give men and women in various lines of enterprise ideas whereby they may succeed; and to suggest new roads to fortune by the employment of capital. The author has been moved to the undertaking by the reflection that there exists nowhere a book of similar character. There have indeed been published a multitude of books which profess to tell men how to succeed, but they all consist of merely professional counsel expressed in general terms. We are told that the secrets of success are "industry and accuracy," "the grasping of every opportunity," "being wide awake," "getting up early and sitting up late," and other cheap sayings quite as well known to the taker as to the giver. Even men who have made their mark, when they come to treat of their career in writing, seem unable to give any concrete suggestions which will prove helpful to other struggling thousands, but simply tell us they won by "hard work," or by "close attention to business."

The author of this book has gone to work on a totally different plan. I have patiently collected the facts in the rise of men to wealth and power, have collated the instances and instruments of fortune, and from these have sifted out the real secrets of success. When as in a few cases, the worn-out proverbs and principles are [12] quoted, these are immediately reinforced by individual examples of persons who attributed their advancement to the following of these rules; but, in general, the suggestions are new, and in very many cases plans and lines of work are proposed by the author which are entirely original, and so far as he knows, absolutely untried. Hence, the work becomes of incomparable value to business men who are constantly seeking new means to interest the public and to dispose of their goods.

Of course, the vast field of action treated of in this work lies beyond the experience of any one man, but the author has talked with business men in every walk in life and gleaned from them the essential facts in their career; in many instances these facts are not the things they have done, but the things they would do if they could begin again, thus giving the reader the benefit both of their success and failure. As a book offering opportunities to the ambitious; presenting openings to those seeking a wider scope for their faculties; affording stimulation to persons of sluggish blood; and giving away trade and business secrets never before divulged; the author feels confident that the little work stands unrivaled, and as such he modestly offers it to the public for its approval.[13]

ONE THOUSAND WAYS TO MAKE MONEY.

CHAPTER   I.

HOW TO GET A PLACE.

You Can Get It—Positions Yawning for Young Men—Any Young Man May Become Rich—Men Who Began at the Bottom and Reached the Top—How A. T. Stewart Got His Start—John Jacob Astor's Secret of Success—How Stephen Girard's Drayman Made a Fortune—$100,000 for Being Polite—How One Man's Error Made Another Man's Fortune—Secret of the Bon Marché in Paris—How Edison Succeeded—A Sure Way to Rise—How a Young Man Got His Salary Increased $2,000—A Sharp Yankee Peddler.

YOUNG men are often discouraged because the desirable places all seem to be filled. But remember there is always room for the right man. Says a New York millionaire: "I hold that any young man, possessing a good constitution and a fair degree of intelligence, may become rich." Says another business man: "I have made a personal canvass of a dozen of the largest business houses in five different commercial and professional lines to see to what extent there exist openings for young men." In only two of the houses approached were the heads of the firms satisfied the positions of trust in those houses were filled by capable men. And in each of these two houses I was told that "of course, if the right sort of a young man came along who could tell us something about our business we did not already know, we should not let him slip through our fingers. Positions can always be created. In four of the houses, positions had been open for six months or more, and the [14] sharpest kind of a lookout kept for possible occupants. These positions commanded salaries all the way from $2,000 to $5,000 a year. In the publishing business, I know of no less than six positions actually yawning for the men to come and fill them—not clerical positions, but positions of executive authority. Young men are desired in these places because of their progressive ideas and capacity to endure work."

Another prominent man who interviewed the heads of several large firms writes in a recent periodical as follows: "It is not with these firms a question of salary; it is a question of securing the highest skill with the most perfect reliability. This being secured, almost any salary to be named will be cheerfully paid. A characteristic of the business world to-day is that its institutions, empires in themselves, have grown to be too large for the handling of ordinary men. These institutions are multiplying in excess of the number of men whose business skill is broad and large enough to direct and command them. Hence, the really commanding business brain is at an immense premium in the market. A salary of $50,000 a year as president of a railroad or manufacturing company at first sight seems exorbitant; but the payment of such a salary usually means pure business. The right or the wrong man at the head of a great business interest means the making or the unmaking of fortunes for the stockholders. Only a single glance at the industrial world is needed to show that here is room for the advent of genius of the first order. This world, seething like a caldron, is boiling to the brim with questions of the most vexing and menacing kind."

Look at the men who reached the top of fortune's ladder, and see under what discouraging circumstances they began. James Fisk, called the Prince of the Erie,[15] rose to that position from a ragged newsboy. Stephen Girard began on nothing, and became the greatest millionaire of his time. Young men, would you scorn to row a boat for a living? Cornelius Vanderbilt plied a boat between Staten Island and New York. Would you tramp the country as a surveyor for a map? Jay Gould began in that way, and forty years later satisfied certain doubters of his financial standing by showing them certificates of stocks worth $80,000,000. Do you fear to have your hands calloused with ax or saw? John W. Mackay, who acquired a fortune of $20,000,000, started in life as a shipwright. Is it beneath your social station to handle butter and eggs? "Lucky" Baldwin, the multi-millionaire, kept a country store and made his first venture by taking his goods overland in a cart to Salt Lake City. Are your fingers too delicate for the broom handle? A. T. Stewart began his business career by sweeping out the store. Do you abhor vile odors? Peter Cooper made $6,000,000 in the glue business.

Tens of thousands are looking for a place. Most of them have had places, but could not keep them. If you follow all the rules below, having obtained a place, you will never need to seek one again. The place will seek you. Employers are in search of the qualities herein to be considered, and they are willing to pay liberally for them. They are qualities that come high everywhere. If you possess them, you can in a short time command your own price. But do not scorn to take the humblest place. Merit, like murder, will out. Be sure you have the winning cards and wait.

1. THE SECRET OF WORK.—Men will employ you if you mean business. When you find men working, work with them. Lend a hand. Every employer[16] would rather employ a busy man than an idle man. When he sees you working, he will watch you. If he likes you, he will make you an offer. A glazier, being refused work at a place where a church was being erected, put down his kit of tools, picked up the broken pieces of glass which the workmen had thrown away, and, laboring just as if he had been hired to work, fashioned the finest church window in the world, and became rich and famous.

2. NATURE'S FURROW.—Plow in nature's furrow. In general, a man is fitted for the thing he likes. Do that which you can do best. What you want to do you are called to do, and what you are called to do you can do. Darwin says that the fittest survive because they

have a slight advantage over those which do not survive. Your liking for an occupation is the advantage you have over those who do not like it. Follow the hint, whether it be to publish a paper or peg shoes. A leading merchant in New York found his calling through having loaned money to a friend. He had to take his friend's store to secure his money, and thus learned his gift for merchandise. The man was A. T. Stewart.

3. General Details.—The best general is General Details. In business life, no matter is small enough to be despised. To master an infinite number of small things is to prepare yourself to master great things. When your employers see that you have everything at your fingers' ends, they will intrust you with larger interests, and greater responsibility means greater pay. John Jacob Astor knew the minutest point about every part of his great business. *That* was the secret of his success.[17]

4. The Prismatic Brain.—Be many-sided, but transparent. Tell your employer where you have failed. Do not try to cover up a fault. Be absolutely honest. You may get along for a time on "shady" lines, but such success is only gained at the expense of ultimate loss. It is absolutely essential that your employer should have the utmost confidence in your integrity. Try by every means to gain that confidence. Court examination. Invite inspection. Remember that his profound belief in you—belief in you when out of business hours as well as in—is your surest stepping-stone to promotion. Character is power. Your success depends as much upon what you are as upon what you know or do. Stephen Girard once trusted his drayman to buy a shipload of tea worth $200,000. He trusted him because he knew his man, and he gave the young man the profits of the transaction, which amounted to $50,000.

5. The Bridled Tongue.—Do not cross your employer in any way. Never dispute with him. You may be sure that you are right, but do not say so. You need not be a Democrat or an Episcopalian because your employer is, but if you are wise you will avoid discussing with him questions of politics or religion. Courtesy pays. Ross Winans, of Philadelphia, secured a business that netted him $100,000 a year simply through his politeness to two Russian agents, to whom others in the same trade had accorded scant courtesy.

6. Studying the Stair Above.—Study, not stars, but stairs. Learn all about the position next above you. When you can point out new methods to your employer, advance new ideas, or suggest new channels of trade or lines of work, you are surely on the way to[18] promotion. Only, be sure that your new ideas are practical. There is no more direct road to the confidence of your employer than for him to see that you understand any part of his affairs better than he does himself. Employ your spare moments in studying the business. While the other clerks are joking, do you be learning. While the students at the boarding-house in Andover were chaffing each other during the wait for breakfast, Joseph Cook would turn to a big dictionary in one corner of the room and look out a word. He climbed many stairs above them.

7. THE MISSING FACTOR.—Your employers are wrestling with a question. They are uncertain whether to invest or not. They are doubtful about the character or standing of some man with whom they are or may become heavily involved. It will be worth thousands to you if you can procure any scrap of information that will help to set them right. A young clerk who discovered an error in Bradstreet's was soon admitted to partnership in his employer's firm.

8. THE MAGNIFYING GLASS.—Make the most of your present position. Wear magnifying glasses. Exalt the importance of every item. Let not the smallest thing be done in a slipshod way. If you are answering letters for the firm, answer them briefly but completely. Remember that brevity is not brusqueness. If you are waiting on customers, treat the small customer just as courteously as the large one. You may be sure that your employer knows the market value of politeness. In the Bon Marché in Paris, the employers determined that something must be done more than was done in other stores so that every visitor would remember the place with pleasure and come again. The result[19] was the most exquisite politeness ever seen in a mercantile establishment, and it has developed the largest business of its kind in the world.

9. THE MICROSCOPIC EYE.—The microscope shows a hundred things the naked eye cannot see. Endeavor to see what others fail to see—new possibilities of sales, new means of profit, new methods of doing things. It was by steadily looking at a thing until he saw what was not apparent to the superficial view that Thomas Edison became the greatest electrician of the world.

10. SCORING A POINT WHEN OFF DUTY.—Do something for your employer when you are out of the shop or store. You may be sure that he will appreciate it. It is a fallacy that he has no claim on you when off duty. Do not give him the idea that you have no interest in the business except to get your salary, and no time to spare him except what you are paid for. Do not watch the clock; do not filch a few moments at the beginning or end of the day's work, and do not ask leave of absence except when absolutely necessary. Do overwork and unpaid-for work, and when you see a point in favor of your firm, fasten to it. Become essential to the place, and you will rise in the place. "I can't spare you," said the publisher of a New York magazine to his advertising agent when another publisher offered him an increase of $1,000. "Let's see—you are getting $5,000 now; I'll make it $7,000."

11. THE STUDY OF MEN.—This is the very key to success. The proper study of mankind is man. The greatest college on earth is the business world. The man who can sell the most goods is the one who knows the weaknesses of human nature, and how to avail himself[20] of them. Your best diploma is a big bill of sale. Sell something to everybody— what the customer wants if you have it; if not, what he doesn't want; but at any rate, sell him something. It is related of a Yankee book-peddler that he sold three copies of the

same book to a family in one day—to the husband in the store, to the wife who was calling at a neighbor's, and to the daughter at home. And not one of the family wanted the book.

Following the above lines, and adding thereto good health and steady habits, you cannot fail to be promoted and to rise to the highest position of responsibility, if not even to actual partnership in the firm. These are the qualities that proprietors are yearning for—nay, actually groaning for, but which are hard to find in the average man. Employers are keeping the sharpest kind of a watch for the right man. It is stated on the best of authority that there are a thousand business firms in New York and vicinity each having one or more $5,000 positions awaiting the men who can fill them. If you have the right qualities or will acquire them, at least a thousand great firms want your services, and posts of responsibility with almost unlimited salary await your hand or brain.[21]

CHAPTER II.

STARTING IN BUSINESS.

Why Men Fail—Luck on the side of Pluck—Marking the Day's Profits Before they Begin—No Diamond Like the Eye—The Man Who Takes His Bank to Bed With Him—The Two Hands of Fortune.

MANY men fail because they undertake a business without considering whether there is room for it; others because they do not thoroughly establish themselves in the place, making no effort to get a constituency; and yet others because they do not keep the goods that are in demand, or do not renew the stock sufficiently quick, or do not present their goods in an attractive way. Such causes of success or failure as are in the line of this work will now be considered. Here are the rules of an old merchant which he would take for his guidance were he to start anew in business:

12. THE MINIMUM BASIS.—Enumerate the entire number of heads of families in the town, village, ward, or neighborhood where you purpose to begin business. Figure out the number of such persons you will require as a minimum basis in order to get on—that is, how many persons or families, spending each on an average a certain amount per day or week at your place of business, you will require in order to make a living. Do not go blindly into your work, trusting to luck. Luck is always on the side of pluck and tact. Determine what per cent. of the people's patronage is absolutely essential[22] to your success. The first step is to ascertain if such per cent. is likely to come to you.

13. THE HOUSE TO HOUSE CANVASS.—Make a personal canvass from house to house. Do not trust the work to your friend, relative, or clerk. Nobody can help you so much as you can

help yourself. Nobody has your interests so much at heart as you have. Tell people pleasantly that you are a new bidder for their patronage. Inform them what you propose to do. Make them to understand that no man shall undersell you, or give them in any way a better bargain. If possible, take a few samples of your choicest goods with you.

14. THE CHOICE LOCATION.—If you become popular, the people will come to you; but at first you must go to them. Your place need not be central or on a corner, but it must be where many people pass. Step out largely and conspicuously. You could make no greater mistake than to rent a shabby place on a back street. Have out all manner of signs, curious, newsy, and alluring. Do not think to sustain yourself by people's sympathies. Men will trade most where they can do best.

15. THE MAXIMUM BASIS.—The maximum basis is the high-water mark. It is the number of persons or families that under the most favorable state of things can be your patrons. All you cannot expect. Kindred, religion, politics, friendships, and secret fraternities, will hold a portion of the community to the old traders. The sharpest rivalry will meet you. Also, you must consider what incursions are likely to be made by out-of-town dealers, and what prospect there is of others[23] setting up business in the place. But you should have an ideal trade toward which you steadily work. Declare daily to yourself, "my gross earnings shall be $—per day," or "—— (so many) persons shall be my patrons." When you fall below the mark, bestir yourself in many ways.

16. THE PERSONAL EQUATION.—Remember that you yourself in contact with your customers count for more than anything else. The weather of the face, the temperature of the hand, the color of the voice, will win customers where other means fail. Make your patrons feel that you are their friend. Inquire about members of their family. Be exceedingly polite. Recommend your goods. Mention anything of an especially attractive or meritorious nature you may have. Join the church, the regiment, the fire company, and the secret society. Become "all things to all men, if by any means you can sell to some." Be everywhere in your place of business. Oversee the smallest details. Trust as little as possible to your clerks. The diamond of success is the master's eye. Remember there is no fate. There are opportunity, purpose, grit, push, pluck, but no fate. If you fail, do not lay the blame upon circumstances, but upon yourself. Enthusiasm moves stones. You must carry your business in your brain. "A bank never gets to be very successful," says a noted financier, "until it gets a president who takes it to bed with him." There was an angel in Michael Angelo's muddy stone, and there is a fortune in your humdrum store. Hard work and close thought are the hands that carve it out.[24]

CHAPTER   III.

MONEY IN TRADE.

What Kind of Advertisements Pay—"Don't Fail to See the Blizzard Saturday Night"—The Keynote of a $20,000,000 Sale—Selling Goods by the Mile—Watches for Bait—How to Get Five-Year Customers—"Trade With Me and Get a House and Lot"—Why Trade at Push and Pluck's?—Bargains in Buttons Often Means High Prices in Broadcloth.

THOUSANDS fail in business every year when an idea put into practical operation would have tided them over the trouble and opened the road to a competence. This chapter will tell you how to succeed. No man with common ability and industry who puts the half or even the quarter of these ideas into practice can possibly fail. The great thing is to make people buy your goods. But to induce them to purchase you must first of all call attention to what you have to sell. Here are a few of the ways in which this is to be done. The following methods will fairly compel the people to trade with you, but you must bear in mind that as soon as the influence of one device begins to flag it must be immediately succeeded by another.

17. THE INTERLINED ADVERTISEMENT.—Advertisements are not read unless persons are looking for something in that line. This is because they are all placed by themselves. Your bid for patronage must be put in the midst of the reading matter if it is to attract general attention. Many publishers will not do this, but your chief and only point in appearing in the paper is to have[25] your advertisement read, and it pays better to insert it in a journal with 5,000 readers who will all see it than in one having 100,000 subscribers, hardly 100 of whom will glance at the advertisement. You can afford to pay handsomely if the publisher will give you a line of black-faced type to eight or ten lines of news.

18. THE PICTURESQUE NAME.—Have a name for your store such as will easily fit everybody's mouth. "The Beehive," "The Blizzard," "The Buttercup," or "The Bonanza," are suggestive titles. Many customers are attracted by the talk of their acquaintances, and it is much easier to tell a friend that you bought an article at "The Hub," or "The Sun," than to attempt the unpronounceable name of a proprietor, or to give a forgotten number. Successful men in several lines of business assert that they owe much of their good fortune to the happy hit of a popular name.

19. THE PICTORIAL WRECK.—A writer with the gift of a lively imagination can write something interesting in the way of a fanciful battle between customers and goods. Head lines, "Great Slaughter in —— (the taking name of your store)," "Wreck of Old Conservatism," "Smash of High Prices," "Ruined by the Rush." Then would follow a graphic description of the charge of customers upon wares in which the store was almost wrecked by the enormous number of people who took advantage of the under-cost

prices. People enjoy this kind of pleasantry, and the impulse to follow the crowd is almost irresistible. A certain New York house grew from a small to a great one by this method of advertising.

20. RED LETTER DAY.—Have a day in which you[26] offer special bargains to the people of a certain town, village or hamlet. Put up flaming posters, announcing "Squashville day," "Jonesboro Day," "Bloomington day."

21. CLASS DISCOUNT.—You may draw numbers of men to your place by this means. Secret fraternities, workingmen's orders, church societies, wheelmen's leagues, will be attracted to you if they know you specially favor them. Fortunes have been made by close attention to these great organizations.

22. THE HONEST FLAW.—Strictly instruct your clerks to tell your customers the precise nature of every article; if the quality is inferior, make them to understand exactly what they are getting for their money; and if there be a flaw, let them be careful to point it out. By such means thousands of people who cannot trust their own judgment in these matters, will be attracted to a place where they are certain to be treated fairly. A. T. Stewart, who began business in a modest store, and who, in the latter part of his life sold $20,000,000 worth of goods every year, declared that this plan was the keynote of his success.

23. THE PREMIUM CLERK.—You need clerks who can induce acquaintances to visit your store, cajole visitors into customers, and coax customers to become larger buyers. If you have a number of clerks and your business will admit of it, offer a monthly premium to the one who brings into the store the largest number of new buyers or into the cash-drawer the heaviest receipts. There are certain kinds of business where this plan will work, and will be provocative of such competition as greatly to increase trade.[27]

24. THE RAILROAD MILEAGE.—Arrange, if possible, with some railroad company to issue mileage tickets as premiums to those who will trade with you. At two cents a mile you could afford to give two miles of travel for every one dollar's worth of goods. At that rate $500 worth of goods would buy a $20 mileage ticket.

25. THE DIAL DOLLARS.—How many figures on the dial of your watch? Twenty-eight, counting the number VI, which is generally either omitted or only partly indicated. Fix a big dial two feet or more in diameter in some prominent part of your store, and announce that when a customer has traded an amount equal to the total figures on the dial you will present him with a watch. Of course, the timepiece would be a very cheap one, but many a parent will trade with you for the sake of getting a watch for his child.

26. FIRST CUSTOMER PACKAGE.—In some periods of the day you will have more custom than you can well attend to, while at other times you will have nothing to do. The following plan will perhaps help to equalize trade, and also give you additional buyers: Suspend a

package in some conspicuous part of your store with the announcement thereon that it will be given free to the first customer in the morning.

27. THE CARPET COUPON.—By a system of large-sized coupons—we will say a foot square —you can put into practice a unique system that will appeal to the heart of every housewife. Publish that you will give a free carpet of a certain size and grade when a fixed amount has been traded. A square foot of a coupon represents a sum of money spent in the store—perhaps one dollar. Every woman by measuring her room can [28] learn how many dollars' worth of goods she must buy before she can have a free carpet.

28. THE HOUSE LOT COUPON.—This is an extension of carpet coupon. A certain amount of purchased goods entitles one to a building lot, which, if in the country, need not be of great cost. Have the particular lots selected and advertised. Another plan is to offer the lot to the largest purchaser within a certain time—possibly five years. This is a good way to hold on to customers.

29. PRICE-TIME GRADE.—If you have the credit system, have also a gradation of prices so as to encourage people to pay at the earliest possible time. A system like this would do— forty days full price; thirty days, two per cent. off; twenty days, three per cent. off; ten days, four per cent. off; cash, five per cent. off.

30. SALES BULLETIN.—People like to buy where others buy. Success brings success. If you are doing well, you may do better. Have a large bulletin board in front of your store, or near it, announcing your sales for the past week. Newspapers boom themselves in like manner by publishing their enormous circulation.

31. BEST REASON PRIZE.—Offer a prize to the one who will give the best reason for trading at Push & Pluck's, and then insert in the form of an advertisement in a leading paper a list of the best reasons. Six months before Christmas offer presents to all who will trade a certain amount before that holiday.

32. BIRTHDAY CALENDAR.—A calendar with the birthdays of your customers (age of course omitted), [29] would attract attention, and the offer to give a present to any one trading a certain amount before his birthday would certainly add to your receipts.

33. CONSPICUOUS PRICE-LIST.—Buyers are caught like fish. Display in your window a list of cut prices. Passers-by who cannot resist the opportunity of a bargain will come in, and often be induced to purchase the goods which are not reduced.

34. THE EARLY DISCOUNT.—In order to equalize the trade of the day announce that you will give a slight discount to persons trading during the dull hours.

35. THE MONEY-SPACE COUNTER.—Determine that every portion of your store shall pay. Have every lineal foot of your counters calculated at a certain rate of profit. If you find a department that does not pay, change methods or your goods, and if still unsuccessful drop it. Many large dealers fail because they keep departments where the expenses are

more than the profits. But if every foot of room pays only a little, the entire store must pay handsomely.

It will be seen in the foregoing how every leading impulse in human nature is appealed to—curiosity and cupidity, honesty and economy, personal flattery and local pride. If, in addition to these powerful inducements to patronage, you combine shrewdness in buying and cautiousness in trusting, if your goods are excellent in quality and generous in quantity, if your place of business is neat and attractive, and your service marked by promptness and politeness; then it is impossible to fail; you have all the elements of prosperity, and are certain to be a great and successful merchant.[30]

CHAPTER IV.

MONEY IN THE INTRODUCTION OF A NEW ARTICLE.

Success of the "Imitation Cigar"—The Dealer's Seeds of Gold are Black—Barnum's Belief in Humbugs—Tricks for Trade—Politics for the Men, Novels for the Women—How the Remington Typewriter was Boomed—A Business Man's Experience in Advertising.

NEW articles in all lines of trade are constantly appearing. Inventors of mechanical appliances, authors of books, proprietors of patent medicines, introducers of something novel in groceries, and promoters of new departures in dry and fancy goods, are all anxious to have the public take their products and pay them in cash. The problem is how to introduce the article. However meritorious it may be, it is useless unless the people find it out. The following are believed to be unique methods of advertising:

36. THE PUZZLE.—Buy some patented puzzle which can be manufactured cheap and scattered broadcast over the land. There is no better way to advertise. If men do not solve the puzzle, they will remember what is stamped on it. The "Get-off-the-earth-Chinese puzzle" enormously advertised its purchasers.

37. THE TOY IMITATION.—Wooden nutmegs and shoe-peg oats have duly advertised the shrewd ways of the people of Connecticut. A man recently made a hit by the "imitation cigar," which is only a piece of wood[31] of the shape and color of a cigar. Every boy wants one. As an advertising medium it was an immense success. Think of something as common and cheap as a cigar, get up an imitation for the children, have your enterprise stamped upon it, and it will go from one end of the land to the other.

38. THE CARTOON.—A caricature of some political person or situation is always taking. Hit off some social craze, or give a witty representation of some matter of passing interest. Drops of ink in this way are seeds of gold, and the harvest will be golden.

39. THE CONJURER.—This is a good way to advertise when the article is a cheap affair which can be shown in the street. There are few things so attractive to the masses as the tricks of the sleight-of-hand performer. Mr. P. T. Barnum uttered at least an half-truth when he said the people liked to be humbugged. For a few dollars you can get an equipment, and in a few days' practice you can acquire enough of the art for your purpose. You can draw a crowd wherever there are people. When you have performed a few tricks, your climax should be a shrewd advertisement which can be worked into the last performance.

40. THE STRIKING FIGURE.—If your goods are on sale in some prominent store, this device is sure to draw attention. Make a figure of some animal or vegetable or other form, if your article will lend itself to such a work. The figure could be some prominent man, or represent an historic scene, or illustrate some popular movement. A dealer in confectionery had in his window a bicycle made all of candy. [32]

41. THE ADVERTISING STORY.—Offer a prize to the one who will write the best story about the merits of your article. The latter must be brought deftly into the story, and the award should be based upon the merits of the literary production and the skill in the use of the advertisement. Every competitor should be required to buy a small number of the articles, and the story should be published.

42. THE WORD-BUILDER.—Another prize might be offered to the one who could compose the greatest number of words from the name of your article or invention. The name ought to include at least a dozen letters, and there should be a set of rules for building words. Every contestant must buy your invention from whose title he is to build words.

43. THE POPULAR PUN.—This is an expensive way of advertising, but an immensely paying one. You make a pun upon some fad of the day, a hit upon some general craze, a piercing of some passing bubble, a political quib. Something of this nature printed several times in the issue of the daily papers would make your venture known to everybody.

44. THE POLITICAL GUESSER.—If your enterprise admits of the coupon system, offer a prize to the one who will guess the successful candidate at the next election, and come the nearest to the figures of his plurality. The contestant must purchase one of your articles, and in this way hundreds of thousands may be sold. Every presidential election is the occasion of the floating of many things by this scheme.

45. THE GEOMETRICAL GROUP.—Some wares, such [33] as fancy soaps and canned goods, admit of a grouping which is very attractive to the eye. Pyramids, cones, circles, and towers, always draw attention. Some mechanical device whereby motion is produced will be sure to draw a crowd to your show window.

46. THE PICTORIAL COMPARISON.—If you are sure of your ground, draw a diagram or other figure, comparing your staple with those of others in the market. In this way the Royal

Baking Powder Company pushed to the front, comparing with heavy black lines its product with the outputs of other companies.

47. THE OPEN CHALLENGE.—And if you are still further confident that you have the best thing of its kind, you may issue a challenge to your competitors. Make it apparent that you are anxious, even clamorous, for a trial of your product against others. By this means you will establish yourself in the confidence of the public. The Remington Typewriter was boomed in this way.

48. THE BOOK GIFT.—Try the religious field. Issue leaflets or tiny books with paper covers, costing not more than two or three dollars a thousand, and offer them as gifts to Sunday-schools or other children's organization. Most Sunday-school superintendents would be glad to give away booklets of this kind if they could be obtained free of charge. The books should contain a bright story, a few pictures, and, of course, a taking presentation of your wares.

49. SUNDAY-SCHOOL SUPPLIES.—In some cases, you might even be warranted in issuing the supplies of a Sunday school, at least for a portion of the year. The {34} books in the last number might not in every case be read, but the picture papers, lesson leaves, and other helps, are all looked over, even if not studied. You could in many cases present them, reserving large advertising space for yourself so as to net a good profit. The class of customers thus obtained would be the very best. Do not hope for large returns unless you are willing to spend money. Money is the manure that creates crops, the blood that makes fatness, the wind that fans fortune, the sap that runs into golden fruit. Money is the bread on the waters that "returneth after many days." It seems like the sheerest folly to spend so much in advertising, but you cannot reap bountifully unless you sow bountifully. "For every dollar spent in advertising," declares a successful merchant, "I have reaped five." {35}

CHAPTER   V.

MONEY IN THE HOME STORE.

How to Make Money at Home—One Hundred Ways to Get Gain in Your Own House—How to Get One Hundred Per Cent. Profit—Make Your Own Goods—Cheaper to Make than to Buy—Anybody Can do It—A Woman as Well as a Man—A Chance for Persons With Small Capital—Three Profits in One Sale.

HOW? On every article sold there is first of all the profit of the manufacturer, then of the wholesale dealer, and finally of the retailer. There is commonly a fourth, that of the freighter. If you keep a retail store, you must pay the man who makes the goods, the man who transports the goods, and the man who keeps the goods in large stock, and all this leaves you only a small margin of profit. In the following plan you avoid all these costs, pay only for the raw material, and make the four profits yourself.

You may begin your sales in your own home. If you have a large room fronting the street and near it, a little alteration will make it a veritable store. An expenditure of $25 should give you a show window and some nice shelves. Have a workroom in connection with your store. If your sales at first are small, you can put in your spare time in the making of your goods, and afterward as your custom increases you can employ help. The following articles are easily made. Many of them are novel, but all are salable if the store is properly managed. [36]

Section I. Household Ornaments.

A home may be rendered attractive by a few simple ornaments that are very cheap. Vines, grasses, etc., add touches of beauty to a home and cost very little. Few people know how to prepare these little curiosities, and many would esteem it too much trouble to get and arrange the material if they did know. But most of these persons would buy them if the materials were prepared, and the vines, etc., ready to grow. You must have models of each kind in full growth in order to excite their admiration, and then you must have others in the initial stage for sale. Take pains to show the models, and explain the method of treating the plants and vines. The following cost little, and can be sold for from 300 to 500 per cent. profit. Some of your patrons will prefer to buy the models outright, and others to grow them themselves.

50. CRYSTALLIZED GRASSES.—Put in water as much alum as can be dissolved. Pour into an earthen jar and boil slowly until evaporated nearly one half. Suspend the grasses in such a manner that their tops will be under the solution. Put the whole in a cool place where not the least draught of air will disturb the formation of crystals. In twenty-four to thirty-six hours take out the grasses, and let them harden in a cool room. For blue crystals, prepare blue vitriol or sulphate of copper in the same manner. Gold crystals can be produced by adding tumeric to the alum solution, and purple crystals by a few drops of extract of logwood. Sell them at twenty-five cents a bunch.

51. LEAF IMPRESSIONS.—Hold oiled paper in the smoke of a lamp, or of pitch, until it becomes coated with smoke. Then take a perfect leaf, having a pretty [37] outline, and after warming it between the hands, lay the leaf upon the smoked side of the paper, with the under side down, press it evenly upon the paper so that every part may come in contact, go over it lightly with a rolling-pin, then remove the leaf with care to a piece of white paper, and use the rolling-pin again. You will then have a beautiful impression of the delicate veins and outline of the leaf. A sheet containing a dozen such leaves should

bring you twenty-five cents; if arranged in a pretty white album, with a different kind of leaf for every page, the selling price should not be less than one dollar.

52. VINE AND TRELLIS.—Put a sweet potato in a tumbler of water, or any similar glass vessel; let the lower end of the tuber be about two inches from the bottom of the vessel; keep on the mantel shelf, and sun it for an hour or two each day. Soon the "eyes" of the potato will throw up a pretty vine. Now with some small sticks or coarse splints construct a tiny trellis, which, if placed in the window, will soon find a customer.

53. THE SUSPENDED ACORN.—Suspend an acorn by a piece of thread, within half an inch of the surface of some water contained in a vase, tumbler or saucer, and allow it to remain undisturbed for several weeks. It will soon burst open, and small roots will seek the water; a straight and tapering stem, with beautiful, glossy green leaves, will shoot upward, and present a very pleasing appearance. Supply water of the same warmth once a month, and add bits of charcoal to keep it from souring. If the leaves turn yellow, put a drop of ammonia into the water, and it will renew their luxuriance.[38]

54. MOSS AND CONE.—Take a saucer and fill it with fresh green moss. Place in the center a large pine cone, having first wet it thoroughly. Then sprinkle it with grass seed. The moisture will close the cone partially, and in a day or two tiny grass spears will appear in the interstices, and in a week you will have a perfect cone covered with graceful verdure. The advantage of this, as well as of the other pretty things in this section, is that they are fresh and green in the midst of winter, and people are attracted to the slice of spring in your window when the outside world is mantled with snow.

55. THE TUMBLER OF PEAS.—Take a common tumbler or fruit can and fill it nearly full of soft water. Tie a bit of coarse lace or cheese-sacking over it, and covering it with a layer of peas, press down into the water. In a few days the peas will sprout, the little thread-like roots going down through the lace into the water, while the vines can be trained upon a pretty little frame.

56. THE HANGING TURNIP.—Take a large turnip and scrape out the inside, leaving a thick wall all around. Fill the cavity with earth, and plant in it some clinging vine or morning glory. Suspend the turnip with cords, and in a little time the vines will twine around the strings, and the turnip, sprouting from below, will put forth leaves and stems that will turn upward and gracefully curl around the base.

57. BLEACHED LEAVES.—Mix one drachm chloride of lime with one pint of water, and add sufficient acetic acid to liberate the chlorine. Steep the leaves about ten minutes, or until they are whitened. Remove them on a piece of paper and wash them in clean water. [39] They are now ready for sale, and all you need do is to arrange a dozen of them on a sheet of black paper, or in a dark-colored album, and expose them in your show window.

58. THE ARTIFICIAL PLANT.—Take the glossy silk stuff known as taffeta. Dye the piece the proper green color before cutting. After it is dried, prepare with gum arabic on one side to represent the glossy surface of the leaves, and with starch on the other to give the velvety appearance of the under side. Use a fine goffering tool to make the veins and indentations. Glue the leaves to the stem, and place to advantage in your store window, where, if you have been skillful, they can hardly be distinguished from the leaves of a growing plant.

If you are moderately successful, procure a book about household ornaments and artificial plants, and you will learn to make many more designs. We have selected these because they are the cheapest and most easily made. All the above, except the albums, should sell for twenty-five cents. Remember that a great deal depends upon your taste in arranging, your manner of explaining, and your adroitness in recommending. You must be so in love with your plants as to be enthusiastic. In general, a lady succeeds in this work better than a gentleman.

Section 2. Tea Dishes.

At almost no cost, you find yourself established in the midst of dozens of clinging vines and pretty plants. Now for the next step. Have a few appetizing tea-dishes in your window. Put out a sign, telling people that you will have every night certain fine and fresh table delicacies on sale. The effect of dainty dishes in {40} close proximity to graceful vines is exceedingly tempting to the appetite.

59. DELICIOUS HAM.—If very neat, you can sell to many families cold boiled ham for supper or lunch. Put the ham in cold water, and simmer gently five hours. Set the kettle aside, and when nearly cold draw off the skin of the ham and cover with cracker crumbs and about three tablespoonfuls of sugar. Place in the oven in a baking pan for thirty or forty minutes. When cold, slice thin and lay temptingly on large white plates. Cost of a ham weighing ten pounds, $1.20. Sales at thirty cents a pound, $3.00. Deduct for shrinkage in boiling and waste in trimming one and one-half pounds, forty-five cents. Profits, $1.35.

60. CHOICE TONGUE.—If successful with ham, you can try a little tongue. Soak over night and cook for four or five hours. Throw into cold water and peel off the skin. Cut evenly and arrange attractively on plates, garnishing with sprigs of parsley. Cooked meats should be placed in the show window under transparent gauze. In hot weather a cake of ice beneath will greatly tempt the appetite of the passer-by.

61. ARTIFICIAL HONEY.—Where honey is high priced, make the following: Five pounds white sugar, two pounds water, gradually bring to a boil, and skim well. When cool, add one pound bees' honey and four drops of peppermint. There is a large profit in this

where the customer is not particular about the quality; but if a better article is desired add less water and more real honey.

You can add a number of other tea-dishes as you learn what will sell. A thing that is salable in one[41] community is often not so in another. You must be guided by the taste of the locality, and when a dish does not sell well try another.

Section 3. Pastry.

Suppose you now try a little pastry. If you can make a superior article, you will have a ready sale, but it is often difficult to introduce the goods. It is sometimes a good plan to donate a cake to a fair, cutting the loaf into very thin slices, and giving them to leading ladies who may be present, superintending the matter yourself, and advertising that you will take orders.

62. ANGEL CAKE.—The whites of eleven eggs, one and a half cupfuls of granulated sugar, measured after being sifted four times, one cupful of flour measured after being sifted four times, one teaspoonful of cream tartar, and one of vanilla extract. Beat the whites to a stiff froth and beat the sugar into the eggs. Add the seasoning and flour, stirring quickly and lightly. Beat until ready to put the mixture into the oven. Use a pan that has little legs on the top corners so that when the pan is turned upside down on the table after the baking, a current of air will pass under and over it. Bake for forty minutes in a moderate oven. Do not grease the pan. This cake should sell for $1, or, cut in twenty pieces, at five cents each.

63. DOMINOS.—If you are located near a schoolhouse or on a street where many children pass, you can do a big business in dominos. Bake a sponge cake in a rather thin sheet. Cut into small oblong pieces the shape of a domino. Frost the top and sides. When the frosting is hard, draw the black lines and make the dots with a small brush that has been dipped in melted chocolate. They will sell "like hot cakes."[42]

64. SOFT GINGERBREAD.—All children like this. Here is an excellent kind: Six cupfuls of flour, three of molasses, one of cream, one of lard or butter, two eggs, one teaspoonful of saleratus, and two of ginger. You can sell this, when light and warm, almost as fast as you can make it.

65. DOUGHNUTS.—These, too, are tempting to children. Four eggs, one half-pound sugar, two ounces butter, one pound flour, boiled milk, nutmeg, cinnamon, and a few drops of some essence. Beat the eggs and sugar and melt the butter and stir it in; then add a pound of flour and enough boiled milk to make a rather stiff dough; flavor with nutmeg, cinnamon, and a few drops of some essence; cut into shapes with tumbler or knife, and fry brown in hot lard. When done, sift on fine sugar. Made fresh every day and placed temptingly in the window, they will sell fast.

After you are well established, you should sell at least two dozen doughtnuts at a profit of a penny apiece, two cards of gingerbread at seven cents profit each, and three dozen dominos at a profit of five cents a dozen. Total profit per day on three last articles in this section, fifty-three cents.

Section 4. Sweetmeats and Confectionery.

If you find that children are your best customers, you may cater yet further to their taste. Remember that your success depends upon your keeping choice articles. It is surprising how children find out the best candy stores, and how quick they are to discern between good and bad stock. By making your own goods, you can sell a little cheaper than the dealers who have to buy.

66. WALNUT CANDY.—This is something which all children like. Put the meats of the nuts on the bottom[43] of tins previously greased to the depth of half an inch. Boil two pounds of brown sugar, one half pint of water, and one gill of molasses, until a portion of the mass hardens when it cools. Pour the hot candy on the meats and allow it to remain until hard.

67. CHOCOLATE CARAMELS.—A favorite with girls. Boil a quart of best molasses until it hardens when put in water. Before removing from the fire, add four ounces of fine chocolate. Pour a thin layer into tin trays slightly greased. When it hardens a little cut into squares. You can sell these as low as thirty cents a pound, and still make a good profit.

68. PEPPERMINT CREAMS.—Take one pound of sugar, seven teaspoonfuls of water, and one teaspoonful of essence of peppermint. Work together into a stiff paste, roll, cut, and stamp with a little wooden stamp such as are bought for individual butter pats.

69. MOLASSES CANDY (White).—All children want molasses candy. Two pounds of white sugar, one pint of sugar-house syrup, and one pint of best molasses. Boil together until the mass hardens when dropped in cold water, and work in the usual manner. Sell by the stick, or in broken pieces by the pound, half, and quarter.

70. BLANCHED ALMONDS.—Shell the nuts; pour over them boiling water. Let them stand in the water a minute, and then throw them into cold water. Rub between the hands. The nuts will be white as snow, and, if placed prominently in the window, very tempting. Sell by the ounce.[44]

71. FIG PASTE.—This always has a good sale. Chop a pound of figs and boil in a pint of water until reduced to a soft pulp. Strain through a fine sieve, add three pounds of sugar, and evaporate over boiling water until the paste becomes quite stiff. Form the paste into a square mass, and divide in small pieces with a thin-bladed knife. Roll the pieces in fine sugar, and pack in little wooden boxes.

72. FIG LAYER CANDY.—One half-pound of drum figs, one pound of finest white sugar, white of one egg, one tablespoonful of cold water. Make sugar, egg, and water into a cream, and mold like bread. After figs are stemmed and chopped, roll a fig to one fourth of an inch in thickness. Place the rolled fig between two layers of cream, pass rolling-pin over lightly, and cut into squares of any desired size. Delicious, if well-made, and always salable.

It is astonishing what vast sums accumulate from the children's pennies spent for candy and sweetmeats. Many cases could be given of persons who have kept small stores, and been supported solely by the little streams of coppers and nickels. Get the children's confidence, learn their names, always have a bright, kind word for them, and bait your hook occasionally with little gifts of sweets. They will flock to you like bees to a flower-garden.

Section 5. Preserves, Pickles, and Jellies.

We put these sweets and sours into one group because they sell best when in proximity. Almost everything depends upon the way they are put up. If the fruit shows artistically through the glass jars, or the pickles are put up attractively in cute little bottles with fresh-painted labels, he must be a stoic indeed who can pass [45] your show-window without a coveting glance. Here are a few of the most popular things in this line:

73. ORANGE MARMALADE.—Take equal weights of sour oranges and sugar. Grate the yellow rind from one fourth of the oranges. Cut all the fruit in halves, pick out the pulp and free it of seeds. Drain off the juice and put it on to boil with the sugar. When it comes to a boil, skim it, and let it simmer for about fifteen minutes; then put in the pulp and grated rind, and boil fifteen minutes longer. Put away in jelly tumblers. Sell large glasses for twenty-five cents; small, for fifteen.

74. BRANDIED PEACH.—The Morris whites are the best. Take off the skins with boiling water. To each pound of fruit allow one pound of sugar, and a half-pint of water to three pounds of sugar. When the syrup is boiling hot put in the peaches, and as fast as they cook take them out carefully and spread on platters. When cool put them in jars and fill up these with syrup, using one-half syrup and one-half pale brandy. This is a very choice brand, and will only pay you where you have customers who are not sparing of their money.

75. OX-HEART CHERRY.—Of showy fruits, none can excel this. To each pound of cherries, allow one-third of a pound of sugar. Put the sugar in the kettle with half a pint of water to three pounds of sugar. Stir it until it is dissolved. When boiling, add the cherries, and cook three minutes. Put up in jars that can be sold for from twenty-five to fifty cents.

76. POUND PEAR.—They hardly weigh a pound a piece, but they look as if they do with their great white [46] bulks pressed up against the sides of the transparent glass. Take the

largest kind, Bartlett, Seckel, or any that have a delicious flavor. Pare the fruit, cut in halves, and throw in cold water. Use one pound of sugar for three of fruit, and one quart of water for three pounds of sugar. When the syrup is boiling take the pears from the water and drop into the syrup. Cook until they can be pierced easily with a silver fork. Fill the jars with fruit, and fill up to the brim with syrup, using a small strainer in the funnel, in order that the syrup may look clear. Sell good-sized jars for fifty cents.

77. GRAPE JELLY.—Jellies in little tumblers take up small room, and they can be grouped in artistic shapes. Here is a good grape: Mash fruit in a kettle, put over the fire, and cook until thoroughly done. Drain through a sieve, but do not press through. To each pint of juice, allow one pound of sugar. Boil rapidly for five minutes. Add the sugar, and boil rapidly three minutes more.

78. SWEET PICKLES—(Apple, Pear, or Peach). For six pounds of fruit, use three of sugar, five dozen cloves and a pint of vinegar. Into each apple, pear, or peach, stick two cloves. Have the syrup hot, and cook until tender. Put up in attractive little jars with colored labels. Jars should sell for twenty-five cents.

79. CHOW-CHOW.—Here is a very taking kind: Take large red-peppers, remove the contents, and fill them with chopped pickles. The red of the peppers against the white of the glass gives a very pretty appearance. Small bottles that can be sold cheap will be the most popular.[47]

80. PICKLED WALNUTS.—Pick out the nuts as nearly whole as possible, and steep in strong brine for a week, then bottle, add spice, and fill with vinegar boiling hot. Put up in very small jars. Have a jar from which to give samples if the dish is not common in the place.

There are a vast number of other fruits, vegetables, and nuts, which you can use as custom shall demand. If you grow your own fruit and do your own work, the result is nearly all profit. If you have to buy the fruit, the selling-price should be such as to give one third profit. This is the per cent. which all manufacturers expect.

Section 6. Toilet Articles.

These have a perennial sale. They are not confined to any season or age. Most of them, especially the French makes, come high, but they are composed of a few simple ingredients, and can be made by any person of ordinary skill. Here are a few of the best selling:

81. ROSE OIL.—Heat dried rose-leaves in an earthenware pipkin, the leaves being covered with olive-oil, and keep hot for several hours. The oil will extract both odor and color. Strain, and put in little cut-glass bottles.

82. COLOGNE WATER.—Take one pint of alcohol, twelve drops each of bergamot, lemon, neroli, sixty drops of lavender, sixty drops of bergamot, sixty drops of essence of lemon, and sixty drops of orange-water, shake well and cork.

83. FRENCH FACE POWDER.—*Poudre de chipre* one and one-half pounds, *eau* (water) of millefleurs one and one-half drachms. Put up in small cut-glass bottles[48] and give it a French name. *Poudre de Millefleurs* will do.

84. NIGHT-BLOOMING CEREUS.—This is a very delicate and fragrant perfume. Spirit of rose 4 ounces, essence of jasmine 4 ounces, tincture of tonka 2 ounces, tincture of civet 2 ounces, tincture of benzoin 4 ounces. Cost $1.65 per pint. Put up in half-gill bottles at fifty cents each, $4.00. Profit, $2.35.

In selling expensive perfumery, remember that the glass is cheaper than the contents, and you should therefore select thick bottles with small cubical space. Tie pretty colored ribbons around the necks of the bottles, and put them, four or six together, in attractive boxes with the lids removed. You must in every way court the patronage of the ladies, and you can in some cases well afford to give a bottle to the leader of a social set with the understanding that she recommend it to her friends.

Section 7. Varnishes and Polishes.

With your plants, meats, preserves, candies, and perfumery, you have already got much beyond your show-window. You now have a "department store" on a small scale, and as you make the goods yourself you ought to be making money. There are some things you can add for which the demand will not be great, but then the cost of making is small. Besides, the goods, put up in bright tin boxes with colored labels and built up in pyramids on your shelves, will give your store an artistic and attractive appearance. Here are a few things that might profitably occupy your spare moments:

85. STOVE BLACKING.—Take half a pound of black[49] lead finely powdered, and mix with the whites of three eggs well-beaten; then dilute it with sour beer or porter till it becomes as thin as shoe-blacking; after stirring it, set it over hot coals to simmer for twenty minutes; then, after it has become cold, box and label.

86. SHOE BLACKING.—Mix six parts of fine bone-black, twenty-eight of syrup or four of sugar, three of train-oil, and one of sulphuric acid. Let the mixture stand for eight hours, then add with vigorous and constant stirring four parts of the decoction of tan, eighteen of bone-black, and three of sulphuric acid, and pour the compound into a little tin boxes. Cost, one cent per box; sell for five cents.

87. FURNITURE CREAM.—Take eight parts of white wax, two of resin, and one pint of true Venice turpentine. Melt at a gentle heat, and pour the warm mass into a stone jar with six

parts of rectified oil of turpentine. After twenty-four hours it should have the consistency of soft butter. Sell in small ten-cent boxes.

88. LEATHER POLISH.—Beat the yolks of two eggs and the white of one; mix a tablespoonful of gin and a teaspoonful of sugar; thicken it with ivory black, add it to the eggs, and use as common blacking. This will give a fine polish to harnesses and leather cushions, and also may be used as a dressing for ladies' shoes.

These are the varnishes and polishes that sell the most readily, but you must not think they will sell without advertisement, recommendation, and display. Label them attractively, and tell just what they will do. It is well to have a little hand press so that you can print your own labels, and also some marking-ink for posters. Use ink freely; and, if you can get the {50} recommendation of some townsman who has tried one of your varnishes or polishes, give it a large display.

Section 8. Soaps and Starches.

Soaps are easily made and very profitable. Several firms have made fortunes in soap during the last few years. You can make just as good an article in your own home and reap all the profits. With starches, take pains to let your customers know that you have different ones for different kinds of goods. Many use the same starch for all kinds of washing. You must show people that your starches are made especially for various kinds of garments, and that the effect will not be so good if the wrong starch is used, or one kind applied indiscriminately to all kinds of goods.

90. GLUE STARCH.—(For calicoes.) Boil a piece of glue, four inches square, in three quarts of water. Put it in a well-corked bottle, and sell for a little more than Poland.

91. GUM ARABIC STARCH.—(For lawns and white muslin.) Pound to a powder two ounces of fine, white gum-arabic; put it into a pitcher, and pour a pint or more of boiling water upon it, and cover it well. Let it stand all night, and in the morning pour it carefully from the dregs into a clean bottle, and cork it tight. Recommend this to your customers, and tell them that {51} a tablespoonful of this stirred into a pint of starch made in the ordinary manner will restore lawns to almost their original freshness.

92. STARCH LUSTER.—This is a substance which, when added to starch, gives the cloth not only a high polish, but a dazzling whiteness. To produce this result, a little piece the size of a copper cent is added to half a pound of starch and boiled with it for two or three minutes. Now we will give you the whole secret. The substance is nothing more than stearine, paraffine, or wax, sometimes colored by a slight admixture of ultramarine blue. You can buy it in quantities for a trifle, and sell it in little balls or wafers at a profit of 500 per cent.

93. HARD SOAP.—Five pails of soft soap, two pounds of salt and one pound of resin. Simmer together and when thoroughly fused turn out in shallow pans so as to be easily cut. This costs little more than the labor and by being able to undersell rivals you should have a monopoly in soap.

94. SAVON D'AMANDE.—This is a celebrated French toilet soap. The recipe is French suet nine parts, olive oil one part, saponified by caustic soda. Toilet soaps are also made of white tallow, olive, almond and palm-oil, soaps either alone or combined in various proportions and scented. The perfume is melted in a bright copper pan by the heat of a water bath.

Section 9. Soft Drinks.

You may now if you have a counter try a few soft drinks. A soda fountain is expensive and perhaps would not pay at this stage, but you might try it when you have more capital and customers. First try.—[52]

95. ROOT BEER.—Get a bottle of the extract, and make it according to the directions. Cost of ten gallons extract and sugar, $1. Put up in pint bottles at five cents a bottle $4. Profit, $3.

96. GINGER POP.—Put into an earthen pot two pounds of loaf sugar, two ounces of cream tartar, two ounces of best ginger bruised, and two lemons cut into slices. Pour over them three gallons of boiling water, when lukewarm, toast a slice of bread, spread it thickly with yeast and put it into the liquor. Mix with it also the whites of two eggs and their crushed shells. Let it stand till next morning. Then strain and bottle. It will be ready for use in three or four days. Profits about the same as the last.

97. LEMONADE AND ORANGEADE.—Get juicy fruit, and allow one orange or lemon to a glass. The tumblers for orangeade should be smaller than those for lemonade. Profits about two and one-half cents a glass.

Have your counter for drinks as near the door as you can. Keep your bottles on ice. Make your lemonade to order, and let it be known that all your beer is home-brewed. Ask your patrons if they like it, and take kindly any suggestions they may make. Let them know you want to please them.

Section 10. Dairy and Other Farm Produce.

If you live in the country, or if your grounds are large enough, you can add immensely to your profits by keeping a cow, a pig, some poultry, and a few hives of bees. You will now need help—a boy to milk your cow, run on errands, and deliver goods; and a girl to help you in the work-room and to assist in the store.[53]

98, Golden Butter; 99, Fresh Eggs; 100, Sweet Milk; 101, Sparkling Honey; 102, New Cheese; and 103, Clean Lard, are among the attractions and the sources of revenue you can add to your already prosperous business. Churn your butter till it is entirely free of the milk, salt it well and put it up in tempting balls, rolls or pats. A little finely-strained carrot-juice will give it a golden color without any disagreeable taste. For poultry, the Wyandottes and Plymouth Rocks are the best year-round layers. Have a sign "Eggs Laid Yesterday," or "This Morning's Eggs." Sell milk by the glass, pint or quart; only be sure it is always fresh. Get a small cheese-press, and if you find a good sale for your cheese, milk, and butter, add to your stock of cows. Find out which of the three dairy products pays the best, and work accordingly. Invite people to taste your good things, and tell them that everything is homemade and fresh. Bees are perhaps the most profitable things in the world, as they entail no expense after the first outfit. Have honey both strained and in the comb as you learn the wants of your patrons. The pig will keep you in meat a large portion of the year, besides supplying to your store a limited quantity of nice white-leaf lard, which should be sold in little bright tin pails.

104. White Pork.—If you do not care for swine's flesh, you can sell it for from twelve to twenty cents a pound. People are glad to buy fresh-killed meat and to pay a good price for it when their ordinary purchases have been many days slaughtered, and often freighted a thousand miles.

105. Poultry to Order.—Do not keep your hens beyond the second year, as they are not so good layers[54] after that age. Have always a stock of fat fowls ready for market. Spring Chickens. Here is another line in which you can invest. A chick costs in feed about twenty-five cents for the season, and they sell readily for a dollar a pair.

Section 11. Garden Vegetables.

If you have a small garden, you can supply your store with fresh vegetables during the season. It is very important that they should be fresh. Having your own garden, you can guarantee that quality to your customers. Take orders for the following day so that the vegetables may come straight from the garden into the hands of the consumer. Here are the six which grocers say sell for the largest profit.

106. Cut-to-Order Asparagus.—Asparagus is at least one-half better when newly cut. Choose the white variety, and tie in small bunches. Sell at fifteen cents a bunch.

107. Quick Market Strawberries.—Pick them fresh every morning. Put them in the usual boxes, and set them on a stand in front of the store. Have one or two large ones on the top of each box, and lay around them two or three strawberry leaves wet with dew.

108. Round Tomatoes.—If possible, have them so fine and large that five will fill a quart box. Sold even as low as five cents a box they are very profitable. This is at the rate of a penny apiece, and a thrifty tomato plant will bear fifty.

109. PINT PEAS.—Peas in the pod are not attractive, but very young peas when shelled and put in little [55] bright tin pails are irresistible. The very sight of them tickles the palate. Rise early, and pick and shell a pint of peas. If they do not sell, you can have them for your own dinner. Do not keep them overnight, as the succulent quality is soon lost after shelling.

110. STRING BEANS.—Nothing easier to raise, nothing easier to sell. You can raise a bushel on a square rod if properly managed. Sell at fifteen cents a half-peck.

111. GREEN CORN.—Sell at twenty-five cents a dozen ears. Be careful to pick before the kernels become large. Have a notice, "Corn Picked to Order."

We have found out from the grocers what garden products sell the best. Now, suppose you have only a single rod of ground (about the size of a large room), and want to know how to plant it to the best advantage. Below will be found a comparative table of what, under generous cultivation, may be expected of each of the above in the way of hard cash from a single rod of soil.

Asparagus (40 bunches at 15 cents a bunch), $6.00; strawberries (33 baskets at 15 cents a basket), $4.95; tomatoes (150 quarts at 5 cents a quart), $7.50; peas (16 pints at 25 cents a pint), $4.00; beans (1 bushel at 15 cents half-peck), $1.20; corn (8 dozen ears at 25 cents a dozen), $2.00.

If you have twenty square rods instead of one, your revenue from your garden may be increased by that multiple, and you will have an opportunity to try all the above sources of profit. Find out what fruits and vegetables sell best in your neighborhood, and plant accordingly. And remember that the key to your success in garden produce is the single word *fresh*. [56]

Section 12. School Supplies.

There are a number of articles in use in our schools which can be made at home. Once let it be known that you can make and sell as good a quality as the imported article, and at a cheaper price, and you will have the patronage of all the schools in your vicinity. Advertise wisely, and in cases where the trustees furnish the things, make a low bid for the entire school supply.

112. BOOK COVERS.—Save all your paper bags, iron them out smoothly, and make them into book covers. Sell them at three cents apiece, or take the contract to cover all the books in the school at two cents apiece.

113. ARTIFICIAL SLATES.—Take forty-one parts of sand, four parts of lampblack, four parts of boiled linseed or cottonseed oil. Boil thoroughly, and reduce the mixture by adding spirits of turpentine so that it may be easily applied to a thin piece of pasteboard. Give three coats, drying between each coat. Finish by rubbing smooth with a piece of cotton

waste soaked in spirits of turpentine. You have an excellent slate or memorandum book, which may be sold for ten cents. Use a slate pencil. Made in large quantities, these are very profitable.

114. CHEAP INK.—Boil one and a half pounds of logwood with sufficient residue water to leave a residue of two and a half quarts. When cold, add one and a half drams of yellow bichromate of potash, and stir thoroughly, and the ink is ready for use. The above will fill twenty-five large ink bottles, which, at five cents apiece, come to $1.25. Cost, 25 to 35 cents.

115. SCHOOL BAG.—Take a piece of cheap white[57] linen and make it into a pretty bag, with a strap to go over the shoulder. Have a colored stamp to put on the initials of the purchaser. Sell for twenty-five cents.

116. PEN WIPER.—Take any cheap material, and cut in three circles of different sizes. Scallop the edges, and stitch together at the center. If the circles are of different color as well as size, it will be attractive to the children, and still more so if the smallest circle has an initial letter. Sell for five cents.

117. CHILDREN'S LUNCHEON.—Thousands of parents would rather pay a trifling sum than be put to the trouble of providing and preparing lunch. Make a little repast cheap and neat. One large or two small sandwiches, a small dish of jelly or a tart, a pickle or a piece of cake. Put in a collapsible paper box, and tie with red or blue ribbon. Cost about six or seven cents. Sell for ten cents.

Section 13. Christmas Presents.

You can do well with these if you are supple with your fingers and nimble with your tongue. Learn what artistic designs are becoming popular, and keep abreast of the latest fads. The fabric called denim is coming more into use every year, and as it is very cheap, and comes in all colors, it is especially suited for making, covering, and adorning all kinds of household handiwork. A ramble through the large metropolitan stores with a request to see the various lines of goods used for trimming and ornamenting will astonish you. The endless varieties of silks, satins, velvets, plushes, linens, laces, feathers, and so forth, should suggest to a lively mind infinite possibilities in the way of made-up articles of market value. Our list below must be taken[58] only as samples of what a fertile mind and ingenious fingers can accomplish.

118. SOFA PILLOW.—Take a piece of India silk of different colors, and let them all taper to a common center upon which a monogram is worked. Relieve the bareness of the white by a running vine and morning glories. A pillow of this kind which cost $3 sold for $8. The varieties of the sofa pillow are almost endless. Get a book of designs and learn to make the Organdy, Butterfly, Duck, Clover, Daisy, Cretonne, Yacht, Mull, Poppy, and many others.

119. JEWEL TRAY.—Cut a circle of delicate écru linen twenty-two inches in circumference, and sew a piece of bonnet wire around it, notching or looping it so as to give an escaloped edge. Have a pretty little motto in the center, and fill the remaining space with snowdrops worked in ivory white, each tiny petal tipped with pale green, and with a long green stem. When properly worked, this is very pretty, and ought to command a good price.

120. AMERICAN FLAG.—Make it five feet in length by three in width, and smaller flags in the same proportion. There should be seven stripes of red bunting, six of white, and a field of blue. On this field stitch forty-five stars of white. Face the inside of the flag with a piece of strong canvas for the admission of the pole. If the stars are of silk, the price should be at least twice that of linen.

121. HAIR-PIN CASE.—Cut a piece of fine white duck in the shape of a square envelope and embroider upon the flap any simple design in wash silk. Close with button and buttonhole. Sell for fifty cents. {59}

122. CHAIR CUSHION.—Take blue denim with dark and light shades happily combined. Let the tint of pale blue be appliqued on, and then worked in different shades of this color with rope floss in long and short stitch. The back may be of plain denim unadorned.

123. LAMP SHADE.—You can get a dozen skeleton frames for a few cents, and French crêpe paper which costs little, and your own cultivated taste and deft fingers will do the rest. A cheap kaleidoscope will suggest an infinite number of designs. One lady made an elegant shade at a cost of $2.50, and sold it for $6.00.

124. BOOK-MARK.—Silk, worsted, and two hours of spare time will give you a pretty book-mark which should sell for fifty cents, at a cost of making (time not reckoned) of only fifteen cents.

125. HANDY WORK-BOX.—Take a pasteboard box and line with denim. Include a tiny pin-cushion, scissors-case, thimble-holder, needle-book, flap, and spool wires.

126. PIN-CUSHION.—Always popular, but the form changes every season. Cover with silk or satin, and overlay with strips of fine linen embroidered in festoons of tiny blossoms. Border with ruffle of lace, and put small rosettes of baby ribbon at the corners.

127. CATCH-BAG.—A convenient receptacle for laundry, schoolbooks, shoes, and many other articles. It should be in envelope form, the dimensions eighteen by twelve. The material may be white linen, upon which you should work a gold border. Make an attachment for hanging on the wall. {60}

128. COURT-PLASTER CASE.—Cut two circles of celluloid two inches in diameter, and four other circles of thin drawing-paper for inside leaves. In these little pockets place pieces of court-plaster, pink, white and black, cut into strips or squares, and held flat and stationary by having their comers thrust into slits cut in the paper. Punch holes in the left

side of the case, and tie with baby-ribbon. Paint or work on outside cover a design of burrs with "I cling to thee," or a design of beggar-ticks with "I stick to thee."

129. POSTAGE-STAMP HOLDER.—Same as above except that the shape is square.

130. PHOTOGRAPH FRAME.—Take a piece of stout pasteboard and turn down the corners. Cut the inside to the proper size, and stitch a piece of chamois over the pasteboard. Tie bits of colored ribbon on the corners. Sell for twenty-five cents.

131. MATCH-SAFE.—Cover a tin box of any shape with one of the lesser inflammable materials such as chamois, and on the front attach a piece of match-paper. Sell for ten or fifteen cents.

132. WALL-POCKET.—Take bamboo sticks or thin strips of wood, and glue them together in the form of a pocket-frame. The sticks should be about two inches apart and the outer lattice-work a little lower than the inner. Wind colored ribbons around the sticks, and have a circular head-piece for attachment to the wall.

133. GLOVE-BOX.—(Easter present). Cover a flat pasteboard box with pale gray linen or delicate blue. Work a spray of passion-flowers on the top, inclosing some suitable motto.

Christmas presents should be in the store at least {61} three weeks before the holidays. As many donors like to attach the initials of the recipient to the present, have prettily worked letters for that purpose, and charge ten cents a letter. Be careful to inform all possible customers of this arrangement, as many will be attracted by that feature. Call attention to this class of goods when your patrons are buying other kinds of your wares, and be always eager to show your latest designs. Remember that taste in this department is as important as the word fresh in Section 10.

Section 14. Miscellaneous Articles.

Here are a few other things to complete the list of one hundred which you can make in your own home. You will discover many others for yourself as your trade increases, and your friends make suggestions. The secret of success is to find out what people want, and then give them a better and cheaper article than they can get elsewhere. You will find your customers' wants changing according to the season or the newest fad. Things which you expected to sell will often be left on your hands. You must be prepared to take advantage of this. Drop the price when the demand falls, and always have in your mind some new article of home manufacture to take the place of that whose popularity is waning. Keep eyes and ears strained for the newest thing. As it was said of a certain burglar that he never saw a lock without the thought, "How can I pick it?" so you should never witness the sale of any article without the query, "How can I make it?" The following are easily made, and some of them very profitable:

134. Hot Gems.—If you can work up a demand for hot gems, you can make a good profit. Take a pint[62] each of flour and milk, an egg, and half a teaspoonful of salt. Beat the egg until light, add the milk and salt to it, and beat gradually into the flour. Bake twenty minutes in hot gem-pans. The quantities given will make a dozen gems. Notice should be given of the hour of the day when they may be expected to be fresh from the oven. Charge twenty-five cents a dozen.

135. Sliced Watermelon.—Nothing so delights the heart of a boy. Cut a large ripe melon into half-slices, rather thick, and lay them on ice in the show window. Cost of melon and ice, fifty cents. Twenty slices at five cents each, $1. Profit, one-half.

136. Toothsome Pies.—Roll two strips of paste for the upper and lower crusts. Place the latter in position after moistening the plate, and fill with the prepared material already sweetened and seasoned. Lay on the upper crust, and make a little slit in the center. Put in hot oven, close draft after fifteen minutes, and bake from fifty minutes to one hour. Charge twenty-five cents for good deep pies.

137. Ice Cream.—You can do well with this in warm weather, if you have a room suitable for serving. One pint of sugar, one of water, and three of cream, the yolks of five eggs and a large tablespoonful of the flavoring extract. Boil the sugar and water twenty-five minutes. Beat the eggs with one fourth of a teaspoonful of salt. Place the basin of boiling syrup in another of boiling water, and, stirring the yolks of the eggs into the syrup, beat rapidly for three minutes. Take the basin from the fire, place it in a pan of ice water, and beat until cold. Add the cream and extract, and, placing the mixture in the freezer, pack around[63] with ice, alternating with thin layers of salt. Turn the crank until the cream is frozen hard.

138. Pork and Beans.—You can make a large profit on pork and beans in places where there is a demand for them. Both are cheap, and you can make a handsome profit on a dish selling for thirty-five cents, the dish to be returned. It is well if you can to make a bargain to supply families once a week on particular days. This dish takes well in all parts of New England.

139. Tomato Ketchup.—Raising your own tomatoes, you can make it at a trifling cost, and reap a profit at ten cents for small bottles. For twelve ripe, peeled tomatoes, take two large onions, four green peppers, and chop fine. Add two tablespoonfuls of salt, two of brown sugar, two of ginger, one of cinnamon, one of mustard, a nutmeg, grated; and four cupfuls of vinegar. Boil all together for three hours, stirring frequently, and bottle while hot.

140. Mince Meat.—Many housekeepers prefer to buy the preparation rather than to be at the trouble of making it. Lean beef, two pounds; beef suet, one pound; apples, five pounds; seeded raisins, two pounds; currants, two pounds; citron, three-fourths of a pound; pounded mace and pounded cinnamon, two tablespoonfuls each; one of grated

nutmeg; one each of cloves and allspice; brown sugar two and one-half pounds; sherry wine, one quart; brandy, one pint. Put up in three-pound cans. The compound should make six cans, and you should charge seventy-five cents a can for so choice a product. You can reduce the expense, if your customers wish a cheaper article.｛64｝

141. DRIED APPLES.—If you have a few apple trees, you will often find it more profitable to dry for future sale than to sell the green fruit. Pare, core, and slice. Lay the slices in shallow pans or on clean boards, and expose to the air until thoroughly dried. Then pack and store for the winter market. You should get at least ten cents a pound.

142. PEANUTS.—No risk of loss on these for they will always sell. Buy from a shipper or wholesale grocer a bag of peanuts and roast them in the oven until they are a fine brown, taking care not to burn. Profits in a bag of peanuts selling at five cents, one-half pint, 100 per cent.

143. CIGARETTES.—Roll a pinch of tobacco in a piece of white paper and scent with any agreeable perfume. More profit than in cigars.

144. TALLOW CANDLES.—Still used in the country, and to some extent by poor people in the city. Take beef and mutton suet in the proportion of one to two. Melt, and fill tin molds in which the wick has been previously inserted. The cost is little beyond the work. Charge twenty-five cents per dozen.

145. LUNG PRESERVER.—(Rock and Rye). Here is the secret of this popular remedy for coughs, colds and lung troubles. Rye whisky, three gallons; syrup, made of rock candy, one gallon. Cost of whiskey and syrup, $3.50. Put up in pint bottles at fifty cents each, $16. Profits, $12.50, or nearly 300 per cent.

146. POISON KILLER.—You may not sell much of this, but it is a useful article to have in the house, and｛65｝ will keep indefinitely. Buy a quantity of powder of aristol, and put it in small pepper-boxes, or in any box with a perforated lid, holding a few ounces. Dust the affected part freely with this, and the effect on the poisoned flesh will be magical. Use for any inflammation. Advertise it in placards.

147. MUCILAGE.—Dissolve gum-arabic in water until the whole is of the consistency of cream, and keep it from contact with the air. Add a few drops of sweet oil to prevent it from souring. The cost is almost nothing. You can sell it at five cents a bottle.

148. POP CORN.—Use a large popper, and when the corn comes out white and hot, add a little molasses to make it adhere, and flavor with some popular extract. Mold it in balls, rectangles, or in any other fancy shape. A bushel of shelled corn which costs a dollar will make 125 balls. These at five cents apiece come to $6.25.

This completes the list of one hundred articles for your store. Observe that they are all made at home, and for that reason the profits are from 50 to 500 per cent., while in the ordinary way of buying from the wholesaler the storekeeper has to be satisfied with from

10 to 20 per cent. You will discover for yourself many other articles which can be made at home and sold at a profit, and you will not confine yourself to homemade goods, but will handle anything for which there is a demand whether you can make it yourself or not. Of course, if you make all the above goods, you will need much help, the cost of which will diminish somewhat the profits, but the design is that you begin on a modest scale, at first doing all the manufacturing yourself, and call in assistance as your business and capital grow. In writing this chapter the author has contemplated a [66] lady as keeping a store of this kind, but a gentleman can do much of the work as well, and some sections of it better. Perhaps the ideal store would be that kept by husband and wife with growing children to assist. Now let us have the experience of a lady who has tried our plan.

Mrs. J—— G—— says: "By the death of my husband I was left alone with three children, Wilhelm fifteen, Gertrude thirteen, and Egbert ten. I had no means, though, fortunately, my little place in the suburban town of T—— was free of debt. It consisted of a neat house and three acres of land. Having a fondness for plants, I cultivated them in curious ways, while keeping my little family together by taking in sewing. One day a lady who was spending the summer in T—— called and inquired what I would take for a pea vine which was growing in a tumbler of water. I was surprised, as I had not thought of making merchandise of my plant pets. She purchased a number of pretty little odd things of vegetable life with which I had amused myself, and suggested that I might earn something by cultivating rare forms of plants. It was a new idea to me. I had not thought there was any money in what had been to me only a pastime, but I increased the number of my plant curiosities, and the lady and her friends bought them all.

"Then my friend said to me, 'Why don't you keep a Home Store? You have so much taste I think you would do nicely?' 'And pray what is a Home Store?' I inquired. 'Oh, it's a store where the things are all made at home.' 'But I have no capital.' 'You need no capital. See, the things are all made at home. Begin with a few tea dishes.' So I bought a ham, sliced it thin, and laid some sprigs of parsley around it. I also made some artificial honey from a recipe in an old cook book. With the money I thus [67] earned, I had my window enlarged into a show-window, and put in a variety of vegetables from my garden, taking care they should be strictly fresh every day. I had such success that, at the suggestion of my lady patron, I began to make a great many other things—pastry, preserves, sweetmeats, and toilet articles. I also purchased one hundred fowls, and served my customers with fresh eggs. My trade grew so that I decided to have a real store, and so, at an expense of about $50, I had my two front rooms made into one and fitted up with shelves and counters. I purchased a cow and a pig on credit, and also two or three hives of bees. The people seemed to appreciate my fresh eggs, milk, butter and honey, and I soon paid all my debts and branched out in several other directions in the way of homemade goods. Hitherto, my three children had afforded me all the help I

49

needed, but now I found it necessary to employ a cheap male laborer to look after my garden, orchard, cow, pig, and poultry, as well as to assist in making some of my goods. I made a great variety of things as new suggestions came to me almost daily, and also, as my customers called for them, I bought what I could not well make myself. Now, after three years' experience, I think I have the most profitable store of its size that can be found anywhere. Here is my account for last year:

ARTICLES.		COST.	SALES.	PROFITS.
Household plants	Seeds	$ .90	$15.25	$14.35
Table dishes	Meats, etc.	12.59	36.94	24.35
Pastry	Materials	53.36	166.05	112.69
Nuts and candy	"	61.66	379.22	317.56
Preserves, etc	"	12.10	49.75	37.65
Toilet articles	"	9.05	19.05	10.00
Varnishes and soaps	"	3.18	15.50	12.32
Soft drinks	"	5.15	31.55	26.40
Vegetables	Seeds	2.50	37.27	34.77
School supplies	Materials	3.70	13.71	10.01
Christmas presents	"	5.25	48.13	42.88
Eggs, honey and the dairy	Keeping stock	75.50	217.00	141.50
Miscellaneous articles	Materials	55.05	291.15	236.10
Goods bought	Price paid	473.02	551.10	78.08
		$773.01	$1,871.67	$1,098.66

{68}

"Deduct from the above the wages of laborer at $20 per month, $240, and I have left $858.66 as net profit for my year's work. The fruit for the preserves and pies was raised on the place, and I was under no expense for tin and paper boxes, these being collected from the houses of my friends. It will be seen that nearly one-third of the sales of my 'Home Store' were of purchased goods on which the profit were only 15 per cent., but so large was the profit on the homemade goods that the total sales were at the gratifying advance of 80 per cent. Besides, I have had the living of my family and hired help. The expense for meats not furnished on the place, and for groceries not kept in the store, together with that for clothes, taxes, and sundries, was $316.05. Thus, I have paid all my expenses, and saved $540 for a rainy day. Pretty good, don't you think, for a woman, and a novice at that? Of course, I have worked hard, sometimes as many as fifteen hours a day, but I have enjoyed it, and think I am on the way to a snug little fortune. Others with more talents, and under more favorable circumstances, I have no doubt could do much better.

"The secrets of my success, if you ask me, are: First, the trading instinct, or the knowing what, where, and when to buy. (I never let myself get out of a stock article). Second, courtesy to all—to the little barefoot colored boy just the same as to the grand madam. Third, economy, both in my family expenses, buying only what I need, and in my store, using in other ways that which will not sell in the original form, throwing nothing away unless it is spoiled and even that giving, as a last resort, to my pig and poultry; and fourth, hard work, making and selling with my own hands everything I can, and carefully superintending everything I cannot." {69}

CHAPTER   VI.

MONEY IN THE HOME ACRE.

Money at Home—What a Single Acre Will Do—Gold in the Soil—How a Dike Made a Klondike—$1,000 at Your Back Door—Nickels in Pickles! Livings in Pickings!—A Fortune in a Fat Slice of Earth—A Great (Grate) Way to Make Money.

THERE are multitudes of people who have a single acre of ground which could be made to yield much profit if they knew how to handle it. Others have an half or a quarter of an acre; not enough, perhaps, to give them a support, but which would add very materially to their income if properly cultivated. In this chapter we tell you what to do with the "home acre," with examples of what others have done with it.

149. MONEY IN PEARS.—Do you know that one acre of the best yielding pear trees will bring more profit than a five-hundred acre farm without a twentieth of the care or capital?

150. GREENBACKS IN GREENINGS.—It is a fact that forty apple trees of the R. H. Greening variety on a single acre have yielded a crop worth $400.

151. PLUMS OF GOLD.—A widow has in her garden twelve plum trees from which she regularly receives $60 a year.

152. THE RASPBERRY ACRE.—"There are repeated{70} instances of $400 and even $600 being made clear from a single acre of raspberries." See Morris' "Ten Acres Enough."

153. PROFITS IN BIG PEACHES.—When ordinary peaches were selling at 25 cents a bushel, a grower received $2 a bushel. This is how he did it. When the fruit was as large as a hickory nut, he employed a large force of laborers and picked off more than one-half the fruit. The rest ripened early, grew large, and were of excellent quality. His net profit that year from eleven acres was between $3,000 and $4,000.

154. EASY TOMATOES.—An easy crop, requiring little care. Says a grower in New Jersey: "My single acre of tomatoes netted a clear profit of $120. I am aware that others have realized more than double this sum, but they were experienced hands, while I was new

to the business." Four hundred dollars per acre has frequently been realized from this crop. One person had four acres from which he received from $1,500 to $2,000 annually.

155. ASSORTED STRAWBERRIES.—Here is the experience of a novice: "I ran a ditch through my wet and almost worthless meadow land, and set it out with strawberry plants. The second year I had an enormous crop. The larger berries were separated from the smaller, and the show thus made by the assorted fruit was magnificent. For 600 quarts I received $300, it being a little early for strawberries in the New York market." It pays to grow early and large fruit.

156. LIVINGS IN LETTUCE.—Fifteen thousand heads can be set upon an acre. These at the average price[71] of $1.50 per hundred means $225 per acre. Five acres of this crop should give a fair-sized family a good living. It is an auxiliary crop and may be sowed between heads of cabbage.

157. SOVEREIGNS IN SPINACH.—There are few more important crops in market. It requires little labor, can be cultivated evenings and mornings by a busy man, and pays about $75 an acre.

158. THOUSAND-DOLLAR CELERY.—Celery may be grown as a second crop after beets, onions, or peas are cleared up. A little reckoning in the number of heads per acre shows that if the grower could get the consumer's price of eight or ten cents a head, it would yield a clear profit of $1,000.

159. FORTUNES IN WATER-CRESS.—"I have no doubt," says a large grower, "that in situations where irrigation could be used at pleasure, or regular plantations made as for cranberries, judging from the enormous price water-cress sells at, picked as it is in the present haphazard way, an acre would sell for $4,000 or $5,000."

160. THE DOLLAR BLACKBERRY.—When the Lawton first came out, so great was the praise of it and the rush to obtain it that many roots were sent through the mail at $1 apiece, and the lucky discoverer netted a small fortune. But any grower has the same chances to discover a new variety, or to improve on his present stock.

161. NICKELS IN PICKLES.—Do you know that the enormous number of 150,000 cucumbers may be easily grown on an acre of land, and that at the low price of[72] $1.50 per thousand this means $225 per acre? The crop also is very easily raised.

162. THE BEET LOT.—You can grow 80,000 roots per acre even when sown a foot apart, yet at $1 per hundred, deducting one-half for expenses, there still results a net value of $400.

163. THE ROASTING EAR.—You can plant an acre of sweet corn, realize $100 for it, clear it off in August, sow the cleared ground with turnip seed, and from the second crop reap another $100.

164. PAYING PEAS.—They are the early kind, marketed before the price falls. If grown under glass so as to be crowded on the market in early June, they will bring $4 a bushel, and at that rate an acre will mean $400. If delayed a month, they will not bring a quarter of that sum.

165. GRATED HORSERADISH.—The root is very easily raised, requires little cultivation, but is quite profitable. Grate finely and put in attractive white bottles with red labels. Give it some fancy name, as "Red Orchard," or "Spring Valley." "Little Neck" clams got their reputation largely in this way. Sell for ten cents a bottle.{73}

CHAPTER VII.

MONEY FOR WOMEN.

One Hundred Ways a Woman Can Earn a Living—A New Way to Remember Your Friends—The Woman with a Pet Dog—Solving the Servant-girl Question—Shopping for Pleasure and Profit—Profits of a Lady Barber—The Business of "Samples"—The Rise of the Trained Nurse—Dollars in Scents—How to Go to Paris Without Cost—Something that will Sell to Millions of Shoppers—How Clara Louise Kellog Got a Start—A Woman Who Sold her Jewels for Newspapers—Women in the Civil Service.

THE field of woman's work has been vastly augmented during the last half-century. From school teaching and dressmaking, which were about the only occupations open to our grandmothers, the number of ways a woman can make a living have increased to over two hundred. To be exact, there are two hundred and twenty-one occupations open to women, out of a total of two hundred and fifty. It is the design of the author to give only those methods which are unique, unusual, and presumably unknown to most lady readers. In a few cases these money-making methods must be considered as only tributary to a larger source of revenue, as when a salaried position or business enterprise is not sufficient for a support, or when a woman wishes to help the family "eke out a living," but in most cases it is expected that the suggestions if followed will be an adequate source of income. Several of these ways may often be united where one is insufficient. There is no need for any woman to marry for the sake of a{74} home. The examples given will enable any lady of the least tact, skill, or enterprise, to secure an independent living.

166. THE SCHOOL STORE.—If you live near a public school, a small store containing candies, school supplies and knickknacks for the children will be found to bring much profit. The store need not be large or conspicuous. A room in a private house will do. Children, like bees, are all fond of sweets. The store need be open only for an hour in the morning, or noon, and at the close of school, so that other work may be carried on at the

same time. A dressmaker, with hours arranged so as not to conflict, could combine very well these two ways of earning a living.

167. THE HAND ALBUM.—Have an album made in usual style, except that the places for pictures are omitted. Smear each page with soft wax to the depth of one-sixth of an inch. When a friend calls, slightly heat a page and request him to lay his hands, palms down, upon it. In that way you can preserve the digits of your friends, and you will be surprised to find there is as much difference in hands as in faces. When your album is full, if you choose you can consult a patent lawyer, and arrange to protect your invention. A novelty of this kind would doubtless be immensely popular, and enable the author to reap a financial harvest.

168. THE NOVELTY BAKERY.—A woman who knows how to make tempting creations in flour can make a good living. Begin by taking your goods to the Woman's Exchange, of which almost every large city has at least one. If your baking is novel, from the Exchange{75} will come demands from private customers, and even orders from hotels. A New England woman, beginning in a small way, in a few months had an income of $33 per week.

169. THE FRONT YARD SNAP.—With a photographer's outfit, go through the better class residential sections of a city or town and take the pictures of the children which you will see in every street, and in almost every front yard. Get a child in a most striking position, on a wheel, or in a swing or hammock, or at play. Secure parent's consent to take the picture. No matter if they declare that they will not purchase, they will yield when they see a pretty picture of their child. Much money can be made at this.

170. THE PET DOG.—Do you know that pet dogs often bring enormous prices? You want the Yorkshire terriers, or the King Charles spaniels, or some of the rare Japanese breeds. A lady in New York counts on $500 yearly as the income from the families raised from one dog, a King Charles spaniel.

171. THE BOX LUNCH.—There is a large field for some one to cultivate in our great office buildings and factories. Thousands would pay for a light lunch which costs five cents, and is sold for ten cents. Rent a small room near a business center. Make known your occupation. Go through the places of business if possible, or if not take a stand near the door, and if your lunch is tastefully arranged, it will find many buyers. After a time you will get regular customers. Profits 100 per cent.

172. THE HAIR-DRESSER.—A refined business for{76} women is the dressing of hair. For $25 you can learn the business. Place samples of all kinds of bangs and switches in the window. They can be sold for a great profit, and if industrious, you can build up in a good neighborhood an excellent paying business, and best of all, it can be done in your own home.

173. TYPO AND STENO.—In many large cities typewriting and stenography may be learned in the Y. W. C. A. Then with a machine and a rented room cheaply furnished a woman is all ready for business. Many women are making $25 per week. One enterprising young lady takes dictated matter in short hand, and then typewrites it at her leisure, thus saving much time to her busy patrons.

174. THE SEWING SCHOOL.—Here is a vast unworked field. If you understand needlework, and have a little business enterprise, you are certain to succeed. Advertise in the papers and get out circulars, stating that for the small sum of twenty-five cents per week you will teach all pupils plain and fancy sewing. Form your pupils into classes, and if you are gentle and patient, as well as skillful at the needle, you will in a short time have the work which mothers are glad to get rid of. And it can all be done in your own home.

175. FLAT HUNTING.—Rent a small office and advertise that for a trifling fee you will exactly suit persons looking for homes, and save them all the trouble. Three or four hours a day are spent in house-hunting, and two in the office. You must have a book with your customers' demands set down in detail, and another book with a careful description of each house to let. A commission might be exacted from both owner and[77] renter. An enterprising woman could in a short time build up a large business in this way.

176. A TEA ROOM.—Hire a counter in a fashionable store much frequented by ladies. Have a sign that fresh tea is sold here, made to order with good cream. Small accessories may be fresh rolls, toasted crumpets, bread and butter, and other light articles of food. Ladies weary with shopping will surely come to your counter to be refreshed. A lady in one of our large cities made a fortune by this means. The requirements are dazzling cleanliness, a smiling welcome, a cheerful place near the door, and hot, fresh tea.

177. DRESS MENDING.—Here is a good field. There is a vast army of women who would patronize a mending office rather than run around the city to find a sewing woman, or use their own limited time in the use of the needle. Have a tariff of prices for mending gloves, sewing on buttons, renewing the sleeves, putting braid around the bottom of dresses, etc. The right woman could earn a good living at this business.

178. LACE HANDLING.—The mending and washing of fine laces is a work that is given to experts, and commands high prices, yet is easily learned. In five lessons at a dollar apiece any lady of ordinary intelligence can learn, or, cheaper yet, one can sometimes give services in return for instruction. You are then in a position to earn a great deal of money. Issue a thousand circulars to the wealthier people of the city, letting them know of your enterprise. This plan combines the three advantages of fascinating employment, good pay, and work done at home.[78]

179. INTELLIGENCE OFFICE on the subscription plan.—Buy a copy of the "Social Register;" send circulars to all persons named therein; announce that you have opened an intelligence office on a new plan. For $10 a year you will keep them supplied with as

many servants as they want, and you will guarantee satisfaction. Make a specialty of securing servants for people going out of town. Thus you will go far toward solving the perplexing question for your patrons, and make an excellent living for yourself.

180. PROFESSIONAL MENDING.—Hotels, boarding houses and bachelor apartments have loud and long calls for mending. Mothers with little ones, professional women, and school-teachers, as well as men, have neither time nor taste for this kind of work. Have an outfit in a small satchel, which should contain a light lunch, a white apron, and various assortments of tapes, buttons, etc. In a short time one would have a regular round of customers. One lady who did this never had to go out of one large hotel for work.

181. THE COLLEGE CRAM.—There is room for a lady with a knowledge of the classics and a faculty for teaching to take boys and young men and carry them over the hard spots in their education. These hard spots, which are known as examinations, conditions, etc., are the bane and bugbear of many a young man's education. In one town a lady earns $100 per month by taking pupils through the intricacies of algebra and Latin.

182. SHOE AND WRAP ROOM.—A room in some fashionable quarter where ladies could go after a journey on the cars and have the dust brushed off their wraps [79] and their shoes polished would doubtless prove remunerative.

183. GENERAL CONVENIENCE ROOM.—The last idea might be combined with this. Have a room in which, for the charge of a dime, one could get a glass of ice-water, could read the morning paper, have his clothes brushed, and look over a map of the city or a directory, and have all the advantages of a toilet room.

184. SICK-ROOM DELICACIES.—Another unoccupied field is the preparation of delicacies for the sick. Bouillon, chocolate, jellies and many other kinds of delicacies could be prepared and placed in a show window in some fashionable part of the town. The conditions of success are exquisite neatness and daintiness. It would pay well, for people stop at no cost in providing for their sick friends.

185. SHOPPING COMMISSION.—If you live at a little distance from the city, a good business may be built up by shopping for your friends and neighbors. By dint of experience you know where to buy, and when your practice is built up you can buy cheaper by reason of larger purchases, and you can give both of these advantages to your patrons. Many women might find here both a congenial and profitable field.

186. SCHOOL LUNCHEON.—Here is another good field. Tens of thousands of schoolchildren have to eat a cold luncheon. Rent a small room near a schoolhouse, and provide bouillon, clam and chicken soups, sandwiches, baked beans, lamb pies, with white and brown bread, plain cake and fruit. You will help to preserve the digestion of myriads of children, as well as fill your own pocket with cash. [80]

187. HATCHING BIRDS.—Buy half a dozen songsters at $1.50 apiece, the females at half that price. Get proper cages, mate the birds, provide soft nests made chiefly of cotton; and with care you can do an excellent business. Birds in good condition mate two or three times a year. One lady, with eighteen pairs of canary birds netted $500 a year.

188. BUTTER AND EGG STORE.—Butter and eggs are two things which every housekeeper wants fresh, but which are difficult to obtain. Get some reliable farmer to supply you at stated dates, and procure a list of customers. Then with a boy to deliver and a push cart for the merchandise, you have little to do but figure your profits. An advantage of this plan is that it gives you the most of your time for other work. The business may be extended almost *ad infinitum*.

189. SARATOGA CHIPS.—These are a sample of what may be done with a single good article by one who knows how. One family has a weekly income of $12.50 from this means.

190. FANCY LAMP SHADES.—Made of crêpe papers they are very cheap, and look almost as well as silk. Any woman of ordinary ability can make them, and they sell readily. She can buy for sixty cents material for a shade which she can sell for $1.25, thus more than doubling her money.

191. BEE-KEEPING.—This is another means of large profit. It can be carried on even in a city where there is a small plot of ground. Fill all the space not occupied by the hives with white clover and such other flowers as your study of bees will tell you they delight in.[81] Buy a book about bees. The advantage of this industry is that the cost of supporting the bees is practically nothing. There is no risk. After the first small expenditure of capital for boxes and hives all is profit.

192. CLEANSING AND BLEACHING.—There are many things too costly to be intrusted to an ordinary washerwoman, and many other cleansing processes that do not come within that woman's sphere. Cleaning feathers, velvets, furs, gloves, silks, and many other articles afford a wide opportunity for one who understands the business. Who can take grease spots from carpets, fruit stains from napkins and table covers, paint from windows, thumb-marks from books, and scratches from furniture? Here is a useful field.

193. FANCY SOAPS.—Fortunes have been made from fancy soaps. The process of making is easy, and the variety of method is so great, and the possible ingredients so many, that there need be no danger of infringing on anyone's trademark. Get a recipe-book and practice on the kinds given in the formulas; then branch out into new kinds. The sale will depend upon your ability. Give your product an attractive appearance.

194. HOME ARCHITECTURE.—Write to the secretaries or agents of church building societies. Many of these societies publish pamphlets, in which, in addition to the designs for churches, will be found many cuts for pretty little parsonages. From these you can compile an attractive little book of home architecture, which would sell to every person

contemplating building a home; and almost every one living in a rented house hopes some day to rear his own domicile. If you have a (82) friend who is an architect, he would procure for you other books of plans.

195. HOME ORNAMENTS.—What is a home without at least a few trifling ornaments? An inventive mind can think of a hundred inexpensive ways of beautifying a room. But most people are not inventive. If, therefore, you have that gift, and can think of a few novelties in lace and embroidered goods which you can make and sell for fractions of a dollar, you will have opened your way to constant and remunerative employment.

196. DOUBTFUL DEBTS.—It is well known that in efforts that require perseverance and persistence women succeed better than men. Grocers, butchers, real estate agents, and in fact almost every business man, has a large number of accounts, a considerable per cent. of which he considers worthless. To any one who could succeed in collecting them, the dealer would give a very large per cent., in some cases even amounting to half the bill. Many of these are really collectible if attempted with the persuasive arts of womanhood. Here is a large and profitable field for a woman having the right qualifications.

197. DRESSING DOLLS.—A fair profit can be made by taking orders for making dolls' dresses, as they can be bought and dressed for about one-half the cost of those already dressed. Persons giving the order should be required to bring the materials for the dress.

198. FRUIT PRESERVERS.—Vast numbers of people are in the country during the fruit season, and cannot "do up" fruits; they must depend on the grocer. Let a thrifty, economical woman who *knows how* equip (83)herself with sugar, fruit, cans and preserve kettles, and she will not long wait for customers if she makes her business known. The second year, her patrons having tested her talents and tasted her fruits, and finding them so much better than "store goods," will flood her with orders.

199. A MUSHROOM CELLAR.—An enterprising woman hired a cellar at a rent of $10 per month, had it fitted up with shelves, placed on these shelves in order, straw, fertilizers, and soil; then put on mushroom spawn, renewing it at intervals, as also at longer intervals the soil. Average sale of mushrooms per week, $31.50. Average expenses, $8.80. Profit per week, $22.70.

200. POULTRY RAISING.—Following is the experience of another woman in raising poultry. She bought forty-five Minorcas, because they lay a large white egg, and are nonsitters and prolific layers. Each hen laid on an average one hundred and sixty-four eggs per annum. She purchased also forty Brahmas for sitters and for fattening. Total expenses for fowls and for keeping, $278.70. Total receipts, $1,144.11. Net profit, $865.31.

201. HOME HOTHOUSE.—Thousands of people will buy plants already started who would not go to the trouble to buy seeds, slips, and pots. There is also a large demand for cut flowers all the year round. Have a cellar for rooting, and a south room for sunning. A

liberal use of cards and circulars, stating what you propose to do, will surely bring custom. The secret of the florists' business is to provide flowers for every month in the year, and to force or retard the flowers that suit the demands of each month. This is a very pretty[84] employment for a woman, and can be done in her own home. There are three hundred and twelve floral establishments in this country managed by women. The work is easy and tasteful to ladies. The elements of success are the habit of early rising, business ability, close superintendence of laborers, intelligent advertising, knowledge of plants, and promptness in filling orders. The best location is near a large cemetery. One florist thus located takes in from $1,500 to $2,000 per month during the busy season.

202. ART NEEDLEWORK.—Here is the way a woman paid off a $600 mortgage on her home, and at the same time attended to her domestic duties. She bought linens stamped with designs, and gave her spare time to decorative embroidery. She disposed of her work at the Woman's Exchange, and at the art stores. Six hundred dollars in spare minutes are not a bad showing. Besides, one could form a class and add the income from teaching. Mrs. Clara Louise Kellogg began by giving lessons in embroidery at the age of fourteen. Before her fifteenth birthday she was earning $30 a week with these classes.

203. NEWS AGENCY.—Keep the daily papers. Almost any lady who will go into the business could count on one hundred patrons; and these by the recommendation of friends could easily be increased to five hundred. One hundred patrons would mean at least $3 per week, and five hundred patrons would mean at least $15 per week. Tact, enterprise, and good service are the qualities needed. If your place is on the main street, and you can make a show-window for periodicals, your income will be much augmented. A woman came to this country and heard of a news stand for sale for[85] $250. She sold her jewels to purchase it. With her two brothers she made it a success, and it now supports three families. "Courtesy and application," she says, "were my capital."

204. WOMEN'S WANTS.—Take advantage of bargain sales—ribbons, silks, lace, and velvets. They can be had, if you watch the papers, at very trifling cost, but wondrous are the shapes into which they can be made by woman's deft fingers. You can make boas, ruchings, berthas, lace bibs, draped collars, belts, etc. Every woman wants these things, and will buy them if they can be found in colors and style required. They can be sold at moderate cost, and at a very large profit.

205. HOME PRINTING PRESS.—Pay $10 for a press, and a like sum for type and other accessories. Print visiting cards, at-home cards, business, reception, and wedding cards, tickets of admission, etc. Give a specimen of your work to every one of your friends, and request their patronage; place circulars with samples and rates in the stores, and solicit the favors of business men. Doing the work in your own home, you have no extra

rent to pay as have printing establishments, and you can do the work much cheaper and still make a profit.

206. SHORT SERVICE BUREAU.—Many people want help in an emergency, and for a short time only. The housewife is suddenly taken ill, a servant without warning leaves, company unexpectedly comes, stoves are to be put up, yards are to be cleaned, gardens dug, snow shoveled, clothes washed, and a hundred other things done requiring short service only. Keep a list{86} of men and women who go out at labor. Know accurately their whereabouts every day. Be ready instantly to supply any one's demand. When it is known that you furnish that kind of service, your office will be in demand, and your patrons well willing to pay.

207. DELICATESSEN ROOM.—Here is a paying business that is not overcrowded, but success depends upon the quality of the goods. Make yourself a specialist in cookery. Homemade pies, plum puddings, orange marmalade, salted almonds, fancy cakes, jellies and jams can be made and sold at a good profit. Bakers and grocers will be forced to keep them when once there is a demand for your goods. This is no speculative idea. Many a woman has not only made a living, but accumulated a snug little fortune by this means.

208. MISCELLANEOUS EXCHANGE.—Many people have no use for some of their possessions, but desire something else; others would be glad to get what these possess. Establish a place for the exchange of typewriters, sewing machines, bicycles, baby carriages, jewelry, bric-à-brac, etc. Charge both parties to the exchange a small commission. This plan has the advantage that it requires no capital, and hence has no risk.

209. CAP AND APRON PLAN.—Here is a plan available near any large hotel. Have a place for the sale of aprons, waiters' jackets, cooks' caps, etc. Get out a great quantity of circulars, stating your plan in an attractive form, and have a boy to distribute them—one upon whom you can rely to hand one to every employee of hotel shop and store. Repeat the circulars every week until your business is thoroughly known. Arrange to keep the articles in repair, and engage the{87} agency of some laundry establishment for their washing; then with the work of selling, repairing and laundrying these goods you will have an established business.

210. KITCHEN UTENSILS.—As a rule you can sell five kitchen utensils where you can sell one book. The former shows for itself; the latter must be exhibited and explained. Send to a large wholesaler for the most modern samples of labor-saving tools for the kitchen. Test them for a few days yourself. Then start out among your neighbors. A housewife will purchase anything that lightens labor if it is only cheap. An enthusiastic person can make many dollars a day selling useful articles for the kitchen. A woman for three months averaged $4 a day selling an improved coffee pot.

211. WEDDING MANAGER.—How many brides shrink from the work of a large wedding, while at the same time feeling under obligations to have one! A lady who has an artistic taste and a knowledge of the best social customs may very properly undertake the management of a wedding. She should know what is proper for the bride's outfit, and how to dress her, how to decorate the rooms, what style of invitations to issue, and in short, all the delightfully perplexing details of a wedding. For this work she has a right to charge a fair sum, and if the wedding proves to be a very pretty one, she is entitled to the credit of it. When once the office of a lady manager is recognized, and the relief afforded to the bride's family appreciated, the fashion will quickly spread, and others will wish to avail themselves of your taste and skill. [88]

212. FOREIGN HOMES.—Here is an example of the pluck and enterprise of an American girl: Miss Mary Widdicomb went to Paris in company with a lady friend, and established a home for Americans in that capital. Her rooms accommodated thirty-five, and such was the success of her venture that she is about to open another apartment. Think of it! You can go to a French city and hear the American language, associate with American people, and have American surroundings the same as if in the United States. Here is an opportunity for young women with small capital to see a foreign country and make money at the same time.

213. LADY BARBER.—There is a school in New York for the instruction of barbers. Three months' apprenticeship will give you a knowledge of the trade. One lady who graduated a year ago from the school now has two assistants, and is earning from $6 to $10 a day.

214. MINERAL COLLECTIONS FOR SCHOOLS.—Dana's Mineralogy gives fourteen hundred places in the United States where rare minerals are found. There are 240,968 public schools, and each one needs a mineral collection. Why has no one thought of gathering these rare stones and selling them to our public schools? At $1 a school, the sale should be $240,698, but many rare collections would bring $5, and even $10 each.

215. TURKISH BATH.—One lady opened a place for Turkish and Russian baths. She went around among her lady friends and acquaintances and secured the promise of a paying patronage. Five promised their patronage every week, eight every two weeks, and twenty-four at least once a month. Thus the sum of [89] $60 per month was assured at the start, and this paid for rent and assistants, with a good margin of profit.

216. TRAINED NURSES.—Trained nurses in our large cities command $25 a week. The duties are exacting, but not difficult. Assistant nurses receive $15. The latter have less responsibilities, and are not required to spend so long a time in training. This is an inviting field for ladies who have gifts and tastes for this work.

217. TRAVELING COMPANION.—If you have a good education and can make yourself agreeable, your services ought not to go long begging for an engagement in this delightful occupation. Watch the advertisements in the daily papers; better yet, insert an

advertisement of your own, modestly stating your qualifications. The remuneration depends upon the wealth and liberality of your employer.

218. Paper Flowers.—This has become a distinct trade. You can learn in a few months. There is a paper flower store in Broadway, New York, which does an immense business. There are great possibilities in this line in every city.

219. French Perfumer and Complexion Expert.—How does this sound?—Madame Racier, French Perfumer. Equip yourself with perfumes, essences, tinctures, extracts, spirit waters, cosmetics, infusions, pastiles, tooth powders, washes, cachous, hair dyes, sachets, essential oils, etc. All ladies like perfumes. Once let it be known that you are an authority on the subject, and you will lack neither patronage nor profits.

221. Guide for Shoppers.—A department store in New York recently made a census of its customers, and from the count kept for a single week it was estimated that 3,125,000 persons passed through its doors every year. This for a single store. But there are thousands of stores. Vast numbers of these people are from the country, and do not know where they can trade to the best advantage. What a field is here for a shoppers' guide! Ascertain what stores make a specialty of certain goods, what ones sell the cheapest in certain lines, and what days they make bargains in certain wares. Show by what routes the places are best reached, where to dine, etc. Fill a little book with just the information a shopper wants to know; call it "The Ladies' Shopping Guide," put it on the market at ten cents, and you can sell millions of them.

222. Bicycle Instruction.—Why, may not a woman teach "the wheel" as well as a man? Many women are restrained from learning through the dislike of falling from the wheel into the arms of a strange man, commonly a negro. A woman's bicycle academy would pay in any large city.

223. Cooking School.—Madam Parloa and Madam Rorer have set the example, and they will be sure to have many imitators. A course of instruction in cooking, costing $10, is a vastly better investment to any young woman than a course on a piano costing $100, or many times that sum. First, learn the art thoroughly yourself and then teach it to others. There is money in this, but it needs taste, tact and work.

224. The Boarding House.—One who has a taste for cooking and a little marketing skill can do well in this somewhat overworked and not always paying business. The gains increase from zero with one boarder, in geometrical progression, until $1 a head is realized with twenty boarders. Profits, $20 a week. With great skill and management this may be doubled.

225. Pen Engraving.—If you have a circle of one hundred friends, and can secure their patronage, you can make a fair living for one person at engraving cards. A lady with a

large calling list should engrave $500 worth of cards a year. Expenses, $25. Remuneration for work, $475.

226. A Ladies' Restaurant.—A restaurant where delicacies pleasing to ladies are made a specialty would surely pay. A lady who recently established one adjoining a large department store has been obliged to enlarge her premises to accommodate her crowd of patrons.

227. A Woman's Newspaper.—One has just been started in a Western city. The editors, reporters, printers, and press-feeders, are all women. Of course it advocates woman's reform. An enterprise of this kind requires considerable capital, and is not without risk, but a woman of ability and experience can make it pay as well as a man, besides the advantage of an appeal directly to her sex in support of a paper conducted in this manner.[92]

228. Advertising Agent.—A lady by her courtesy, tact, and gentle address, is especially fitted for this work. All our great newspapers and magazines pay large salaries to successful agents, for, as a rule, the advertising department is the one that pays the dividends of the business. The shopkeepers and others who, by reason of repeated solicitations give the cold shoulder to the male agent, would listen at least respectfully to a lady. On the whole, this field presents to ladies who have the right qualities better opportunities than to men.

229. The Civil Service.—This is now open to women. There are more then ten thousand of these places to be filled every year. Clerkships range from $600 to $3,000. Very few fall below $1,000. These places, according to the Civil Service Law, are filled by competitive examinations. There are thousands of bright young women who secured these places, not through any governmental pull, but by sheer merit in examinations. Get a book entitled "Civil Service," by John M. Comstock, Chairman of the United States Board of Examiners, for the Customs Service in New York City, and published by Henry Holt & Co. This book will give you a complete table of the positions open, the salaries attached to each, and a list of questions required to be answered.

230. Post-Prandial Classes.—Few, even among educated women, are masters of themselves to the extent of being able to rise before an audience, and without previous preparation express themselves clearly and creditably on whatever subject may be under discussion. A woman in New York, a member of Sorosis, made a reputation for bright, witty, after-dinner speeches.[93] As she earned her living by newspaper work, a friend said to her, "Why don't you add to your income by teaching other women how to say a few graceful words in public?" She caught at the idea, and organized classes in the hitherto untaught art of post-prandial speech-making, and had capital success, earning $500 by it in one season.

231. WOMEN DRUGGISTS.—The neatness of women, their delicacy and attention to details, qualify them admirably for the drug business. At the Woman's Infirmary, New York, the apothecary department is entirely in the hands of ladies. Drug clerks receive on the average of $9 per week. There are few lady proprietors, but there is no reason why there should not be more, as the business is very profitable.

232. ALMANAC MAKERS.—Of late years many of the great dailies issue yearly almanacs. The mass of matter which goes to make up these publications can be collected as well by women, who have gifts for details, as by those of the other sex. In one publication house a woman is paid $30 a week to manage one of these almanacs, and in another $20 for the compiling of an index for the daily paper.

233. WOMEN LECTURERS.—Women of talent have earned a competence and almost a fortune on the platform. Lucy Stone was sometimes paid as high as $260 for a lecture, and Anna Dickinson also received large sums. The lady who hopes to succeed in this field must have fluency, the gift of oratory, self-poise, and a certain dramatic or magnetic power.

234. MAGAZINE CONTRIBUTORS.—In this work women are paid as much as men, and their facile pens are often[94] able to turn out equal and even superior work. The Harpers pay $10 a page; the Atlantic Monthly, $6 to $10; the North American Review, $1.50.

235. WOMEN PHYSICIANS.—Says a recent publication: "There is a real necessity for women physicians; there are many ladies who prefer them, and in some cases will consult no other. There are now over one thousand lady physicians in the United States, but the number will soon be doubled, and even trebled. Several of these lady physicians are making over $2,000 a year." One of them says: "I have several well-to-do families whom I charge by the year. I charge $200, if they are people who are considered well off; less, if they are poor."

236. PAPER BOX MAKING.—Hundreds of women are making paper boxes, but as employees, not as proprietors. A woman made the first orange box in California. Seeing that it was a good thing, and that there would soon be a demand for others, she built a factory, and is now turning out fifty thousand boxes a year.

237. HORTICULTURE.—Here is an example of what a California woman can do. A widow having four boys purchased thirty-six acres of land in San Jose, and under her personal care, aided by her boys, planted the tract with apricot, cherry and prune trees. For four years she did all the pruning, a difficult task for a refined and delicate woman, accustomed as she had been to luxuriant ease. Her prune trees alone netted $2,700 in one year.

238. VOCALISTS.—A lady with a good voice is certain[95] of making a living, some have made fortunes with it. The demand is wide and various. If your taste does not incline to

the stage, there is still a large field in the church. All large churches, and many small ones now, have paid choirs. The leading vocalists are commonly well paid. There are a great number of altos and sopranos in New York and Brooklyn, and in the fashionable suburbs, who receive $1,000 a year, or an excess of that sum. And this is an excellent compensation when it is remembered that the singer has nearly all her time in which to pursue some other vocation.

239. Packing Trunks.—This is a Paris occupation carried on exclusively by women. You leave your order at the office of the transportation company, and say when you want a professional packer. She comes, and is paid fifty cents, and sometimes $1 an hour for her services. She has genius for folding dresses so that they can be carried all over the world without a wrinkle. She wraps bonnets in tissue paper. She tucks away bric-à-brac in a way that makes breakage impossible. This industry might be introduced profitably into this country.

240. Women Costumers.—Costumes for the stage are now gotten up mostly by men. A woman of taste and ability could make a success of this business. Many rich ladies would consult them in matters of personal wardrobe.

241. Express Office.—A woman can sit in an office as well as a man. One woman in Boston tried it four years ago, beginning in a modest way. Now she has three offices and five teams in constant use.

242. A Fancy Bakery.—An elegant and educated young woman in San Francisco took a dingy, dying little bakeshop, with sickening sights and smells. She put it in order. In two months she had cleared $700, and in four months $1,800. Another woman in Brooklyn has just opened a bakery under very flattering prospects. She works on the plan of exquisite neatness, trimming her windows like those of a fancy goods' dealer, and wrapping her bread in tissue paper.

243. Women Grocers.—There are not many women in the grocer business, but there is no reason why there should not be. A woman grocer in a Western State who has been established since 1860, has a business worth $80,000 a year.

244. Food and Medicine Samples.—Proprietors of patent medicines and foods will give you a large commission to introduce their inventions into homes, and if successful, you will soon be employed at a good salary. These proprietors often pay ladies to introduce samples at country stores. The storekeeper will give you room rent free for a few days, with the understanding that he alone has the sale of the article in the place.

245. Samples in Stores.—Ladies of tact and good address are receiving fair salaries in the introduction of new articles. Every inventor is anxious to introduce his goods, and every storekeeper is equally desirous to sell. Call upon the proprietor of some new article of household use, secure territory, and then solicit space in a country store. After three or

four days in one store you should go to another, or perhaps to the next town. You may have to begin on a commission,[97] but if successful you can soon command a salary.

246. Samples from House to House.—Others find ample remuneration in introducing new articles from house to house. We know a little lady in Brooklyn who is paid well for giving away samples of a new baby food. This is much more pleasant work than that of importuning people to purchase.

247. The Woman Beautifier.—Whatever is of the nature of beauty appeals to the heart of woman. A lady who has the secret of making other women beautiful cannot fail of success. After making a study of your business, advertise that you understand the art of removing moles, wrinkles, warts, wens, birthmarks, tan, freckles, and superfluous hair. If successful in pleasing one or two leaders of fashion, you will have plenty of custom.

248. The Manicure Parlor.—The manicure business is yearly increasing. For $15 you can learn the business. Implements will cost you $10 more. With the capital of $25 you can begin business, and, if ladylike in appearance and gentle in touch, you can build up a big business in the right neighborhood. Any lady would prefer in this art to patronize one of her own sex. Get out cards and circulars and scatter them freely. There is room for many women to excel in this field. One lady who entered upon this work two years ago says she is on the road to a fortune.

249. The Massage Treatment.—Another lady is having great success with the massage treatment. She has now more than seventy regular patrons. This[98] method of cure is easily learned and readily applied. Hardly a lady among your acquaintances is in good health. It is a proverb that no woman is well. A vast proportion of these cases are nervous and will yield to the massage treatment. If you have strong muscles you could readily achieve a large practice by this system, especially in summer resorts and places where invalids flock.

250. Ice Cream Parlor.—This is not new, but possesses possibilities of a good living where the field is not overworked. There are five things necessary to success, and in the following order of importance: An attractive place in a clean, fashionable locality; good and generous plates of cream; unexcelled neatness; polite service; and popular prices. We have known a lady commencing business on these principles to oust quickly an older establishment run on slacker methods.

251. Flower Packets.—Buy quantities of flower seeds of all varieties. Put them up in very small envelopes, a few seeds in each one, advertise that you will send samples for a penny a kind, ten for six cents, twenty-five for fifteen cents, fifty for twenty-five cents, etc. A large mail envelope will hold fifty or more of the smaller ones containing seeds.

252. Lady Caterer.—A woman has a fine chance to succeed as a caterer. Her taste in arranging tables should at least make her hold her own with business rivals of the opposite sex. Mrs. A. B. Marshall, a woman caterer of London, often manages a supper for one hundred guests.

253. DELICACIES FOR INVALIDS.—This is a new field[99] which is being worked with much promise. "Mrs. Kate Teachman," as she is known in the New York *Sun*, is working in this line with great success. She says: "Of course, if you want this sort of thing you must pay for it—sixty-five cents for a pint of broth, seventy-five cents for a pint of puree, sixty-five cents for a half-pint of jelly, twenty-five cents for chopped chicken sandwiches."

254. INSECT POWDER.—A California woman who now owns four hundred acres of land has a history that ought to inspire other women with a belief in their ability to get on in the world. In 1861 her husband died, leaving her with a debt of $1,400, three children, and a small farm mortgaged. Within five years she had paid the mortgage by taking boarders, raising chickens, and doing whatever offered. In 1877 she began to raise pyrethrum, the plant from which insect powder is made, some years having one hundred acres planted with it. Now she has from fifty to eighty employees of both sexes, and is said to be worth half a million dollars.

255. RICE CULTIVATOR.—A few years ago a young Iowa girl-squatter, with her sixteen-year-old brother, took up a government claim in Louisiana, and went to planting rice, the first crop of which paid her $1,000. She lives in a three-room cottage, and has a few fruit trees, plenty of good fences, and a sea of waving rice-blades. Her nearest neighbor is another girl-farmer who also settled a government claim, and is bossing an orchard that is giving her a comfortable living.

256. YEAST CAKES.—Here is what one woman did: Being thrown on her own resources, instead of[100] following the beaten path of custom, she engaged in something novel. She made yeast cakes. Gradually her trade increased until she was obliged to hire help, and in time had to build an addition to the house to provide room for her thriving business. She now makes a good living, finding her work congenial as well as profitable. Here is her recipe: Take one dozen hops and boil two or three hours, remove from the fire and strain through a sieve, adding boiling water until there are three or four quarts of the liquid. Then thicken with canaille until quite stiff; and one-half tablespoonful of ginger and one-quarter cup of molasses; let it stand until cool, add one-half cup of salt yeast, or one cake of lard, and in the morning stir down with a little fine cornmeal. Let it rise again, then mix with cornmeal, roll, and cut with a cutter. This rule makes one hundred cakes. They sell for seventy-five cents per hundred, and retail for one cent apiece.

257. PHYSICAL CULTURE.—There are twelve million young women in the United States. The great majority of them have an ailment of some kind; in fact, it is almost impossible to find a perfectly healthy woman. Physical culture will add years to one's life. An eminent physician has estimated that twenty-four million years, or an average of two years each,

can be added to the lives of our young women by simple bodily exercise of one hour each day. Get a book, study a chart, employ a teacher; then, after a thorough course go about among your friends and form a class. Induce your pupils to bring other pupils. Advertise, lecture, give class exhibitions. Charge $5 a quarter for a class of twelve; $4 for one of fifteen; $3 for one of twenty. Mr. John D. Hoover, of Los Angeles, Cal., says: "When I entered a college of oratory, I was almost[101] penniless. I took a special course in physical culture, with a view to teaching that art. It is now eighteen months since I left the college, and during that time I have earned in clear cash from teaching physical culture the sum of $20,960. I have 1,507 pupils. My sister also has been very successful in teaching since she graduated, and has made quite a large sum of money."

258. HOUSE CLEANING.—Enterprising men have taken up the work of house cleaning with considerable success, but the business can be managed better by a woman than by a man. If your patrons are not too many, you can personally superintend the work in each house yourself to the great satisfaction of the lady, who would commonly prefer to have it managed by one of her own sex. If your business increases so as to require your presence in the office, you can send a lady assistant to superintend the work. Have a fixed price per room where there is no extra work, such as painting, kalsomining, and paper hanging. In the latter case it is better to take the work by the job.

259. SELLING OYSTERS.—Here is the way a woman with five little children gets a living: She hires a boy to open the oysters, which she then puts up in little pint pails and takes from house to house. She has many customers whom she serves regularly on certain days. Sales per week, fifty pints, or twenty-five quarts. Boy's wages, $1. Net, $3.

260. PIE CART.—Hear what another woman says: "I have a little pie cart. It is nothing but a pie-crate mounted on wheels. I bake every morning ten pies and in the afternoon I sell them hot from door to door.[102] I make about seven cents on a large pie, and four cents on small one." Average earnings per day, fifty cents.

261. MEN'S NECK TIES.—As every man, at least every well-dressed man, wears a tie, which must be renewed several times a year—white lawns every day—the number in demand is enormous. First learn the business, and then if you can sell them a little under the manufacturers' price you are sure to dispose of all you can make. One girl earned $12 a week in this way.

262. DANCING TEACHER.—The natural grace of women fits them better than men to be teachers of this art, especially to be instructors of young girls. Dancing teachers charge on the average $15 a quarter. There are several very successful lady teachers.

263. HABERDASHER.—The selling of small articles of the dress and toilet is profitable if the location is good and the competition not too severe. Where one cannot purchase the articles outright, she can sell on commission. Dealers in small wares of this kind often take in from $12 to $20 a day, of which on the average, one-sixth is profit.

264. LADY ARCHITECT.—There is no reason why women should not succeed in this occupation, since it is one in which taste is a chief requisite. Several young lady graduates of college have entered it recently, and with flattering success. Architects charge about three per cent. on contracts.

265. LOST AND FOUND AGENCY.—In every large city numbers of articles are lost by the owners and found by others every day. A single New York paper contains[103] daily from ten to twenty advertisements of lost articles. Open a small office, advertise in the "Lost and Found" column of the paper that you will receive any articles that may be found, and charge the owner a small commission. The agency could be carried on in connection with some other light business.[104]

CHAPTER VIII.

MONEY FOR BOYS.

Seven Ways to Get a Place—The Way a Boy Should Advertise—Openings Everywhere for the Right Kind of Boys—Beating the Booksellers—Stories About Smart Boys—Twenty-five Hints to Hang Your Fortune On—How a Towheaded Country Boy Became a Great Editor—A Barrel Full of Postage Stamps—How a Poor Boy Became the Richest Man in the Country—The Journey from Nothing to Forty Millions—The Best School in the World—The Beginnings of Great Fortunes.

BOYS, you can do it! What! get rich? attain to fame? Yes, both. "But I have no chance." Neither had Humphry Davy, nor Jay Gould, nor Henry Wilson. But the first became one of the greatest of scientists; the second, the richest man in the country; and the third, vice-president of the United States.

"The best school is the school of adversity," said Rousseau, who, from a waiter in a restaurant, became the most noted man of his age. The boy, Horace Greeley, wandered up and down the streets of New York, asking of printers if they "wanted a hand," and was everywhere laughed at and turned away; and the boy, George W. Childs, worked for $2 a week as a clerk in a book store, saved money, bought the Philadelphia *Ledger*, and became a millionaire.

"I have no capital," you say. But you have ten servants (fingers) to work for you. Daniel Manning, ex-President Cleveland's Secretary of Treasury, started as[105] a newsboy. John Wanamaker, the great merchant, commenced in a book store at $1.25 a week. Fred Douglass, the colored orator, began life as a slave without a cent. And P. T. Barnum, the world-famed showman, rode a horse for ten cents a day. No chances! You have *five* on each hand. No capital! It is the *blood* that fights and wins. If you have no opportunity, make it. Do not wait for something to turn up; *turn* something up. Be a match for events.

The world's great and rich men have forced their way to success at the bayonet points of their fingers, and with the iron pry of an unconquerable will. Boys, here are a few hints for you:

Section   1.   How   a   Boy   can   Get   a   Place.

SEVEN WAYS TO GET A POSITION.

266. FREE SERVICE.—Make friends with a clerk. Offer to go with him on the delivery wagon. He will be only too glad of your assistance. The next step will be to help in odd jobs about the store. After a little familiarity with the business, you will find an opening. Your friendly clerk will have a sick day, or a leave of absence, or a vacation. The employer knows you have assisted the clerk, and will gladly give you his place for a day or a week, and from temporary employment it is but a step to a permanent place.

267. SPECIAL DEPARTMENT.—Make yourself familiar with a particular department of the work of shop or store. Suppose you take a pound of tea. It will surprise you to find out how many things you can learn about so insignificant a thing as a pound of tea. Ascertain the different brands; what markets they come from; where they are raised; how they are manufactured; in what quantities they are shipped; what[106] are the fluctuations in price; who are the largest dealers; in what section of the country the trade is chiefly carried on. A study of these things will suggest other branches. A year given to a study of this kind, and you will know more about tea than the most trusted employee, whose knowledge is commonly of a superficial kind. Then, if you have an opportunity, you can surprise the merchant with a knowledge of his business, and he will be sure to give you a place as soon as he has an opening. One merchant says: "I always have a place for a person who can tell me anything about my business I don't know myself."

268. SHOW SUPERIORITY OF GOODS.—A man occupied his spare moments in measuring the linear feet of advertisements contained in the different Sunday papers, and sent the result to the one which had printed the most. Go around among customers and find what brand of goods they like the best. Then report to the makers of these brands, and you may be sure they will take an interest in you if they see that you take an interest in them.

269. ADVERTISING.—Here is an advertisement for the right kind of boy: "A brisk-footed, up-to-date boy, not afraid to work, will take a place at low wages for the sake of learning the business." Here you have four qualities in two lines—quickness, intelligence, industry, and low wages—the four things men are looking for, and such an advertisement will not wait long for a reply.

270. INFLUENCE.—Great names are mighty. Introduce yourself to the greatest man in your town, and tell him your qualifications and ambitions. Do not be[107] afraid of him. A truly great man is more willing to do a real kindness to a meritorious boy than you think.

Robert Lennox, an old-time New York merchant, one Sunday at church saw a timid young person looking anxiously around as if for a seat. "Come with me," said Mr. L., "and I will give you a seat." The next day the young man took a letter of recommendation to the store of a merchant. "Can I get a small bill of goods to begin business with?" he inquired. "I will trust anybody that Robert Lennox invites into his pew," was the reply. "I owe all my success in life," said Jonathan Sturges, "to the invitation of Robert Lennox to sit in his pew." With the great-and-good-man's indorsement you will find places waiting for you.

271. A TRIAL WEEK.—All many boys want is a chance. When you apply in vain for a place, tell the proprietor you are sure that he needs you, and that you will come a week for nothing (better a month if you can afford it). If you really have the merit you think you have, it will be strange if you cannot displace some indolent or indifferent employee.

272. COMMISSION.—Offer to sell the dealer's goods on commission. You must leave a deposit to cover the worth of the goods. Take the articles to your friends and tell them you are trying to get a place. In most cases, if the goods are cheap, they will try to help you, and you will be able to make an excellent report to your employer. When he sees that your service means money in his pocket, he will be eager to employ you at a salary.

Section   2.   What   Boys   Can   Do.

TWENTY HINTS FOR BOYS.

273. THE BOY MAGICIAN.—For fifty cents you can [108] buy a book entitled "The Parlor Magician," containing one hundred tricks for the drawing room. A few weeks' practice should make you master of these arts, and then with your outfit you are ready for a money-making tour. It is best to take along a friend, as in some of the most clever tricks you will need an assistant.

274. THE GLASS-BLOWER.—For twenty-five cents you can get a book with full instructions in the curious art of glass-blowing. The wondrous forms you will be able to produce, the pleasure of the work, and above all the money derived from the sale of your products, will delight the heart of any boy. There is money in glass-blowing after you have mastered the art, but if you would make a business of it you must apprentice yourself for a time to a master of the trade.

275. THE DIME LUNCH.—There are thousands of business men and clerks in our large stores and offices who would prefer to pay ten or fifteen cents rather than go out to a restaurant. Especially is this the case in rainy weather. Pretty boxes with tasteful lunches could be prepared at a small cost, and taken through the places of business. The important item is attractiveness.

276. CANCELLED STAMPS.—In every large city there are dealers who will pay you for canceled stamps. Ordinary stamps bring about ten cents per thousand, but rare ones bring very high prices. Ask all your friends for their canceled stamps. In a store in New York there are several barrels full of postage stamps collected by boys. Each barrel contains a million. {109}

277. THE BOYS' PRESS.—Do you know you can get a printing press with complete outfit, a full font of type, and one hundred cards for $3? You can make money easily by printing cards and doing other small press jobs. Charge fifty cents, seventy-five cents or $1 for cards, according to the quality of paper and amount of printing.

278. SAW AND SCROLL.—Most interesting articles, both of use and ornament, can be made by the scroll-saw. Some have earned boys' fortunes in making these curious articles, and there is as much pleasure in making them as in getting the money for them.

279. THE MAGIC LANTERN.—The very best lantern and slides can be obtained for $6. From that figure the price runs downward to fifty cents. Purchase a good one and give parlor exhibitions at a charge of five cents admission. As you become more expert, you can increase your price. If you are a success at the business, your services will be in demand for more pretentious entertainments, where you can make $5 or more in a single evening.

280. CANDY MAKING.—What can please a boy better than candy making. Offer your services free for a short time to a confectioner. When you have learned the trade, which you can do in a little while, commence the business on your own account in a small way. Beginning with those sweets which are easily made, you can extend your art as your business increases until you have a good trade.

281. ODD JOBS.—"I push baby carriages through the park at five cents apiece," says a Chicago boy. "I {110} clean and oil bicycles," says a New York lad. "I stand on the Boulevard and pump up tires," declares a third. "I buy a dozen lemons and a pound of sugar and sell lemonade on all holidays and at times of parade," says an enterprising schoolboy. "I carry bundles and valises from the train, and make often fifty cents a day," says a Boston youth. "I hang up a slate on the front gate and take store orders for neighbors," says a bright village lad.

282. GENERAL EMPLOYMENT AGENCY.—Inform a hundred or more families in a particular district that at a certain hour of the day you will be there to carry messages, roll out barrels of ashes, go on errands, mail letters, black boots, and do whatever work they may require. If the work is sufficient to warrant it, a business partnership of boys may be formed, so that while one is engaged another can go on his usual rounds, and thus insure punctuality.

283. COLLECT MAGAZINES.—Almost every one takes a literary magazine, and some take two or three. After a time they become refuse on their hands. Many persons would gladly give you a truck-load. But these are worth money, and second-hand dealers who sell them at five cents apiece will give you three cents for them.

284. VACANT LOT.—If you live in the city, get the owner of a vacant lot to give you the privilege of raising vegetables. With a little experience you can easily raise from $50 to $100 worth of vegetables on a lot 20 × 100 feet. This will go far to eke out the support of a large family.{111}

285. BICYCLE TEACHING.—Here is a field for a stout lad of fifteen years. There are thousands of modest young ladies and men, especially elderly gentlemen, who would like to learn to ride a wheel, but do not like the publicity of a riding academy. Issue some neat cards and circulate them from house to house with the information that for the sum of $1 you will teach any one to ride. Most people have a back yard where such instruction could be given. Having no rent to pay, you could easily afford to take them for that price, as you have the advantage over the professional instructor, both of cheapness and privacy. There is a lot of money in this for the right kind of a boy.

286. FIRST-COST SALES.—When public attention is aroused upon any subject, consider how you can turn it to account. Here is what a boy thirteen years old says: "When 'Coin's Financial School' came out and the people were talking about it, I wrote to Mr. Harvey, the author, and got a lot of the books and sold them all before they got into the book stores here. I have made in this and like enterprises $500." Like opportunities were presented in our late war, with the Dewey buttons, battleship pictures, etc. Keep your eyes open. Opportunities to make money are all about you. The alert boy makes the successful man.

Boys, there is gold in all the mountains, pearls in all the seas, and money in every street. Elijah Morse at fifteen years of age bought a recipe for stove polish, paying $5 for the materials. He peddled it in a carpetbag, and from this small beginning grew the celebrated "Rising Sun Stove Polish," whose huge factory covers four acres at West Canton, Mass., and whose proprietor is immensely rich. Cornelius Vanderbilt was a poor{112} boy without a cent. When he died his estate was valued at $40,000,000.

Boys, there is a fortune for you. It is not to be found, but made by hard work. Write on your banner, "Luck is a fool. Pluck is a hero."{113}

CHAPTER

MONEY IN AGENCIES.

The Omnipresent Agent—What He Says and What He Sells—Power of the Successful Drummer—The Five Secrets of the Book Agent—Five Thousand Dollars Commission on a Patent—How Seven Men Carry $7,000,000 Insurance—A Man Who Receives $5,000 a Year and Does Nothing—How Teachers Pay for Their Positions—Searching for a $10,000 Preacher—The Matrimonial is Often a Matter-of-money-all—A New Way to Get Good Servants—The Farm Supply Company.

FEW occupations offer such inducements for persons with little or no capital as that of the agent. There are two classes of agencies. In one, as a book or patent agency, the agent works for one or two persons at a fixed commission and needs no capital. In the other, as that of servants and of supply companies, the agent is also in a certain sense a principal; he obeys no one's orders, fixes his own commissions, and makes his profits directly from the public. Here are a few points for agents:

287. BOOK AGENCY.—The book agency depends partly upon the kind of book, but chiefly upon the kind of man. The right man selling the right book can make enormous wages. An agent selling a commentary on the Bible made sometimes $25 in half a day. An agent for the "People's Encyclopædia" earned $3,000 in one year, and spent only about half the time in the work. Many agents for "Memoirs of General Grant" earned from $10 to $20 a day. Ordinarily, an[114] agent should be satisfied if he can make from $3 to $5 a day. From this sum must come his expenses. Book agents receive from 25 to 45 per cent., according to the nature of the work. Forty per cent. is considered excellent compensation.

288. THE PATENT AGENCY.—Considerable business is now done in the selling of patent rights. The agent studies the lists that come out weekly in the "United States Patent Gazette," and sends his circulars to those who have secured patents. The agent will charge from five to ten per cent., if he can arrange with a patentee for the sale of the patents. In other cases, he charges a fixed sum, which is paid in advance, and is considered an equivalent for his services whether or not he is successful in effecting a sale, on the same principle that doctors and lawyers are paid whether they gain or lose a case. In extent and profit, the business varies from the itinerant vender with half a dozen patents in his valise to the established business house with sub-agencies in all parts of the world. What the profits are in the latter situation may be judged from a single case in the former, where a traveling man received as commission on a single patent sold the sum of $5,000.

289. COMMISSION MERCHANTS.—A vast business is done in the sale of general merchandise on commission. Foreign houses have their agencies in this city. Also much of the produce of the farm and of the products of manufactures are disposed of in the same

way. Take a case of the former kind. A man hires an office in New York and storage in a warehouse. Then he sends circulars to Westerndealers, stating that he is prepared to take their stock or grain on commission. When he can make quick sales he saves the expense of storage,[115] but rental in a warehouse is necessary in holding for futures. He receives in one day 100,000 bushels of wheat at seventy-five cents per bushel, which, after paying freightage, he sells at one half of one per cent. profit. Gain of one day, $500. He will not receive so much every day, and some days he will have to sell at a loss; but, taken altogether, there are good chances of wealth in the commission business.

290. INSURANCE AGENCY.—Insurance, both fire and life, is a mine of wealth, and has opened wondrously during the last few years. The present magnitude of the business is shown by the statement that there are $2,500,000,000 invested in life insurance in the United States, while the fire insurance agents last year wrote more than $16,000,000,000. There are seven men who have an aggregate of $7,000,000 on their lives. But the business is yet in its infancy. The field of life insurance is not nearly covered, and if it were, ten million persons will come to maturity during the next ten years, all of whom may be considered as candidates for insurance, and all the policies will have to be renewed in a short time. Insurance agents receive as commission from ten to twenty-five per cent. Some companies secure to their agents a regular percentage on the premium so long as the policies continue in force. If, therefore, an agent gets fifteen per cent. commission, and the company receives $10,000 per year as premiums from the policies he has written, his share will be $1,500; and thus he enjoys an annuity without any further work for a long period of time. The larger old-time companies, also, have general agents whose positions are still more lucrative. Many of them are in circumstances of affluence, and have very little to do. In fact, it is in the insurance business as in many other[116] occupations, that as one rises the salaries are larger, and the actual work, aside from the responsibility, is smaller.

291. TRAVELING SALESMAN.—In some houses a traveling salesman is allowed a standing commission on all goods bought by firms whose custom was secured through his influence. As the commission continues as long as the customer continues the trade at that house, some agents, after a few years of active work are enabled to retire on incomes of $2,000, $3,000, and in some cases of $5,000 a year. The business done by drummers is immense. Three hundred million tons of goods are shipped by them yearly, and the business amounts to nearly $2,000,000 a day.

292. SUPPLY COMPANIES.—A supply company differs from an ordinary merchants' firm in that it does not keep goods in stock. It is a mammoth general agency for procuring whatsoever you desire. Specimens only are kept in the store, and from these the customers make selections. The advantage of supply companies is the saving of large rentals, of expensive clerk-hire, and of loss or damage in the long keeping of goods, and, most of all, of risk in unsalable articles, and in the fall of prices. Thus, a supply company

can undersell an ordinary dealer, and if alert and prompt can make vast profits. Another great advantage is the smallness of the capital required. Here are great opportunities for bright young business men of limited means.

293. AGENCIES FOR TEACHERS.—The number of teachers in the public schools in the United States is 400,325. The matter of engaging school teachers varies in different States, and often in different parts of the[117] same State. Sometimes it is done by county superintendents, often by the Board of Education, but most frequently by the school trustees, commissioners, or committees. One going into the business of a Teachers' Agency must ascertain the particular method in every part of the country, and learn the name of the persons authorized to act in that capacity. Then he should issue circulars by the hundred thousand. For the eyes of applicants, he should use the advertising pages of the newspapers. Teachers should be charged a commission upon their salaries in something like the following order: Five per cent. on first year's salary, three per cent. the second year, and one per cent. the third year. After that it may be allowed to lapse. The contract should be rigorously drawn, and, where possible, payments should be collected in advance. There are great profits in the business when systematically and vigorously conducted. One agency in the eastern part of the United States is receiving commissions from ten thousand school teachers. Owing to frequent changes, the majority of these are paying five per cent.; but if we suppose the average to be only the amount payable the second year—$3 commission—the income would be $30,000.

294. CLERICAL AGENCY.—Here is an opportunity for an unoccupied clergyman of wide clerical acquaintance. There are thousands of vacant pulpits and other thousands of ministers anxious for calls. Establish an agency through whose medium the supply shall meet the demand. Your list should comprise the names of all churchless pastors, together with those desirous of change; and their experience, qualifications, education, family, age, personal appearance, together with other interesting information, should be properly tabulated[118] for the inspection of church committees. Candidates should be graded according to the catalogue, and sent out in order as pulpit candidates. As clerical engagements are commonly much longer than those of teachers, it is right that you should receive a larger per cent. for your services. If a church pays its pastor a salary of $10,000, and you are successful in the search for an available man for its pulpit, it would hardly be a presumption for you to charge $500 for your services.

295. MATRIMONIAL AGENCIES.—These should be conducted with the greatest care, and only by the most conscientious persons, on account of the great responsibilities involved. They are, however, capable of vast development, and of immense good. In Massachusetts alone there are seventy thousand females in excess of the males, while in Illinois the men preponderate to the number of fifty thousand. Your task of bringing together the unmated is a most delicate one, and you should accordingly be well compensated. Where there is much wealth on either side, your commission may be

expressed in three figures, and even in four. One thousand dollars is a small sum for a man to pay who secures an accomplished wife and a happy home. We have known several marriages made in this way to turn out exceedingly well.

296. AGENCY FOR SERVANTS.—This is not new, but you might revolutionize it by a new plan. Written recommendations are worthless, because almost every one will compensate the disappointment of the discharged servant by a certificate of good behavior, in the writing of which the elasticity of the conscience is more or less drawn upon. Instead of accepting a valueless paper, let an employee of the office personally[119] visit two or three of the places where the servant has been employed. The lady of the house will tell you many things she would not write in the letter. This will consume time, but the compensation is in the better class of service you will be enabled to offer. When it is known that you make personal investigation, sifting out the useless and offering only first-class help, your patronage will be vastly increased, and you can charge much higher commissions. Tell your patron that at the end of a month she may pay you $10 if satisfied; and most people would prefer to do that than to pay a half or quarter of that sum in advance with small guarantee of fitness.

297. AGENCY FOR FARM HANDS.—There are thousands of idle people in the great cities who would gladly go on farms for a portion of the year. If they make personal application, they are commonly regarded by the farmer as tramps. Besides these, there are thousands of emigrants arriving in search of work. Many of them are valuable as farm help, having tilled the soil at home. An agent who has a keen knowledge of human nature, and knows how to ask questions, sifting out the useless and the vicious from the valuable and the virtuous, can through proper advertising in agricultural papers, send at least a thousand of these men into the country every summer. Through an arrangement with the farmer by which $5 of the first month's wages shall be withheld and forwarded to the agent, the sum of $5,000 as commission for these one thousand laborers is secured. But the energetic agent ought to do far better than this.[120]

CHAPTER   X.

MONEY IN PROPRIETARY COMPOUNDS.

Proprietary Kings and How They Acquired Power—Patent Medicine Secrets Given Away—Where Perry Davis Found His Recipe—The Parent of the "Killers"—Men Who Made Their "Pile" in Pills—Fortunes in "Bitters"—Electricity, or "Mustard Plasters"—The Story of a "Discovery"—How a Man Made a Fortune With an Indian Cure—"What's in a Name?" The Mighty Lubec—Tons of Drugs Taken Every Day—Triumph of "Soothing Syrup"—A New Patent Medicine for Every Day of the Year—The Man Who Took Everything.

OWNERS of proprietary compounds have built up great fortunes in the sale of their concoctions. Our drug stores are filled with patent medicines, and millions of "cures" are sold annually. The names of some of these, such as Hostetter, Brandreth, and Mother Winslow, have become household words, proving how largely and universally their medicines have sold. The story is told of one credulous hypochondriac, who, on the theory that of many shot some one is likely to hit, actually took every kind of patent medicine in the world, or at least of every sort he had heard about. As there are more than three hundred and sixty diverse concoctions, this genius must have taken a different kind for every day of the year, or else have extended his experiments through a long period, which seems impossible under the circumstances. It is said that Perry Davis obtained his famous "Discovery" in the form of a recipe in an old newspaper which he found in an outhouse. This was the foundation of one of the[121] largest fortunes in patent medicines, and it was the parent of all the "Killers." The men who have made their piles in "pills" may be counted by the hundred. Perhaps the "Soothing Syrup" success is the most signal example of "*multum in parvo*." It is sold by the million bottles, and yet it is nothing but a little paregoric dropped in some sweet mixture. "Lubec" is a mighty name, but anybody can be a Lubec so far as the question of perfumery goes. Among the anecdotes of medicine venders we have only space for one or two. A man was crying up the virtues of an electric belt, and it was found that he had adroitly attached a strip of mustard plaster to the magic band, and this when heated by contact with the warm skin produced redness and an itching, which were supposed by the too trusting patient to be the effects of the healing electricity. Another man has made a fortune with an "Indian Plant." He travels about the country with what he advertises to be a "troop of Indians," giving performances and hawking his "cures." The "Indians" are New York toughs, and the "medicine plant" is a common pasture weed. We give no sort of countenance to these frauds, but, dismissing them all, there are still both profit to the patient and profit to the maker in the taking of proprietary medicines. To succeed in this line one should first have an article of genuine merit, and then advertise lavishly. Below are given some recipes quite as good as those that have made fortunes for their possessors, and in some cases the exact formulas of these widely renowned medicines are given.

298. HEALING OINTMENT.—One of the most celebrated of ointments is composed of these simple ingredients: Butter, lard, Venice turpentine, white wax and yellow[122] wax. Here is a rule for another ointment: Fresh butter, three-quarters pound; beeswax, four ounces; yellow resin, three ounces; melt together; add vinegar of cantharides, one fluid ounce; and simmer the whole with constant agitation for ten or twelve minutes, or until the moisture is nearly evaporated; then add of Canada balsam one ounce; express oil of mace, one drachm; balsam of Peru, ten or twelve drops; again stir well, allow mixture to settle; and when about half cold pour into pots previously slightly warmed, and allow it to cool very slightly. There is nothing else but to put on your label and expose for sale.

299. SPASM KILLER.—Acetate of morphia, one grain; spirit of sal volatile and sulphuric ether, one fluid ounce each; camphor julep, four ounces. Keep closely corked in a cool place and shake well before use. Dose, one teaspoonful in a glass of cold water as required.

Here is another: Spirits of camphor, two ounces; tincture of capsicum, one ounce; tincture of guaiac, one-half ounce; tincture of myrrh, one-half ounce; alcohol, four ounces. This is Perry Davis' famous medicine.

300. ANTI-MALARIA.—One ounce each of Peruvian bark and cream of tartar, cloves one-half drachm reduced to fine powder. Dose, one and one-half drachm every three hours.

301. HOSTETTER'S BITTERS.—Here is the recipe for the famous bitters: Calamus root, two pounds; orange peel, two pounds; Peruvian bark, two pounds; gentian root, two pounds; colombo root, two pounds; rhubarb, eight ounces; cloves, two ounces; cinnamon, four ounces; diluted alcohol, four gallons; water, two gallons; sugar, two pounds.[123]

302. TOOTHACHE EASE.—Liquor of ammonia, two parts; laudanum, one part; apply on lint.

303. CANDY DIGEST.—Lump sugar, one pound; water, three ounces; dissolve by heat; add cardamom seeds, ginger, and rhubarb, of each one ounce; when the mixture is complete pour it out on an oiled slab or into moulds.

304. COUGH LOZENGES.—Lactucarium, two drachms; ipecacuanha, one drachm; squills, three-fourth drachm; extract of licorice, two ounces; sugar, six ounces; make into a mash with mucilage of tragacinth, and divide into twenty grain lozenges.

305. LOVERS' HAIR OIL (Makes the hair glossy).—Castor oil, one pound; white wax, four ounces; melt together; add when nearly cold, of essence of bergamot, three drachms; oil of lavender, one-half drachm; essence of ambergris, ten drops.

306. PURGATIVE POWDER.—Equal parts of julep and cream of tartar, colored with a little red bole; dose, a teaspoonful in broth or warm water two or three times daily.

307. CONSUMPTION WAFERS.—Two parts each lump sugar and starch in powdered form; powdered gum, one part; made into a lozenge mass with vinegar of squills, oxymel of squills, and ipecacuanha wine, equal parts, gently evaporated to one-sixth their weight with the addition of lactucarium in proportion of twenty to thirty grains to every ounce of the powders, the mass being divided into half-inch squares weighing about seven and one-half grains.[124]

308. BEEF, IRON AND WINE.—Here is a recipe for Liebig's famous extract: Beef juice, one-half ounce; ammonia citrate of iron, 256 grains; spirit of orange, one-half fluid ounce; distilled water, one-half ounce; sherry wine sufficient to make sixteen fluid ounces. Dissolve the ammonia citrate of iron in the water; dissolve the extract of beef in the sherry wine; add the spirit of orange and mix the solution.

309. SPRING TONIC.—Calamus root, two pounds; orange peel, two pounds; Peruvian bark, two pounds; gentian root, two pounds; colombo root, two pounds; rhubarb, eight ounces; cinnamon, four ounces; cloves, two ounces; diluted alcohol, four gallons; water, two gallons; sugar, two pounds.

310. DR. PIERCE'S GOLDEN MEDICAL DISCOVERY.—Here is all there is of Dr. Pierce's Golden Medical Discovery. It is no doubt a good thing, but you can make it yourself. A one-dollar bottle holds 220 grains of a brownish-colored, clear liquid, consisting of fifteen grains of pure honey, one grain of extract of acrid lettuce, two grains of laudanum, 100 grains of diluted alcohol, with 105 grains of water.

311. BED-BUG EXTERMINATOR.—Corrosive sublimate, one ounce; muriatic acid, two ounces; water, four ounces; dissolve, then add turpentine, one pint; decoction of tobacco, one pint. Mix. For the decoction of tobacco, boil two ounces of tobacco in one pint of water. The mixture must be applied with a paint-brush. If well applied, this is a sure destroyer of bed-bugs. It is a deadly poison.

312. CATARRH CURE.—One-half gram of carbolic acid; one-half gram of camphor; and ten grams of[125] common salt; which are to be dissolved in four-sevenths of a liter of water and injected into the nostrils. You can call it the "Excelsior," for it is excelled by none.

314. OINTMENT FOR CHAPPED HANDS.—Camphor, sixty grs.; boric acid, thirty grs.; lanolin and white vaseline of each one-half ounce.

315. COD-LIVER OIL EMULSION.—Yolks of two eggs; powdered sugar, four ounces; essence of oil of almonds, two drops; orange flower water, two ounces. Mix carefully with an equal bulk of cod-liver oil. This is a delicious emulsion. Of course, the dose is double that of the clear cod-liver oil.

316. BEAUTY WATER.—(To remove freckles). Sulpho-carbonate of zinc, two parts; glycerine, twenty-five parts; rose water, twenty-five parts; spirits, five parts. Dissolve and mix. Anoint twice daily, keeping the ointment on the skin from one-half to one hour, then wash off with cold water. Wear a dark veil when exposed to the sun.

317. COUGH MIXTURE.—Syrup of poppies, syrup of squills, and paregoric, each one-half ounce. Mix.[126] Dose, a teaspoonful in a little warm water night and morning, or when the cough is troublesome.

318. DR. SAGE'S CATARRH REMEDY.—Here is the famous secret: One-half grm. of carbolic acid; one-half grm. of camphor and ten grms. of common salt; which are to be dissolved in four-sevenths of a liter of water and injected into the nostrils. Its reputation is believed to be well deserved.

319. DIARRHEA MIXTURE.—Wine of opium, one fluid ounce; tincture of valerian, one and one-half fluid ounces; ether, one-half fluid ounce; oil of peppermint, sixty minims; fluid extract of ipecac, fifteen minims; alcohol enough to make four fluid ounces. This is the

formula for a most celebrated patent medicine. The dose is a teaspoonful in a little water every two or three hours until relieved.

320. BLOOD PURIFIER.—Equal to the best selling compounds. For a bottle holding 220 grms., take fifteen grms. of pure honey; one grm. extract of poisonous or acrid lettuce; two grms. laudanum; 100 grms. of diluted alcohol; with 105 grms. of water. Make large quantities in like proportion.[127]

CHAPTER   XI.

MONEY IN REAL ESTATE.

> The Costliest Spot on the Western Hemisphere—A Mile and a Half of Millionaires—The Kings of the Earth—Why Some Rich Men Do Not Live in New York—The Country Fool and the Knowing Ones—How Coney Island Was Born—The Story of a Great Land Sale—Rents in Apartment Houses—The Fifty-story Office Building—The Man Who Gave a *Carte Blanche* Decoration Order, But Won't Do it Again—The Western Land Bubble—Good Farms Going to Waste—The Jersey Flats.

No class of men have made greater or securer fortunes than dealers in real estate. W. C. Ralston, James Lick, and J. J. Astor, are examples of persons who have accumulated vast sums through investments in land. The *points* of real estate are: First, a sound title; second, a keen foresight of the wants and the roads of civilization; third, a careful inspection of the neighborhood where a contemplated purchase is located; fourth, a thorough knowledge of market values of this kind of property; fifth, non-professional advice, in the disinterested judgment of men thoroughly familiar with property and prices. Other considerations are the rate of taxes of various kinds, imposed or likely to be imposed upon the property. Tax methods in large cities are often ways that are dark. For this reason, George Gould, the multi-millionaire, and Mr. Rockefeller, the Standard Oil magnate, have disposed of their urban properties.

321. CITY PROPERTY.—A mile and a half of millionaires![128] Midway between the East River and the Hudson there lay a few years ago a neglected tract of land which could have been bought for a few hundred thousand dollars. To-day it is the wealthiest mile and a half on the Western continent. One hundred million dollars would not purchase the ground alone. Forty years ago a piece of land which is now almost "down-town" was called "Eno's Folly," because he paid for it what was supposed to be an extravagant sum. It is now the site of the Fifth Avenue Hotel. The tide is still running up, but you must now go to the Bronx, or even further for cheap city property. It is, however, the most secure of all investments. Nothing is more certain than that the property in the

annexed district of New York is bound to advance. So also with real estate in all city suburbs.

322. Pleasure Resorts.—Less than forty years ago a man, simulating country simplicity, sauntered along Coney Island and astonished the owners by inquiring the price of what was supposed to be worthless land. They, thinking him crazy or a fool, named a thousand dollars, or five times what it was supposed to be worth. He accepted the offer on the spot. A million dollars would not buy the land to-day. The supposed countryman's "folly" has been repeated many times since. The owner of Bergen Beach has made a fortune in this way during the last two or three years. As cities grow, pleasure resorts must be found. Buy a bit of seashore and make it into a Bergen Beach or a Bowery Bay. Or, purchase a grove within easy distance of the city, and make it into a pleasure park. In either case, railroads or trolley connection is indispensable, but with these and plenty of enterprise and money you cannot fail to reap a large harvest. [129]

323. New Town Sites.—Large fortunes have been made by men who had the sagacity to see a potential factor in the meeting of two rivers, or the projection of a railroad. The question for investors in real estate is, "Where is the population going?" Keen observers note the drift, get ahead of the tide, and are ready to sell lots when the people arrive. Whitestone and Morris Park on Long Island were built in this way. It is a good investment, not quite so safe as city property, but paying more handsomely where the projector is fortunate in his location.

324. Western Lands.—Fortunes have been made and lost in Western lands. The facts are that some sharpers have been booming lands that are hardly worth the taxes. Persons who have bought "corner lots" in "promising" Western towns have been surprised to learn that the towns were not built, or even surveyed, and that often the site was located in the midst of an impenetrable swamp where a town was impossible. However, lands along the line of railroads, or places which have harbor facilities on the banks of rivers are good investments.

325. The Apartment House.—The apartment house, which is a kind of evolution of the flat, is becoming a feature of life in large cities. The question whether it is a paying property will receive light by the consideration of the rents received by the owners of a building of this kind in New York, the Knickerbocker at Fifth Avenue and Twenty-eighth Street. This is a typical apartment house, and the tenants may almost be said to buy their rooms, for there are several who give $100,000 for a ten-years' lease, and even small bachelor apartments on the tenth floor command $1,000 a year. [130]

326. The Sky Scraper.—There is no limit to the extent of a building in height. Some are twenty stories, one is thirty, and it is reported that a sky-scraper fifty stories in height is projected. Do they pay? Here is the account of a modest one of only nine stories, the Mills Building on William Street, New York. The cost, with land, was $2,500,000. It is

175 × 150 feet. It contains 400 offices, has 1,200 tenants, and pays an annual net rental of $200,000, or eight per cent. It is related of Mr. D. O. Mills, the owner, that in completing his magnificent residence on upper Fifth Avenue, he gave a *carte blanche* order to a decorator, and departed with his family to California. On returning he was delighted to find the place transformed into an Aladdin's Palace, but his joy was somewhat modified at the presentation of the bill which amounted to $450,000.

327. THE JERSEY FLATS.—Right over against property whose taxable value is $3,000,000,000 lies another property worth literally nothing. Step over from Manhattan Island, where every foot of land needs to be overlaid with silver round-moons for its purchase, to New Jersey, and you will find 27,000 acres of marsh lying under the very nose of the metropolis—land hardly worth a song. Why is this? Simply because capitalists have not been wise enough to improve this great waste. In Holland, by a system of diking, land in a similar condition is now covered by great warehouses and factories, and cannot be bought for hundreds of millions of dollars. Here is the opportunity for capitalists. Why invest money in far-off gold fields when you have a Klondike here at the very threshold of the metropolis? "The first step," says the State geologist, "is to build an embankment and a pumping station. [131] The cost will be about $1,000,000. The main ditches should be made, and the whole area laid out in twenty-acre farms, and sold on the express condition that each plot shall be immediately ditched and brought under cultivation." If we put the cost of ditching, and of other incidental expenses at $500,000, we have a total cost of $1,500,000. Then, if we estimate the worth of the land at only one-fourth the average price of land on Manhattan Island—which is the average worth of land in Jersey City—we have a value for the total 27,000 acres of $50,000,000. Profits, $48,500,000.

328. ABANDONED FARMS.—There are 4,300 abandoned farms in New England alone. These with a little expense could all be made profitable. Some are selling, buildings complete, as low as $700, and even $500. Many of these abandoned farms, costing $1,000, could, at the expense of another $1,000, be put in a highly thrifty condition and sold for $4,000. An Abandoned Farm Company will some time be organized with chances of good profit. [132]

CHAPTER XII.

MONEY IN THE FINE ARTS.

Some Things Everybody Ought to Know—An Institution that Teaches "Without Money and Without Price"—A Woman Who Earns $3,000 a Year—The Old Glue-Maker's Gift to Women—How a Little Girl Earned $300—A

THIS is one of the most enjoyable as well as one of the most remunerative occupations. One of the noblest things which Peter Cooper ever did was to found a Free Art School for Women. Not only is it absolutely free to all women, but opportunities are afforded for meritorious pupils to earn no mean sums during their period of instruction.

329. CRAYON WORK.—A teacher in the Cooper Institute says: "During the previous year forty of my pupils in art have made $7,000, or $175 each, while learning the art of crayon-photography. Every year one hundred women on leaving the Cooper Institute make from $400 to $1,200 a year by art work."

330. DRAWING.—One graduate of the Cooper Union is now receiving from $2,000 to $3,000 as a teacher of drawing in the New York public schools, and another has been appointed manager of a decorative art society [133] in New Orleans, with a salary of $150 a month, and opportunities to earn as much more by private tuition.

331. PHOTOGRAPH COLORING.—"A little girl," says Mr. Cooper, "came to my house to thank me for what she had learned at the Institute." "I have earned $300 coloring photographs," she said with enthusiasm. The coloring of photographs gives employment to many hundreds of young women, and there is no prospect that the market will become glutted.

332. OIL PAINTING.—A man in middle life met Mr. Cooper on the stairs of the Institute. "My daughter," he said, "makes $1,300 a year by teaching painting, and I never earned more than $1,200 myself." The chief points of oil painting are a *good tooth* (a canvas which will take color from a brush readily), perspective, fineness of touch, delicate perception, an eye for shades of color, and a bold, free hand. Oil paintings bring from $5 to $50,000, according to merit.

333. WATER COLORS.—Paintings in water colors are popular because less expensive than those done in oil. Good work in this department is, however, well paid. Much depends upon the subject and its treatment. It is said that the artist, Mr. John LaFarge, sold about $15,000 worth of water colors last year.

334. WOOD ENGRAVING.—A young woman from California sat on the sofa of Mr. Cooper's library. "I have come to thank you," she said. "I feel as rich as a queen. I have thirty pupils in wood engraving."

335. BOOK DECORATION.—Publishers of books, and especially of magazines, pay large prices for decorations [134] for the covers, title pages, and other important parts. The secret of success is in the design. If you can find a happy idea, you will get a large price for it. Of course, the point in most cases is to illustrate the subject-matter. A unique conception, happily worked out, will give both fame and money.

336. DYEING.—This may not be thought one of the fine arts, but it requires a skill hardly inferior to that of the painter or sculptor. There is a large field in the recoloring of tapestries, silks, and woolen goods. The requisites of success are taste, a good eye for color, knowledge of dye-stuffs, and indefatigable industry in finding a market.

337. DESIGNS.—These are constantly in demand. Wall paper manufacturers, dressmakers, architects, builders, home decorators, carpet manufacturers, fine-art workers, all want designs. An ordinary kaleidoscope will furnish you thousands of suggestions every day. From these select a few of the best and work them on a fine, white drawing paper. Have a separate folio for each department of drawings, and advertise what you are doing. If you have a real talent for the work, and a show-window, you cannot fail of success in any large town.

338. ENGRAVING ON GLASS.—By the use of the wheel this becomes easy work. The chief fields for its operation are in summer resorts where people wish to carry away a souvenir of the place. One who knows how to display goods can do a very profitable work in the season.

339. EMBROIDERY.—This is one of the simplest of the[135] arts. The only capital required is a ball of worsted, the only tool a needle, and the only instruction a few elementary rules that can be quickly learned. The demand depends upon the skill. A small store can be cheaply stocked, and its contents sold at a good profit if the articles are unique.

340. LACE MAKING.—Our valuable laces are chiefly imported, but there is no reason why work equally good should not be done at home. An immense field yet to be developed is American-made needle-point lace. Get a book on the subject and study it theoretically. Then take lessons of a maker. The book will give you suggestions and enable you, after you have learned the business, to strike out in various directions independently of your teachers.

341. DRAWING IN CHARCOAL.—This is a rapid, facile, and effective method for sketching. The drawings are more especially in demand in summer cottages, tents, and in whatever places lodgings are temporary, and where lodgers dislike the trouble of shipping costly paintings. You can find a ready market for good work at any mountain or seaside resort.

342. PAINTING ON CHINA.—This is becoming very popular. Few kinds of art pay better than china-firing. The outfit will cost from $15 to $50, according to the size of the kiln, but the pleasure and profit will be worth many hundreds of dollars. If you live in a country town, put your wares in a prominent store, and they will be sure to attract attention.

343. PORTRAIT PAINTING.—This is profitable if you can secure sufficient custom. The difficulty is to get[136] the flesh tones, the expression, and the proper degree of illumination. Last year, there were thirty young women in Cooper Institute learning the

art, and one-fifth of the number were earning from $5 to $12 a week, even during their tutelage.{137}

CHAPTER XIII.

MONEY IN MANUFACTURE.

> How a Blacksmith Got Rich—The Story of Pullman—The Story of the Columbia Bicycle—A Recipe for a Fortune—A Mica Secret—How to Make Marble—Another Great Secret Given Away—Rubber as Good as Goodyear's—A Way to Smash the Trusts—Wanted—A New Railroad Car—Sidney Smith's "Wooden Pavement."

VAST profits accrue from manufactures, but the best returns for investments in this line are realized when the manufacturer is able to make a new article, or to make an old article by improved means. David Maydole, a village blacksmith, was requested to make for a carpenter a hammer as good as he could make it. He made a better hammer than had ever before been seen, and the carpenter's mates all wanted one. The village storekeeper ordered two dozen. A hardware dealer, passing through the place to sell his wares, left an order for all the blacksmith could make. The hammer-maker built a large factory, and this was the humble origin of the celebrated Maydole hammer, and the foundation of a great fortune. Another fascinating chapter on manufacture is the "Story of Pullman," which reads like a fairy tale, but is all strictly true. Mr. Pullman began in a small way to build parlor cars, making one or two as an experiment. The traveling public were quick to appreciate the luxury, and Mr. P. had to enlarge his works again and again. {138} He built the town of Pullman, which is now valued at $30,000,000, and the capital stock which now has a market value of $60,000,000, has paid dividends with the regularity of a government loan.

344. BICYCLE FACTORIES.—These have proved veritable bonanzas during the past few years. In 1878, Col. Albert A. Pike began the manufacture of bicycles, making fifty that year. To-day he has a phenomenal business, employing a capital of $5,000,000 utilizing four factories in Hartford, Conn., and making 600 bicycles a day.

345. DOUBLE PROFIT FURS.—Here is a way to make a double profit from the skins of animals: Soak the furs in limewater till the hair is loosened, then wash and hang it up to dry. Lay it on a board with the hair side up and apply a solution of glue, care being taken not to disturb the natural position of the hairs. When the glue is dry and hard, hold the hairs so firmly as to allow the natural skin to be peeled off. Now you can apply the artificial skin by pouring over the hairs liquid India-rubber, boiled drying-oils, or other waterproof substances, which on drying will form a continuous membrane supporting

the hairs. The glue is then removed by steeping the fur in warm water. This plan has the double advantage that the fur so prepared is moth-proof, and the old skin can be used for the manufacture of leather.

346. MICA SHEETS.—Large sheets of mica command a great price. There are only a few places where the mineral can be mined in sheets of one foot square or larger, but the vast heaps of waste mica can be utilized by building up the sheets artificially. This can be done[139] by treating it with shellac. There are fortunes in waste mica quarries for those who know how to utilize the countless tons of fragments. The field is especially promising in North Carolina and Georgia, where immense quarries abound.

347. ARTIFICIAL MARBLE.—There is room for profitable investment in the manufacture of any article which is procured from nature at great expense. This is the case with marble. It is scarce at best; the quarries are remote from the centers of population, and the mining and transportation make it a very costly article. Marble can be manufactured by imitating nature's processes—the percolating of water through chalk. The popular verde antique can be made by an application of an oxide of copper. The slices of marble are then placed in another bath, where they are hardened and crystallized, coming out exactly like the real article. In Italy, a fine black marble is made from common white sandstone. The manufacture is carried on by the owners of the local gasworks, who thus reap a double profit from their plant. Here is a hint for American manufacturers.

348. ARTIFICIAL WHALEBONE.—Whalebone is in great demand. It is worth from $3 to $4 per pound. No artificial substance has as yet been found to take its place, but we are surely on the eve of that discovery. No one substance is at the same time so hard and so elastic, but experimenters will yet find a combination which will answer the purpose. One has already been found which draws the surplus demand when the genuine article cannot be obtained. The inventor who can advance another step and produce an exact imitation[140] will have the whalebone market in his hands. This field is rich with possibilities.

P. S.—Since writing the above we have the secret. Here it is: Treat the rawhide with sulphide of sodium, remove the hair, immerse the hide twenty-six to thirty-four hours in a weak solution of double sulphate of potassa, and stretch it upon a frame or table, in order that it may not contract in drying. The desiccation is allowed to proceed in broad daylight, and the hide is then exposed to a temperature of fifty to sixty degrees. The influence of the light, combined with the action of the double sulphate of potassa absorbed by the skin, renders the gelatine insoluble in water, and prevents putrefaction, the moisture being completely expelled. Thus prepared, the skin is submitted to a strong pressure, which gives to it almost the hardness and elasticity which characterize the genuine whalebone, with the advantage that before or after the process of desiccation any color desired may be imparted to it by means of a dye bath.

349. ARTIFICIAL INDIA RUBBER.—A man while experimenting recently with cottonseed oil for the production of a varnish, obtained to his surprise, not a varnish, but a rubber. By its use, with fifteen per cent. of genuine rubber, an article can be produced so exactly like the real as to defy detection. The process is so simple that a patent is not obtainable. So, manufacturers, the field is open. Rubber is high and in great demand.

350. ARTIFICIAL CAMPHOR.—Here is another trade secret. The genuine camphor is scarce. The artificial is made in England, shipped to Hamburg, and then re-shipped to England as the real article. Here is the way [141] it is made: Pass a current of dry hydrochloric acid gas through spirits of turpentine cooled by a freezing mixture. The liquid deposits crystals, which are dissolved in alcohol and precipitated by water. The separated crystals are drained and dried. They are perfectly colorless, with an odor like camphor. At the ordinary temperature, its vapor tension is sufficient to cause it to sublime like ordinary camphor in small brilliant crystals in the bottles in which it is preserved. It is insoluble in water, and gyrates when on the surface of that liquid like true camphor.

351. CAR BUILDING.—Some day another Pullman will arise, but with developments in car building in a totally different direction. We quote from a recent magazine article: "The time is sure to come when a new railroad genius will arise and make an end of the game of brag between American general passenger agents. This reformer will probably substitute light and easily cleaned bamboo seats for those now in use; he will save a good deal of the money now spent in useless ornamentation, and spend it in better ventilation and lighting; and he is likely to design frames and trucks much lighter, and at least as strong and durable, as those which carry the average day car of the present time. It is possible, too, that he may accomplish a good result by lowering the center of gravity of the prevailing type of passenger car, thus preventing it from rolling at high rates of speed, and obviating the supposed necessity of placing two or three tons of old rails in the floor to keep it steady." It is perhaps needless to say that such a man as Mr. Pullman or Mr. Wagner will become a multi-millionaire through this much-needed reform.

352. THE TRANSVERSE WOODEN PAVEMENT.—One [142] day the celebrated wit, Sidney Smith, was talking with some vestrymen of the church of which he was a member about laying a wooden pavement around the sacred edifice. "Well," said the famous jester, "we have but to lay our heads together and the thing is done." But here is a pavement which some capitalists will one day lay their heads (funds) together to produce, and it will be no joke. It has been ascertained that the most durable pavement is made from blocks of wood sawed transversely about twelve inches in thickness. The larger and smaller blocks are fitted together, the smaller interstices being filled with wooden wedges. Here is a chance for some enterprising firm. [143]

CHAPTER   XIV.

MONEY IN MINING.

The Earth a Vast Treasure-box—$300,000,000 from the Comstock Lode—A Short Story of Three Millionaires—Opportunities in Mica Mining—Fortunes in Salt Wells—$10,000 for Locating a Mine—Not a Cent of Capital Needed—The Gold Belt of the United States—Two Men's Earnings with the Pan—What Michigan Boys are Doing—Big Dividends in Tin—A Man with an Income of $2 a Minute.

THE immense importance which minerals play in our industries and the glittering fortunes made by delving into the earth, are faintly indicated by the fact that the output of last year aggregated the almost unthinkable sum of nearly $1,000,000,000. Profits in mining come mainly from four sources. The buying of mining lands with a view to sale, prospecting for the purpose of selling claims, placer-mining, and mining by machinery. Here are a few of the most promising roads to the earth's hidden wealth.

353. NEVADA SILVER.—The Comstock lode produced in three years $100,000,000, of which $30,000,000 went for cost and working expenses, and $70,000,000 for profits. Altogether $300,000,000 have been taken from that celebrated mine. In the African mines there are sixty-nine companies. In 1896 the lowest dividend of any of these companies was 10 per cent., and the highest 350. In 1897 the lowest was 10 and the highest 500 per cent. The accounts of the way that such men[144] as James Flood, James G. Fair, and William Sharon obtained their wealth from silver mines reads like the fascinating story of a popular novel.

354. ALUMINUM, THE NEW MINERAL.—"The product of aluminum in the United States," says a mining expert, "should be three million pounds in 1900." The present price is from thirty-five to fifty cents per pound. It is found chiefly in Georgia and Alabama at the foot of the Appalachian system, but there is no known reason why it should not be discovered in other parts—the mountains of Tennessee, North Carolina, and Pennsylvania.

355. NORTH CAROLINA MICA.—In the mountains of North Carolina are found the best mica dikes in the United States, but the methods of mining are crude and bring small profit. Here is an opportunity to make a vast fortune by the producing of mica with machinery such as is used in extracting other minerals.

356. KANSAS ZINC.—Zinc is a mineral which has a great future. It is being used largely in place of tin. There are many zinc mines, and especially in the Western States, as yet undeveloped. One acre in Galena, Kansas, produced $250,000.

357. MISSOURI COTTAS.—For clay go to Missouri. It is found in 90 out of the 114 counties of the State. From this mineral three companies in Kansas City are manufacturing sewer-pipes and working on an invested capital of $1,000,000. They have an annual output

worth $1,100,000, or more than 100 per cent. profit, less, of course, the cost of production. The sewer-pipe industry will vastly increase with the growth of cities. [145]

358. NICKEL MINES.—Nickel is a metal for which there is a constantly increasing demand. Aside from the vast number of nickel-plated articles, it has recently been found that steel, alloyed with a small percentage of nickel, makes the hardest substance known which can be produced on a large scale. It is bound to be used in future for the shells of our ironclads. In North Carolina and in Oregon, are large deposits of this valuable ore awaiting the hardy miner or bold speculator.

359. MEXICAN IRON.—Near the city of Durango, Mexico, are the largest iron mines in North America, but as yet entirely unworked. There are 10,000,000 square feet in sight, sixty per cent. of which is metallic iron. An opportunity for capitalists.

360. TENNESSEE LIMESTONE.—In the foothills of the Cumberland Mountains are ranges of blocks—lower Carbonifererous and Devonian shales, and impure limestone, but the rocks of the basin proper are pure limestone. This limestone when pulverized makes the best phosphate, and is worth $18 a ton. A mining authority states that with proper working it ought to produce at least 200,000 tons of rock per annum.

361. FORTUNES IN COPPER.—Forty-eight per cent. of the copper of the world is in the United States and Canada. The price is $200 a ton. Almost all the mines of the Lake Michigan region are making profit, but the industry is yet in its infancy. When it is known that a mine has been made to pay which contains less than one per cent. of copper, it can be seen what fortunes are in the mines that pay from forty to fifty per cent., and there are some that pay even more. [146]

362. GERMAN AMBER.—In Memel, Germany, a dredging company pays the government an annual rental of twenty-five thalers a day for the privilege of dredging in the Kurische Hoff, near the village of Schwarzarts. But it is not to be supposed that this is the only spot where amber is to be found. It will doubtless yet be discovered in this country.

363. AFRICAN DIAMONDS.—Diamonds in vast numbers are found in the beds of many South African streams, but if you have capital you may develop an industry like that of the De Beers Company, which is paying forty per cent. per annum.

364. TASMANIA TIN.—A single company in Murat Bischoff has paid more than $7,000,000 in dividends to the fortunate owners of a tin mine.

365. GEORGIA SAPPHIRES.—In 1872, Colonel C. W. Jenks, of Boston, picked up one hundred of these valuable stones at Laurel Creek, Rylang County, Georgia, a single gem of which was sold for $25.

366. ROCK SALT.—Rock salt is found in Syracuse, New York, and in Michigan, also in Louisiana, and in South Eastern Arizona. It is believed that if these mines were bored deeper, potassium salt—a salt hitherto not found in the United States—would be

discovered, and home plants take the place of foreign imports. Here is a chance for enterprising men.

367. ASBESTOS POCKETS.—A profitable pocket of asbestos was found a few years ago on Long Island not far from Brooklyn. Present supplies come from Sal Mountain, Georgia, and from Wyoming. It is believed that the serpentine rocks in Western North Carolina, {147} as well as similar rocks in California and Oregon, contain rich deposits of this mineral.

368. PROSPECTS IN PLATINUM.—This is a metal of very great importance. It has not thus far been found in large quantities in the United States. The most promising field is the North Pacific Slope, following the line of the coast mountains. Some day, it is thought, that rich platinum mines may be discovered there equal to those in Russia, and, of course, the early prospectors will reap large fortunes.

369. PETROLEUM WELLS.—"Petroleum," says a leading article in the *Electrical World*, "is the coming fuel." It is believed by many that the excitement over the discovery of oil fields in Pennsylvania in 1865 will be repeated on a much larger scale in oil regions yet to be discovered in the far West. At present, the mountains of Wyoming appear to be the most promising field. To sink an oil well costs $500 on the average. On Oil Creek, Pennsylvania, a few wells have been struck which yielded 3,000 barrels a day. One of the quickest ways to accumulate a fortune is to prospect for oil, and when a rich vein is struck to buy as much land as you can. A young man named Johnny Steel once owned nearly all the land where the Pennsylvania oil wells were discovered. His income was over $1,000,000 a year, $30,000 a day, or about $2 a minute. But, verifying the adage that "a fool and his money are soon parted," he not only spent all this enormous income, but also squandered the entire principal, and came at last to work as the driver of an oil wagon on the very oil farm he had once owned.

370. GOLD DISCOVERIES.—Draw a line from Colorado{148} Springs, Colorado, north to Laramie City, Wyoming. From these two points draw straight lines one thousand miles to the west and inclose the parallelogram. You have inclosed what is known as the great gold belt of the United States. Nearly all the gold has been discovered within these comparatively narrow limits. Cripple Creek produced $8,000,000 in four years. A man who walked into that place three years ago to save his stage fare is now taking out $100,000 a year from his mines. Dawson City, way up in the frozen British possessions, promises to do as well as any gold discovery in the United States. Two men, the Thorpe brothers, cleaned up with their pans $13,000 in eight weeks. This was but a very small part of the immense amount of gold found in an insignificant creek, but there are at least five hundred creeks on the branches of the Yukon River, many of them no doubt as rich as the one that gave Dawson City its fame.

371. PROSPECTING FOR MINES.—"How many undeveloped mines are there west of the Mississippi, which, if developed, would be valuable properties? There may be ten thousand. It is far more likely that there are a million." Extract from "Mines and Mining Industries in the United States." The same authority also says that a prospector who has spent a year in locating a mine should receive $10,000 from a capitalist as his share. Mark this, you who think mining has no prospects, except for men of wealth.{149}

CHAPTER   XV.

MONEY IN PATENT RIGHTS.

> Nearly 100 Patents Issued Every Day—The Easiest Way to Get Rich—Crystallize Your Idea Into a Coin—Six Billion Dollars of Capital Based on Patents—Great Returns for American Genius—What a Patent is Worth—A Million Dollar Patent Discovered by Accident—A Fortune in a Needle's Eye—The Man who Invented the "Donkey," and What He Made by It—What "Pigs in Clover" Netted the Lucky Inventor—How to Get a Patent —What to Invent for Profit.

PROBABLY no enterprise has yielded so great profits with so little capital as the work of the inventor. The small outlay, resulting in mammoth fortunes, has often consisted in little more than the set of stools and the cost of the patent. Of course, there must be brains and hard thinking. The sale of articles protected by patent rights is a stimulus to invent them, and has been the source of fortunes for more people in the United States than in any other country in the world. The United States Patent Office issues every year about 25,000 patents, and the number is constantly increasing. Nor are the patentees in all, or even in a majority of cases, men of genius, or persons who have been learned in the occupations in which they have achieved distinction. The greater part of them have been issued to persons in humble walks of life, who made their lucky discovery either by accident or by close application of thought.

In every department of human industry there are possibilities of improvement. He who can find a cheaper, quicker, or better, way of doing anything will get rich.{150} Cyrus H. McCormick thought out a better way of cutting grain than with the old scythe. The result was the McCormick harvester, known all over the world. His patents made him a millionaire. Charles Goodyear accidentally mixed a bit of rubber and sulphur on a red hot stove. The result set him to thinking. He discovered the process of vulcanization, which is the basis of the great rubber industry throughout the world. His patents made him enormously rich. Elias Howe wondered if there could not be some better way of sewing than by the bone and muscle of weary woman's hand. He tried and tried in vain. At last he had a dream in which he saw a needle with the eye at the point instead of at the head. He awoke exclaiming, "I have it!" The result was the sewing machine. Mr.

Howe received every year more than $100,000 royalties on his patent needle. Eli Whitney, watching some slaves cleaning cotton, set to work to find a better way. He invented the cotton-gin by which one machine performs the labor of five thousand persons. This invention reaped for him untold wealth.

These were men of genius, but there are inventions which, being simple, lie apparently within the reach of all men. Mr. Parker, whose invention of the tobacco box fastening, is nothing but a "bulge and a dent," and which it would seem any child might have thought out, made an immense fortune. Another inventor obtained a patent for a washing machine, and sold it in about fifteen months for $50,000. A man obtained a patent for a windmill, took a model through the Western States, and in eight months returned with $40,000 in cash. Probably the simplest device of all which has afforded amusement for millions is the game of the "Donkey Party," which is nothing more than the picture of a tailless donkey placed upon the wall. The game costs[151] less than one cent, but millions are annually sold. A copyright costing $5 insured this windfall to the inventor. The "Parlor Target and Dot" patent brought $35,000. The chief examiner of the Patent Office says: "A patent, if it is worth anything, when properly managed, is worth and can easily be sold for from $10,000 to $50,000."

According to an estimate by the Commissioner of Patents seven-eighths of the manufacturing capital of the United States, or upwards of $600,000,000 is based upon patents, either directly or indirectly. A very large proportion of all patents prove remunerative; this is the reason so many are applied for, and so many millions of capital invested in their workings. There is scarcely an article for amusement, convenience, or necessity, in use to-day that has not at some time or other been the subject of a patent either in whole or in part. The sale of every such article yields the inventor a profit. If we purchase a box of matches a portion of the price goes to the inventor; if we buy a bicycle the chances are that we pay royalty to a dozen or more inventors at once.

There are gold mines in every walk in life. There are fortunes hid in the smallest and meanest of things. So far from the field being exhausted, more inventions are now being patented than ever before. The world is inexhaustibly full of nuggets for him who can find them. Every sphere of enterprise is like the children's play of "hide the thimble." Friend, shall you be the first to spy the golden rim? The cost of a patent in the United States is about $60. This includes the government fee, and that of a patent attorney. The way to get a patent is first to think it out; then make the design and take it to a lawyer who makes a business of procuring patents. The government does not now request[152] a model, but it requires a drawing and a specification, and these must be prepared by some competent attorney, in the legal form prescribed. The following are a few suggestions in the various departments of toil where inventions are needed, or where the pry of the brain will disclose the flashing ore.

372. A Non-Puncturable Bicycle Tire.—Any improvement in the universal wheel means a fortune to the inventor. The Dunlap tire sold for $15,000,000.

373. A Bicycle-Holder Attachment.—One that will make it stand upright when not in use. There is a fortune here.

374. The Bicycle Umbrella-Holder.—It should not be difficult to fit to the wheel a small attachment for holding an umbrella. The device should be made so as to allow the umbrella to turn at an angle. Most bicyclists would want this invention.

375. A Bicycle Cyclometer Clock.—A small clock or a watch to be fixed to the front part of the bicycle with cyclometer attachment, so as to give the time of day, the number of miles traversed, and the rate of speed.

376. The Double-Power Bicycle.—One in which the hand or the foot may be used in propelling, to be employed alternately, the one as a rest for the other, or jointly, as when pedaling against the wind or uphill.

377. The Folding Wheel.—One that can be carried lightly on the shoulder and packed in small space for storage or shipment.[153]

378. A Bicycle Support.—A contrivance for holding the wheel in place when the rider stops but does not wish to dismount. A large sale guaranteed.

379. The Cushion Saddle.—The chafing, painful experience of many bicycle riders would be obviated if some one would invent a saddle top as durable as leather, and yet affording a much softer seat.

380. A Bicycle Guard.—One which will enable a lady with a long dress to ride without fear of her skirts being entangled in the wheel. Almost every lady in the land would ride a wheel if this difficulty could be obviated.

381. A Combination Bicycle Lock.—One million bicyclists want a cheap lock which can be operated without a key and fastened to any object.

382. A Bicycle Trunk.—One made of light material and adapted to carrying on the rear of a wheel.

383. The Unicycle.—The wheel of the future will doubtless be single. The man who is the first to invent a practical unicycle will reap a gigantic fortune.

384. A Bicycle Cover.—One which will protect the frame and handle bars when the rider is overtaken by rain, and one which can be packed into a very small compass.

385. A Package Holder.—One adapted to be kept on the bicycle frame. As all bicycle makes are nearly uniform in size, this invention should be an easy one.[154]

386. HANDLE-BAR CYCLOMETER.—Let the indicator or dial face be fixed to the handle-bar instead of the wheel. Every bicyclist would want it.

387. THE ALL-SELLING WHEEL.—A pneumatic bicycle tire with a non-puncturable coating would easily bring a million, and might even rival the popularity of a Dunlap.

388. TOE-AND-HEEL CLIP.—An appliance to the bicycle pedal which would hold the heel as well as the toe, and which would not increase the difficulty of mounting, would have immense sales.

389. THE EXTENSION BICYCLE.—A wheel which may be made as convenience requires into a tandem or single wheel by addition or removal of parts would be in great demand.

390. A BICYCLE SHOE.—A sole adapted to be attached to an ordinary shoe, and with means for retaining a hold on the pedals.

391. THE STIRRUP PEDAL.—A pedal which is shaped like a stirrup, holding the foot and doing away with toe-clips.

392. THE HOME BICYCLE.—The use of the bicycle in certain hours every day has become indispensable to the health of thousands, but there are many rainy and inclement days as well as weeks and months in the winter when it cannot be used. Invent a home bicycle by means of which one can have all the exercise of the ordinary wheel in all kinds of weather.

Section 2. Money in Building Contrivances.

393. THE ORNAMENTAL FLOOR.—Ornamental floors,[155] for ballrooms, summer hotels, and all rooms where carpets are not indispensable.

394. THE SECURE WINDOW BLIND.—The present appliances for holding back the window blind permit it to shake to and fro, giving unpleasant noises in the night. There is needed a device that will hold it securely in place.

395. THE SELF-LOCKING WINDOW.—Doors are made self-locking; why not windows? Who will invent a means by which the shutting of a window at the same time locks it?

396. THE ADJUSTABLE BLIND.—A mechanism by which a blind or shutter can be worked from within. A toothed wheel with crank inside the window, and a connection by an iron rod with the shutter whereby the blind or shutter can be held wide open, can be closed, or held in any position whatever, by simply turning a crank.

397. THE DOLLAR DOOR CLOSER.—The automatic door closer made the inventor rich, but it is expensive; we want a door closer that can be fastened to every door and sold as low as $1.

398. SECTIONAL WINDOW.—A window built in horizontal sections of two or more with a spring or casing to hold it up—much cheaper than weights.

399. ADJUSTABLE STORM DOOR.—Devise a simple door which can be readily brought into place in time of storm, and which will be unnoticed or not seem unsuitable when not needed.

400. A HINGE LOCK.—A hinge which operates as a[156] lock, when the door is closed, and can only be opened by a key. Operated the same as a spring lock, but with less mechanism.

401. THE DOUBLE WINDOW.—Here is a plan for window ventilation. It is the idea of a French physician, but he has not patented it. Have a double window with openings at the bottom of one, and at the top of the opposite one through which the air comes in freely without any one feeling it. The plan is said to possess simplicity, efficiency, and cheapness. Let the American carpenter take notice and profit thereby.

402. HOT-BLAST FURNACE.—A small hot-blast furnace for drying walls. Builders who have to wait days for walls to dry call for such a machine.

403. THE WEIGHTLESS WINDOW SASH.—When the window can be opened the desired width and kept there without the aid of a rope that finally breaks and involves trouble and expense, a great want will be supplied.

404. A FLOOR COVER.—Carpets are expensive; matting is not elegant. Discover something in place of both, cheap and ornamental, and you will reap one of the richest financial harvests of the century.

405. SASH BALANCE.—A system by which the force which holds the lower sash up may exactly balance the force which holds the upper sash down, both sashes being opened at the same width, and thus insuring both the outflow of impure air and the inflow of fresh.

406. PAINTING MACHINES.—Why may not painting as well as so many other modern arts be done by machinery? Something on the order of the garden-hose and spraying nozzle could do the work of the painter[157] more rapidly, cheaply, and with less risk of life and limb. Inventors, give us a painting machine.

407. THE PNEUMATIC WATER TANK.—Instead of the unsightly water tank on the top of isolated buildings or country dwellings, with its liability of leakage and destruction of property, why not have a water tank in the cellar operated by means of compressed air? By being placed in the cellar or underground, there would be the additional advantage of having the water drawn cool and fresh. In winter also, it would be much better protected from freezing than when placed on top of a building. Some one will find money in a pneumatic water tank.

408. THE WOOD-PULP FLOOR.—Floors have been accused of great sins. If the timber is not thoroughly seasoned they warp; if the boards are not properly laid they creak; and the cracks are all at times filled with injurious dust and dangerous germs. Why not invent a wood-pulp floor which shall have no warps, and no cracks, and no creaks? Dry the pulp to powder to facilitate transportation, mix with a small amount of cement, to increase the resistance of the floor, and then after making it a gelatinous mass pass it between rollers. When dry, paint it to imitate oak or other wood. Besides avoiding all the inconveniences and annoyances of the ordinary floor, it will be soft to the foot, and though somewhat more expensive than the entire boards, it will yet be the floor of the future in all comfortable homes.

Section 3. Money in the Kitchen.

409. THE CHEAP WASHER.—For all the many washing machines, most of our women in middle-class and lowly life are still bending painfully over the old[158] tubs. What is needed is a cheap washer that everyone will buy.

410. A MEAT CHOPPER.—One which has a large number of small blades dividing the meat ten or twenty times with one stroke, where now the large blades divide it only one-fourth or fifth that number of times. The scroll bread-knife netted a princely revenue to its fortunate inventor.

411. AUTOMATIC STOVE-DAMPER.—One to take the place of the heedless servant, and close when the state of the fire warrants it. Thousands of dollars' worth of coal could annually be saved to housekeepers by this device.

412. POTATO EXTRACTOR.—Apply the principle of the glass lemon-squeezer to the raw potato and you have not only a new invention but also a new preparation of the common vegetable. The potato in the form of the raw pulp can be cooked in various ways, and will have a decidedly new and agreeable flavor. As a salad or a dressing it would be invaluable.

413. KNIFE SHARPENER.—One for the kitchen use, that could be sold for twenty-five cents; almost every housekeeper would want one.

414. COLD HANDLE.—A separate handle which could be instantly applied to utensils on the stove and remove them without burning the hands waits to enrich the inventor. The cold-handled smoothing-iron brought much money to its inventor.

415. THE ELECTRIC STOVE.—Cooking by electricity will be the domestic feature of the next century. There is a rich field here awaiting some inventive brain.[159]

416. FRUIT-JAR HOLDER.—A device for holding fruit jars during the preserving process so that the can will neither burn the hand nor spill the fruit.

417. CAN OPENER.—All the women are crying for an effective can opener. Those on the market are not satisfactory. They must be made to sell very cheap. A gold mine in a can opener.

418. ODORLESS COOKING VESSELS.—An attachment whereby the odors of cooking will be carried into the chimney instead of out into the room.

419. COAL-FILLED FLAT-IRON.—Construct a hollow flat-iron so that it can be filled with live coals, and thus keep in proper heat much longer than those now in use.

420. AUTOMATIC SOAPER.—A washboard so arranged that the soft soap is fed to the clothes by the simple act of rubbing.

421. DISH-WASHING MACHINE.—A dish-washing machine which can be sold for $5. There are plenty of machines on the market, but they are too expensive for use, except in hotels or in rich households. A cheap machine could be sold in every house.

422. A STOVE ALARM.—Proper cooking requires the heat of the stove to be kept equable. Invent a contrivance by which when the heat exceeds a certain degree an alarm will be sounded.

423. THE ELASTIC CLOTHES LINE.—Save washerwomen and housekeepers the nuisance of tying and untying of hard knots by inventing the elastic clothes line.{160}

424. COMBINATION LINE AND PIN.—If the old-fashioned line is to be used, why not invent a cheap clasp which remains permanently on the line, and is capable of being moved in either direction. Clothes pins are lost, broken, or not at hand when required.

425. A FRUIT PRESS.—A cheap press which will be as much a part of every furnished kitchen as a range. Every housewife needs one for the extracting of juices.

426. THE CAN-SLIDE.—The opening of hermetically sealed cans is one of the difficulties of life. All can openers so far invented are more or less ineffective. A vast fortune awaits a man who will invent a can-slide which will effectually keep the food air-tight, and which at the same time may be easily opened.

Section 4. Money in the Parlor.

427. THE CHAIR FAN.—A slight vertical motion of the foot is much less tiresome than a lateral motion of the hand. An ingenious man could attach a fan to a chair so as to cool the face by the action of the foot.

428. ROCKING-CHAIR FAN.—A fan to be attached to the top of a rocking-chair and operated by the motion of a rocker.

429. CHRISTMAS-TREE HOLDER.—A device for holding the tree upright in any spot without further support. Would sell once a year by the million if made for twenty-five cents.

430. Picture-Frame Fastener.—A device such that every one can frame his own picture, the parts of the frame being attached without hammer or nails. [161]

431. Adjustable Head Rest.—One that can be attached to any chair and adjusted to any position.

432. Imitation Coal Fire.—The asbestos back-log was quite a hit. Now let some one invent a fire where gas may be used in the same manner, but the representation be that of red, live coals.

433. Music Turner.—A piece of music has only a few leaves. It is easy to arrange a series of markers between each leaf with a handle for turning. It may be an ornament as well as a convenience.

434. Roll-Front Fire-Screen.—It is to be constructed on the principle of the roll-top desk, with the difference that it rolls sidewise from one side or from both sides of the fireplace.

435. Removable Rockers.—A chair with rockers easily adjustable, so that it may be a rocker or an ordinary chair as desired.

Section 5. Money in the Bedroom.

436. A Noiseless Clock.—Many nervous people are annoyed by the ticking of clocks. Who can invent one which will perform this work silently?

437. A Narcotic Pillow.—Will not some one give us a pillow composed of the dried flowers or leaves of soporific plants? The nervous, overworked persons who could thus get a night's sound sleep would bestow upon the lucky inventor the money which he now expends in drugs.

438. The Electric Fire Igniter.—In almost every household some one on a winter's morning shivers over [162] a cold stove and suffers much till a fire is well started, but if the fuel were laid over night and the stove equipped with an electric wire running to the bedroom, one could press a button with the satisfaction of soon entering a warm kitchen. Such a device would pay the inventor well.

439. Bedclothes Fastener.—A clamp or clasp which shall fix the cover to the board so that children shall not kick or pull the clothes off in their sleep.

440. The Easy-Working Bureau.—Who will contrive some device by which a bureau drawer will open readily and evenly at both ends? The present working of these drawers is a vexation of the soul.

441. The Extensible Bedstead.—A bedstead that can be extended to accommodate two or three persons, or when room is wanted contracted to the use of one person.

442. MOVABLE PARTITION AND FOLDING BED.—Some one should invent a partition that will form a part of the wall of a room, and which will inclose a bed when the latter is not in use. In the economy of space which forms so important an element in the construction of city houses, it is strange no builder has not yet thought of this.

443. AN ATTACHABLE CRIB.—A combined bed and crib so arranged that when the crib is not in use it may be folded in or under the larger bed of an adult.

444. PULSE INDICATOR.—Hardly one in a hundred can take the beats of his own pulse. The first thing the doctor does is to feel your pulse. Invent an instrument[163] so delicate that its clasp on the wrist will accurately tell the pulse.

445. DRESS-SUIT HANGER.—The device for a dress coat should be extended to other parts of a gentleman's wear. Give us a dress-suit hanger which will cause the suit to appear when not in use very much as it does when on the body of a man.

446. THE ANTI-SNORER.—It should not be difficult to invent a simple mouth or nose attachment to prevent the intolerable nuisance of snoring.

447. THE VENTILATED MATTRESS.—Housekeepers take pains to air their beds, but the mattress remains for years a mass of unventilated feathers or hair, and a fruitful soil for the deposit of disease germs. A kind of honeycombed mattress might be constructed, through the holes of which the air could circulate freely. It might be possible on this plan to have the spring and mattress in one piece.

Section 6. Money in the Cellar.

448. A FURNACE FEEDER.—Every householder would buy an automatic feeder for the furnace, thus saving the arduous labor of shoveling coal. There should be a bonanza in the right invention.

449. ICE MACHINE.—The study of the large ice machines now in use, with a view to produce one on a scale so small and cheap as to be introduced into every household has boundless possibilities of wealth for a fertile-brained inventor.

450. STOVE ASH-SIFTER.—The waste of coal in unsifted ashes is enormous, but the process of sifting is[164] disagreeable. What is needed is an attachment beneath the grate by means of which the ashes will be thrown into one pan and the unconsumed coals into another. An immensely paying invention.

451. JOINTED COAL CHUTE.—Much time could be saved in unloading coal if some one would give us a coal chute jointed so as to be swung at an angle, thus avoiding delay where the driveway is too narrow to permit the straight chute to be inserted properly.

452. COMBINED PAN, CAN, SIFTER AND ROLLER.—A useful article would be the pan beneath the grate of the furnace, which could be used also as a can containing a sifter and provided with rollers so that it could be easily transferred to the street.

453. ASH BARREL.—Much annoyance is caused, especially on windy days, by the blowing of ashes from the carts of the ash gatherers. This might be avoided by the construction of a patent ash barrel which could be transferred to the cart and exchanged for an empty one, on the same principle as oil cans are exchanged by the venders.

Section 7. Money in the Library and Schoolroom.

454. A PAPER BINDER.—One that will bind newspapers and other periodicals, and which can be sold for twenty-five cents. Those on the market are too expensive.

455. THE CORRESPONDENT'S DESK.—A desk with compartments specially arranged for correspondents would save much time and annoyance on the part of letter-writers. Paper, pen, ink, envelope, postage[165] stamp, answered letters, letters requiring immediate reply, and letters which require time for consideration, would then be relegated to the most fitting place, and be available when wanted.

456. BOOK DUSTER.—There is needed some simple attachment to a bookcase whereby the dust which has gathered on the books may be quickly removed when one wishes a volume without soiling of the hands.

457. THE PORTABLE LIBRARY.—A useful device would be a combined box and bookcase, so that in packing for removal the books need not be disturbed, the doors of the bookcase serving as a lid for the box.

458. POCKET LUNCH BASKET.—A lunch basket which can be folded and put in the pocket when empty. Ten million school children want this article.

459. THE MULTIPLE-LEAVED BLACKBOARD.—A blackboard attached to the wall and opening outwardly with several leaves so that it can be used by a number of pupils at once, and when not in use can be folded back so as to occupy a small space.

Section 8. Money in Meals.

460. BUTTER AND CHEESE CUTTER.—A device which cuts butter and cheese into small square blocks. It should be shaped like a caramel-mold with sharp edges, cutting ten or twelve blocks with a single insertion.

461. PAPER TABLE CLOTH.—The constantly increasing use of paper for new articles is a feature of the times. We have paper napkins, but why could not a paper be manufactured of a little better quality so as to serve for a tablecloth?[166]

462. SCROLL-EDGE MEAT KNIFE.—The scroll-edge bread knife is being manufactured as fast as possible, the factories running night and day. Construct a meat knife on the same principle, with difference only sufficient to secure a patent, and a fortune is yours.

463. CARVING-KNIFE HOLDER.—A small wooden or wire frame with depressions for knife and fork when not in use would conduce to cleanliness and save much vexation on the part of those who carve.

464. LAMP COOKER.—A wire frame with hooks on the bottom for clasping a lamp-chimney could be placed on the top of a lamp, and would make an excellent patent cooker for light dishes. Think of the convenience of cooking your supper on your lamp chimney!

465. WINE TABLETS.—Here is an idea for the trade. We have lemonade tablets; why not those of wine? The grapes should be pressed in the ordinary way, and then by means of a knife transferred to an apparatus where they can be evaporated in a vacuum, the vapor to be drawn off by a pump and condensed. As soon as the mass has the consistency of a syrup it is to be mixed with the pulp. Thus a sort of marmalade is produced, containing eighty per cent. of grape sugar. Makers of the lemonade tablets have done well, but the inventor of the wine tablets would have an immensely larger market.

466. EXTENSION TABLE.—Difficulty is experienced with the present extension table. The boards are not at hand when wanted, and frequently will not go into place readily. A table is needed in which the boards fold underneath, and can be readily brought into place by the turning of a crank. {167}

Section 9. Money in the Business Office.

467. THE KEYBOARD LOCK.—A combination lock on the principle of the cash register. Instead of carrying certain combinations of numbers in your brain, you simply remember a definite order of keys, and push them in turn as you would in playing a light air on the piano. This patent would be a great improvement on the present system, and contains barrels of money.

468. AUTOMATIC SAFE OPENER.—Run by clockwork, and set so as to open automatically at a certain hour of the day, and impossible to open at any other time.

469. PAPER BINDER AND BILL HOLDER.—A flat stick, concave at each end, so as to hold a large number of elastic bands. Slip a band over each bill, and you may have a hundred or more papers preserved in compact form.

470. BOOK LOCK.—A pocket contrivance which can be attached to the edges of a book. Notebooks, diaries, and private correspondence, could then be guarded during the momentary absence of the writer. A great sale predicted.

471. THE PERPETUAL CALENDAR.—A calendar which will show on what day or month any event fell or will fall for all time.

472. THE LIGHTNING ADDER.—It is possible by a system of keys to invent a machine which will set down almost as quick as lightning the sum of any column of figures, thus dispensing with much of the service of a bookkeeper.[168]

473. COPYHOLDER.—Typewritists want a copyholder capable of being adjusted to any size of manuscript and which can be sold as low as twenty-five cents.

474. ENVELOPE MOISTENER AND SEALER.—Construct a narrow brass or iron plate, one-fourth of an inch wide and shaped like the flap of an envelope. A shallow vessel of water is placed underneath, into which by the manipulation of a screw, the plate is occasionally dipped. Above the plate is fixed a second plate which acts as a sealer, and which operates with a screw-head.

475. MULTIPLE LOCK.—A device for locking with one movement all the drawers in a desk or bureau.

476. OFFICE DOOR INDICATOR.—One to be operated instantly and easily, showing that the occupant is out, and with a dial face to indicate when he expects to return.

477. AUTOMATIC TICKET SELLER.—It is entirely feasible to have an automatic ticket seller which will both date and deliver tickets. A machine of this kind has been fixed in the Hammerton Station at North London, and is said to work satisfactorily. But there is room for improvement on the part of brainy inventors.

478. PERFORATED STAMP.—The chief of the London Stamp office said the government was losing $500,000 a year through the dishonest practice of removing stamps from official papers and using them again; and he offered a large sum or a life office at $4,000 a year to any one who would invent a stamp which could not be counterfeited.[169]

Section 10. Money in the Packing Room.

479. NONREFILLABLE BOTTLE.—Such a bottle is an absolute necessity to beer and liquor manufacturers, sauce and patent medicine makers, yet no one has yet supplied the demand. Here is a chance, and there are millions in it.

480. THE COLLAPSIBLE BOX.—A box that cannot be refilled for fraudulent purposes. Must be so built that it cannot be opened without destroying it. It would be purchased by every maker of confections.

481. BOTTLE STOPPER.—There are mines of wealth in a cheap substitute for cork. An inventor will some day make a fortune by the inventing of a paper stopper.

482. COMBINATION CORK AND CORKSCREW.—A bottle stopper which can be removed by simply turning it around like the top of a wooden money-barrel made for children. Must be made to sell cheap.

483. THE COLLAPSIBLE BARREL.—A barrel arranged in a series of parts each one above smaller than the one below, and so contrived that when not filled the parts sink into each other like the pieces of a field glass. A barrel of such convenience for reshipping would be bought by the hundred thousand, and would be full of gold for its inventor.

484. SELF-STANDING BAG.—A device whereby bags will stand alone with wide-open top while being filled, thus dispensing with the services of an extra man. All shipping merchants would pay largely for such a bag.

485. BARREL FILLER AND FUNNEL CUT-OFF.—Barrel filling by the ordinary funnel is slow. Provide[170] four openings at the bottom instead of one. A small rubber hose will connect the opening of each barrel, and a cut-off or a string attachment at the end of each hose cuts off the flow when the barrel is full, and permits the contents of the hose to be carried back to the barrel and thence into one of the unfilled barrels, thus avoiding waste.

486. FOLDING CRATE.—The transportation of fruit and other produce would be greatly facilitated and cheapened if some one would invent a folding crate. An empty crate occupies as much room as a full one.

487. PAPER BARREL.—Who will invent a paper barrel which will be as serviceable as the present wooden one, and have the advantage of being light? It would have a universal sale.

Section 11. Money in Articles of Trade.

488. THE TRADESMAN'S SIGNAL.—An automatic device for letting the grocer, butcher, baker, etc., know when he is wanted, saving time both to the household and trade. Sure to sell.

489. BARREL GAUGE.—A dial with hands to be attached to a barrel or keg to indicate the amount of its contents.

490. ELASTIC CHIMNEY.—An elastic glass chimney which will expand with the heat and not break would sell by the million.

491. AIR MOISTENER.—A apparatus for moistening the air in the room. It should avoid the objectionable feature of all present devices which sprinkle minute drops of water to the damage of goods. All large manufacturers and proprietors of large stores, where many[171] workmen and clerks are employed will pay handsomely for such a machine.

492. AUTOMATIC LUBRICATOR.—Every wheel, axle, pulley and joint, in labor's great beehive needs oil. A vast amount of valuable time is consumed in the work. Invent an oil-can which will work automatically, and you can name your own price.

493. Short-Time Negative.—A process by which the negative of a photographic camera may be developed almost instantly instead of consuming the time now required. An immediate fortune is assured to the discoverer of this art.

494. Drying Apparatus.—An invention by which dry air could be produced in abundance so as to dry clothes or be employed in the preservation of fruits would make its deviser independently rich.

495. Rotable Hotel Register.—A revolving frame for a hotel office, so that the register is alike accessible to the clerks within and the guests without.

496. Glass Dome.—The inventor of the little glass bell for hanging over gas jets made a fortune, but as the gas fixture is commonly attached to a movable bracket it does not always occupy the same place. A glass dome which shall be a part of the gas fixture would be a great improvement and bring much money to the inventor.

497. Round Cutting Scissors.—A scissors or shears that will cut round as well as straight. It would be bought by every one who uses a needle.

498. Casket Clamp.—Three thousand people die every day in this country. Undertakers want a clamp[172] which will keep the casket from moving in the hearse either laterally or longitudinally.

499. Self-Winding Clock.—An arrangement such that when the weight of the clock touches a certain point it will set in operation a mechanism which will wind. The prize for perpetual motion has never yet been awarded. Possibly the solution is in the self-winding clock.

500. Dose Stopper.—A thimble-like contrivance which shall act both as a bottle-stopper and a cup to contain the exact dose.

501. Faucet Measure.—A device for measuring the quantity of liquid that passes through the faucet. Invaluable for store-keepers.

502. Automatic Feeder.—A feeding rack so constructed that the hay or grain will be fed automatically with a cut-off when the proper amount has been given.

503. Coupon Cash Book.—At present persons who pay cash are charged the same as those who trade on credit, a practice which is manifestly wrong. A cash-book should be made so that those who pay immediately for goods should receive a rebate. Every merchant would purchase a quantity of these books, since the great bane of merchandise is bad debts.

504. Gas Detective.—A device to be placed on a gas fixture to ascertain instantly whether it leaks. Often there is an odor of gas when it is difficult to tell whence it proceeds.

505. PAPER TOWELS.—Paper towels having the quality of cloth, yet designed only for a single use, will[173] doubtless be a feature of the near future. They will "make" their first maker.

506. WATER FILTER.—A cheap device for use in every household, one which could be attached to the water faucet, and which would insure pure water. It would sell enormously.

507. PNEUMATIC FREIGHT TUBE.—If small packages for store and post office use can be sent by tubes, why may not the principle of compressed air be extended so that grain and fruit may be transported thereby, thus saving the great expense of handling and of car freightage? Some day the greater part of our freight will be carried by this means, and he who is first in the field will coin a mint of clean dollars.

508. STORM WARNING.—Apply the principle of the barometer to a large glass globe, placed on the top of a public building, by means of which the contained liquid shall be colored red on the approach of a storm; or construct an instrument which will give forth a sound when bad weather is to be feared. Such an invention would be wanted everywhere.

509. HEAT GOVERNOR.—If a regulator could be placed upon heat pipes so as to keep the heat at a desired temperature, the inventor would reap untold millions. Florists, poultry raisers, and in fact every housekeeper needs this device.

510. AUTOMATIC OIL FEEDER.—An invention which will feed oil to a lamp at a uniform rate, and which is provided with a cut-off whereby the supply can be stopped when the light is extinguished.[174]

511. PAINT BRUSH FEEDER.—A brush with a reservoir of paint so that when the painter finds the uplifted brush growing dry he has but to reverse it in order to have it replenished.

512. INSIDE FAUCET.—The outside faucet is awkward and interferes with cartage. One which could be worked on the inside by a button on the outside is demanded. Improvements in faucets have made two or three inventors rich, but the right one is yet to come.

513. HOUSE PATTERNS.—Thousands of people like to plan for themselves the building of their homes. At present the only means provided is that of pencil and drawing paper. Wooden blocks adapted for the purpose, and ready-made joints would fill a long-felt want.

514. EXTENSION HANDLE.—A handle which may be applied to any kind of a brush, and which will enable painters, window-scrubbers, and others who have to work at high elevations, to do their work from the ground.

515. WIRE STRETCHER.—Thousands of tons of wire are manufactured annually, but the wires often are slack. Invent a cheap, simple device which will keep spring beds even and wire fences taut.

516. PRICE TAG.—A price tag which can be instantly attached to a piece of goods. Merchants would buy it by the thousands if made for a trifling cost.

517. THE HANDY VISE.—In the course of time a hundred things need fixing in every house. What is needed is a small vise which can be readily attached to a kitchen table, and which would not cost over fifty cents. {175}

518. FOLDING LADDER.—A light ladder which is portable and extensible would pay well.

519. SMOKELESS FUEL.—A kind of kindling which will be as ignitable as wood, but which will not smoke. The inventor will have money to burn.

520. FINGER-RING GAUGE.—A cylindrical piece of metal to which are loosely attached a number of rings of the same material, serving as a gauge to measure the finger, each ring differing from the others by a slight fraction.

521. LAUNDRY BAG.—Hotel keepers want a bag adapted to the carrying of washing, so as to avoid the unsightly baskets of washerwomen. A large ornamental bag should be constructed with apartments for different kinds of wearing apparel.

522. SOLE CEMENT.—A cement which could take the place of pegs, nails, and threads in the manufacture of shoes would revolutionize the trade and make money for the patentee.

523. GOODS EXHIBITOR.—On an upright column attach a number of steel or wooden rods radiating like the spokes of a wheel, and made to turn by clock-work machinery.

524. SHOE STRETCHER.—A metal frame made adjustable to any shoe by having its parts extended or depressed and worked by a tiny crank. The extension of the frame when the crank is turned stretches the shoe.

525. CORK EJECTOR.—A simple means by which the cork can be ejected from within would supplant all prevalent methods and bring wealth to the inventor. {176}

526. LEMON SQUEEZER.—A squeezer of a new type, having a tongue to pierce the fruit, and making a hole just large enough for the juice to be extracted by the squeezer, but not large enough for the pulp to escape. The only squeezer which presses the lemon without cutting it in half. The inventor of the glass lemon squeezer made a large fortune.

527. SPRING WHEEL.—A wheel with inner and outer rim, and the space between filled with springs would afford much easier riding than the present method.

528. THE PLURAL CAPSULE.—Capsules made so as to be divided in order that one-half or one-quarter the quantity can be taken.

529. THE DOSE BOTTLE.—This might be called the neck measurer. A bottle whose neck holds exactly the dose, and an arrangement for closing the lower end of the neck when it is full.

530. FISHERMAN'S CLAW.—A large, steel claw somewhat on the principle of a net, but with many advantages, might be invented. The claw when opened should cover three or four square yards of water. It closes with a spring attached to the handle. Quite as much sport in this as with the hook and line. The right article ought to have great sales.

531. POCKET SCALE.—A little scale capable of being carried in the pocket, so as to be instantly at service in weighing small articles would be appreciated and purchased by almost every one.

532. TOY BANK AND REGISTER.—There is needed for the holding of children's money a bank with a device{177} attached for registering the amount which it contains. A cheap device of this kind would be a great improvement on the present toy bank. The inventor of one of the principal banks for children now in use is said to have made half a million dollars out of his invention.

533. THE PAPER MATCH.—"The time-honored scheme of rolling up a piece of paper and using it for a lighter could be utilized by an inventor in the manufacture of matches," says the *National Druggist*. "The invention would revolutionize match manufacturing, because the wood for this purpose is constantly growing scarcer and more costly. The matches would be considerably cheaper than the wooden ones, and also weigh less, a fact which counts for much in the exportation."

534. ILLUMINATED TYPE.—Here is an idea which if properly worked ought to put the inventor on the high road to fortune. Why could not our newspaper-type, by the use of phosphorous, after the manner of the illuminated watch dial, be illumined so that the print could be read in the dark? Illuminated type may be a newspaper feature of the coming century.

535. PAPER BOTTLES.—If a paper bottle could be made as serviceable as glass, its many other advantages would make it an El Dorado for the inventor. Its lightness in transportation and its freedom from breakage would cause it to come into general use. Especially on shipboard, where bottles are constantly broken by the roll of the vessel, would such an invention be hailed with joy.

536. THE PAPER SAIL.—"Paper sails," says the *Railway Review*, "are meeting with considerable{178} favor. They are cheaper than canvas sails, and they are soft, flexible, and as untearable as the original article." There is room for invention here. Treated with the proper solutions, it may be that paper will entirely displace cloth in the wings of our ships.

537. STREET SWEEPER.—A device like the present carpet sweeper to be used on paved roadways will command a large sale.

538. PHOSPHORESCENT STREET NUMBERS.—Who has not been vexed in trying to locate an unfamiliar house in the dark? In many streets not one number in a hundred can be seen in the night. Contrive some means of illuminating these numbers, and you will confer a boon to others and reap a reward for yourself.

539. BUGGY TOP ADJUSTER.—A contrivance for raising or lowering the buggy top so that it can be readily operated from the buggy-seat.

540. SHOULDER PACK.—Men persist in carrying in their hands that which could be borne between the shoulders with much less strain. Who will give us a convenient pack to be carried upon the back?

541. ADJUSTABLE CART BOTTOM.—A cart with device for lowering the bottom to the ground or nearly so, for the easy reception of the goods, with jack for raising the same when loaded. Every merchant, carter, and expressman would hasten to possess himself of this invention.

542. NAILLESS HORSE SHOE.—A rubber shoe, which[179] can be easily adjusted to a horse's foot without nails. The advantages would be many and the sales numerous.

543. ELASTIC RING.—An elastic ring for hitching horses. One with snap buckle for opening so as to receive both the bridle and the object to which it is to be attached. As the ring is elastic, it will fit any hitching post or tree. It would be welcome to everybody who owns a horse.

544. HEEL CYCLOMETER.—An indicator fixed in the heel of a boot or shoe so that each step records itself, and by which the pedestrian is enabled to tell the distance he has covered.

545. WHIP LOCK.—A cheap device to be placed in the whip-stock of a carriage for securing the whip against theft. If it could be sold for ten cents every driver would have one.

546. REIN-HOLDER.—A contrivance attached to the dashboard and which holds the reins securely in position and prevents them from being switched under the horse's tail.

547. AUTOMOBILE.—The horseless carriage is sold at prices ranging from $1,800 to $3,000. Josef Hofman, the great pianist, says he is confident he can build one for $300. Here is a great opportunity for mechanical electricians.

548. THE LOW TRUCK.—It would be a great advantage to carters if a truck could be constructed whose body would be much nearer the ground than the one in present use. Great expense as well as expenditure of[180] muscle would be saved if by some arrangement the cart body could be as low as eighteen inches from the ground.

549. Automatic Horse-Fastener.—The man will make a fortune who can devise some means whereby the rider can fasten his horse and unfasten him without alighting from the vehicle.

550. The Foot-Cycle.—Persons who know the ease and exhilaration of skating as compared with walking will be interested in an effort to invent a foot-cycle which will do for the foot on the ground what the skate does on the ice. The roller-skate does this in a measure, but it is adapted to hard surfaces only. What is needed is something in the order of a miniature bicycle—a machine capable of going over surfaces hard and soft, in fact, a sort of bicycle skate. Here is vast room for a fertile inventor.

Section 13. Money in Farming Contrivances.

551. A Corn Cutter.—A machine to run between the rows and cut the stalks on each side would sell to every farmer; and there are 4,565,000 farmers in the United States.

552. Frost Protector.—A chemical combination whose product when ignited is chiefly smoke. All farmers suffer from late and early frosts. They would pay liberally for a smoke producer which would protect their crops, for it is known that a very little smoke acts as a mantle to keep off the frost. They should be made cheap so that half a hundred might be placed to the acre. Farmers are the most numerous class of people, and fortunes await those who can invent anything for their benefit.[181]

553. A Farm Fertilizer.—Wanted—a fertilizer more powerful and less bulky than those in use. We have condensed meat extracts for the table; why not better condensation of food for the farm? Chemists will find no better paying employment for their brains than in this direction.

554. A Postless Fence.—For posts substitute a windlass at each corner of the field so as to keep the wires taut. If the field is large or irregular, more windlasses would be required, but they could be manufactured at a cost much less than that of posts.

555. Automatic Gate Opener.—Fix an iron bar or rail with a spring contrivance in such a way that the pressure of wagon wheels on one side of the gate releases a spring and causes the gate to fly open, while the pressure on the opposite side causes it to close. The arrangement of the contrivance on one side is of course the reverse of that on the other.

556. Corn Planter.—A long, hollow cylinder filled with seed corn and having rows of holes placed at regular intervals for dropping the kernels, and wedge-like or plow-shaped pieces of iron between the rows so as to throw up a light covering of soil, would plant easily twenty-nine acres a day. Such a simple contrivance would cost only a few dollars, and would command a ready sale to agriculturists.

557. THE ALL-SEED PLANTER.—A device like the above, the wheels and gearing remaining the same, but with the cylinder fixed so as to be readily detached, and other cylinders substituted, having the rows and sizes of holes adapted to the planting of any kind of seed. These sets of cylinders would make the machine much[182] more expensive than the one in the former article, but it would be much cheaper than separate machines for different seeds.

558. FERTILIZER DISTRIBUTOR.—One constructed on the plan of the street-sprinkling cart would make much of the farm labor easier than it now is.

559. BONE CUTTER.—Farmers want a cheap bone cutter—cost not to exceed $5—by which bones and sea-shells can be cut into small bits for fowls. Bone is an egg-producer, but no cheap means has been invented for utilizing this kind of refuse.

560. BUCKET TIPPER.—A bucket with an attachment at the bottom connecting with a finger-piece at the top, so that the bucket can be tipped and its contents emptied without the wetting of the hands.

561. POST HOLE DIGGER.—A four-sided metal casing is driven into the ground by a sledge-hammer. A small handle sunk in one side of the casing pulls a metal plate through the earth at the bottom, thus making an earth-filled box. Two more stout handles on the top are for lifting the digger and its contents. A digger which could be made for $5 would sell by the ten thousand.

562. WELL REFRIGERATOR.—Farmers often keep articles in the well; but if an accident to the rope occur, the articles of food are often spilled, thus spoiling the water in the well, and entailing great annoyance and expense. Invent a way by which a well may be a safe ice-box.

563. MULTIPLE DASHER CHURN.—A churn which is[183] constructed on the principle of the common egg-beater, and which is operated from the top instead of the side or end. A fortune in this.

564. FRUIT PICKER.—An open bag fixed at the end of a long pole with a shears operated by a string in the hand of the picker.

565. PORTABLE FENCE.—A fence in which the posts are made of steel or iron two inches in diameter, and tapering at the end so as to be readily driven into the ground. Such a fence may be carried in a wagon and set up anywhere in a few minutes.

566. POULTRY DRINKING FOUNTAIN.—A round wooden dish with a large cone occupying the central space, except the narrow channel near the rim. This will prevent the fowls from getting their feet in the water and fouling it, while at the same time the cone is a reservoir of supply. There should be a faucet allowing the water to drip slowly so as to keep the channel filled.

567. POULTRY PERCH.—A movable perch, with an erect post and numerous projecting arms. It has the advantage that it can be removed and cleansed.

568. MOLE TRAP.—One of the greatest pests of the farmer, and the most difficult to catch is the mole. Invent a trap whose upper part shall be somewhat like an old-fashioned hetchel, full of sharp spikes; the under part is a platform, and releases a spring when the mole steps upon it.

569. SEED SOWER.—Apply the principle of the revolving nozzle in the lawn sprinkler to a machine for the sowing of seed.{184}

570. MILKER AND STRAINER.—Construct a pail in two parts, the upper part to receive the milk directly from the cow while a strainer separates it from the lower part. Thus the milk can be taken from the barnyard already strained.

571. PAPER MILK CAN.—In time milk cans will probably be constructed of paper. The saving in cost of transportation would cause every farmer to hail the construction of such an invention.

572. PLANT PRESERVER.—"A German chemist," says *Merck's Report*, "has prepared a fluid that has the power when injected into the tissue of a plant of anesthetizing the plant. The plant does not die, but stops growing, maintaining its fresh, green appearance, though its vitality is apparently suspended. It is also independent of the changes of temperature. The composition of the fluid is shrouded in the greatest secrecy, but as the process is not patented the secret may be discovered and utilized by another investigator."

Section 14. Money in the Mails and in Writing Materials.

573. THE REVERSIBLE PACKAGE.—There is needed a package or paper box in which legal papers or merchandise sent for approval can be turned inside out and remailed to the sender. Such a device would have a large demand.

574. COPYING PAPER.—A paper used for duplicating manuscripts would command a ready sale. The carbon paper now employed is very expensive.

575. WORD PRINTING TYPEWRITER.—Some typewriters have as many as fifty keys. A small increase in{185} number would cover the words in common use. Many words can be omitted, and yet the sense be conveyed. Letters or postal cards, consisting of one, two, or three lines could thus be written in one moment.

576. TRANSPARENT INK BOTTLE.—Produce an ink-bottle of which the glass shall not be so opaque as the one in common use and in which the depth of the ink is clearly seen, thus avoiding the too deep dipping of the pen, with the result of blots on the page and stains on the fingers.

577. DOUBLE POSTAL CARD.—The United States Government would no doubt consider favorably a postal-card made double, so that one part could be readily torn from the other and remailed, the one part containing the message and the other left blank, save for the sender's name and address.

578. THE SAFETY ENVELOPE.—An envelope such that it is impossible for it to be surreptitiously opened without the fact being discovered. The government seeks such an envelope.

579. COMBINATION COVER AND LETTER.—An envelope to which is attached a half-sheet of paper which folds in the cover, thus making only one piece.

580. ALWAYS READY LETTER PAPER.—There is room for a device whereby letter paper can be fed out to the writer as desired, so that the pen or machine may travel continuously without stopping for new sheets.

581. INK REGULATOR.—An inkstand provided with a tiny wooden disk which floats on the surface of the ink. The slightest touch of the pen depresses the [186] disk and permits the pen to be filled, and at the same time prevents it from dipping too far, and thus making an unsightly daub on the holder and fingers.

582. THE PEN FINGER.—Might not a device be attached to the forefinger which could serve the uses of a pen? Think what ease and speed would be gained if one could write directly with one's finger instead of employing the entire hand.

583. PEN REST.—There is room for a device which shall rest upon the paper and support the pen while the latter is writing. Those who do every day a vast amount of writing would appreciate this invention.

584. PERPETUAL PEN SUPPLY.—On a slight elevation have an inkstand with an opening at the bottom to which is attached a small piece of hose, the other end being connected with a hollow pen holder, thus insuring a perpetual flow of ink. A saucer on the writing table containing a tiny cup or several tiny cups holds the pen or pens in an upright position when not in use, care being taken that the pens in that position are higher than the reservoir, so as to cut off the supply.

585. LETTER ANNUNCIATOR.—Constructed on the principle of nickel and slot. The weight of the letter in the house letter box pushes up into view a red card, thus announcing the presence of mail matter at a distance, and avoiding the opening of the box in vain.

586. ENVELOPE OPENER.—Most people open envelopes at the end, often with trouble and awkwardly, but almost every envelope has one of the flaps a little loose near the corner. A small flat piece of steel with ivory [187] handle such as could be disposed of for ten cents, would be salable.

587. MAIL STAMPER.—A stamper constructed upon a letter box so that it would be impossible to insert a letter without at the same time stamping it. The United States Government would pay a large sum for such a device.

588. ROTARY STAMPER.—A wheel broad enough to contain the name desired, and which is operated by taking the handle and drawing or pushing the wheel over the matter to be stamped. It would be ten times quicker than the ordinary way.

589. INVISIBLE INK.—An ink which is invisible, and must be treated by some chemical to make it appear. It would be invaluable to those carrying on a secret correspondence.

Section 15. Money in Dress.

590. BACHELOR'S BUTTONS.—Invent an eyeless and threadless button, somewhat on the style of the envelope-clasp. The million or more bachelors would surely buy them.

591. SHOE FASTENER.—Some device is needed for the quicker and surer way of fastening shoes. The button is inconvenient and the tie is unreliable. The Foster kid glove fastener made the inventor a man of millions.

592. A TROUSERS' GUARD.—One which will effectively prevent the wear at the bottom. Trousers commonly give way first at the end of the legs. The trousers-wearing world is vexed by garments frayed at the bottom.[188]

593. TWENTIETH CENTURY SHOE.—It will be one without laces or buttons. The upper can be taken off or put on instantly when desired, and yet be waterproof. There is a gold mine in that shoe.

594. COMBINATION TIE AND COLLAR.—A time saver which can be adjusted instantly, and yet be separable when desired. You would not have lost the train but for the delay in fixing your collar and tie. Thousands of minutes saved every day mean as many thousands of dollars in the pockets of the fortunate inventor.

595. SPRING HAT.—Not a hat to be worn only in the spring, but a hat with a padded spring on each side, so that it will fit closely in all kinds of weather, and whether the hair is long or short.

596. THE REAR-OPENING SHOE.—A shoe in which the foot could enter from the back instead of from the top would have the double advantage of ease of adjustment and elegant appearance. The buttons or lacings would then all be upon the sides. There is a possibility of much money here.

597. DETACHABLE RUBBER SOLE.—An invention whereby a rubber sole may be attached to an ordinary shoe in wet weather, or to the shoes of base ball and tennis players to prevent them from slipping.

598. THE INSTANTANEOUS CEMENT.—For the last-named invention as well as for hundreds of other cases, there is required a cement which will set in a minute. The man who will produce it can live at his ease the rest of his days.

599. ELASTIC HAT PIN.—A flexible pin provided[189] with a clasp at the head so that the pin may be bent around and secured, thus lessening the danger from that formidable weapon.

600. STARCH-PROOF COLLAR BAND.—Shirts first wear on the collar. Millions of otherwise perfectly sound garments have to be thrown away because the collar band is worn out by the use of starch in ironing. Here is the inventor's opportunity.

601. DRESS SHIELD.—Ladies are often inconvenienced in keeping their dresses out of the mud, both hands being occupied. A dress shield attached to the dress does the work.

602. SLEEVE HOLDER.—An elastic cord passes between the fingers with a grip at each end for holding the sleeve of a coat while an overcoat is being donned.

603. THE CONVERTIBLE BUTTON.—The button which can be so contrived as to be made into a flower holder when required would have an unlimited sale.

604. PAPER CLOTHING.—Many of the Japanese wear paper clothing. The idea might be extended to warm climates, and in the summer season to our own climate. Will not the time come when we shall hear of "Moses' Patent Paper Trousers," and "Isaacs' Patent Paper Coats?"

Section 16. Money in Personal Conveniences.

605. THE POCKET UMBRELLA.—Few things are in more common or universal use than the umbrella, and yet what a cumbersome, awkward thing it is. Who will invent one that can be folded, packed and pocketed? A Mr. Higgins, by the invention of the sliding thimble[190] for umbrellas received $100,000 cash as royalties on his patent. A pocket umbrella should realize for its inventor much more than that.

606. THE MILLION MATCH.—A slow-burning match, which will burn four times as long as the ordinary one. Such a device contains a million dollars, for it would drive all other matches out of the market. "A Hungarian named Janos Irinyi, the inventor of the lucifer or phosphorus match, sold his patent for $3,500."

607. FINGER-NAIL PARER.—A fine blade, especially adapted to the rounded shape of the finger-nail. It may be attached to an ordinary penknife.

608. THE WATCH PAD.—A small watch set in the center of a square pocket pad, so that the engagements for the day may be marked upon a paper opposite the time fixed. The pad should have a sufficient number of leaves to last a month or more. When all have been torn off, the watch can be attached to a new pad.

609. POCKET BILL HOLDER.—Within a flat, leather case, suitable to be carried in the pocket, construct a device for holding bills for collection on one side and for bills for payment on the other. Every business man wants it.

610. EXTENSION UMBRELLA.—An umbrella capable of extension in one direction so as effectually to shelter three persons. It must be made on a radically different plan from the kind now in use.

611. PORTABLE DESK.—A desk which can be conveniently carried under the arm, hung upon a nail when{191} it is not desired for use, and in unfolding presents a stand and all the materials for writing.

612. FLOWER HOLDER.—A spring between the ends of pieces of wood will cause the opposite ends to press firmly together. These ends will press firmly to the lapel of the coat, and the coil of the spring will hold the stem of the flower.

613. HAT LOCK.—A device for securely locking a hat in a public place so that it can be removed only by the owner; a coat lock also would be useful.

614. SPRING SHOE HEEL.—A spring inclosed within the leather of the heel so as to facilitate walking. It would be of special aid to the sick and the feeble.

615. SELF-IGNITING CIGAR.—Some day an inventor will make a stupendous fortune by a cigar which can be ignited by simply rubbing the end, as a match is now rubbed in lighting.

616. SPRING KNIFE.—A pocket knife in which the blade can be opened by touching the spring, thus avoiding the vexation of broken finger-nails.

617. PHOSPHORESCENT KEY GUARD.—A device which will serve the double purpose of covering the hole when the key is not in use and for finding the hole when the key is inserted.

618. KNOT CLASP.—An effective clasp which will securely hold a knot. Parcels are constantly becoming untied and shoes unlaced when an effective clasp would prevent it. It must be very cheap.{192}

619. SINGLE MATCH DELIVERY.—A penny-in-the-slot machine for use in cigar stores, but operated free of cost. The machine should deliver but a single match at a time.

620. WATCH HEAD CANE.—A small watch fixed in the head of a cane would be a great convenience to walkers.

621. BOOK CASE CHAIR.—An easy chair, provided with a small rack for books on each arm. Specially adapted for invalids.

622. COIN HOLDER.—A device by which coins are in sight in a traveler's purse, and by touch of a spring he can cause to fall the exact coin he wants. Very convenient for ferries, cars and cabs.

623. THE POCKET PUNCH.—A simple punch by which with a pressure on a pocket one could secretly make a record every time he paid out money, and thus keep an account of his daily expenses without resort to bookkeeping.

624. MOUTH GUARD.—If you can invent a mouthguard which will be both simple and ornamental and prevent contamination when drinking at public fountains or in partaking of the communion cup in churches, you will confer much favor upon the community and reap large funds for yourself.

625. PARCEL FASTENER.—A hook and eye capable of instant insertion in the wrapping of paper parcels would be sold by the million.

Section 17. Money in Household Conveniences.

626. THE WARNING CLOCK.—A clock which will[193] give notice of its wants when it is nearly run down. A simple device which it should be easy to contrive and quick to sell.

627. A SLOT GAS MACHINE.—One which will operate a certain length of time by the payment of a nickel and automatically close when the money's worth is consumed. It would be invaluable for small consumers.

628. REVOLVING FLOWER STAND.—A clock-work device so that all plants in a cone or pyramid could get their share of a sun-bath.

629. WINDOW SHADE SCREEN.—The inventor would make a fortune who could devise something for windows which would be a shade or screen or both as occasion required.

630. BABY WALKER.—A light frame, mounted on four casters, partially supporting the baby and permitting him to propel himself in any direction. Only the four posts need to be made of wood. For the rest, two or three light pieces of cloth are sufficient. It should not cost over fifty cents—better at twenty-five cents. Every mother with a baby would want one at the latter price.

631. DETACHABLE SHOWER BATH.—Every house should be equipped with a shower-bath, but few have one which can be readily attached to and removed from the supply pipe of the bath room. A cheap article would have an almost universal sale.

632. CARPET BEATER.—Every husband would buy a machine that would beat carpets and thus save himself that drudgery or the expense of hiring a man.[194]

633. CARPET STRETCHER AND FASTENER.—Unite in one device a stretcher and fastener, thus doing away with the mischievous tack and the damage of piercing the carpet.

634. STEP-LADDER CHAIR.—A chair so contrived that it may be thrown into a short step-ladder. A greatly needed device for the house.

635. A WINDOW FLY-GATE.—Apply the principle of the fly-trap to the window screen. In this way the flies in the house may pass out, but those without will not come in.

636. DOUBLE WINDOW SHADE.—It is often desirable to shade the lower half of a window for the sake of privacy, while the upper half is left open to let in light, but the present window shade covers the wrong half of the window. Construct a shade which will be fastened to the bottom and work up to meet the other, or else a single shade which works exclusively from the bottom.

637. FOLDING BABY CARRIAGE.—One which will occupy no more room than an ordinary chair. Perhaps your ingenuity could make an article which would be a chair and a baby carriage combined.

638. A SCRUBBING MACHINE.—The handle just above the brush passes through a cylinder holding two or three quarts of water, the bottom of the cylinder being pierced with holes so that the brush is supplied with water.

639. CATCH-ALL CARPET-SWEEPER.—A sweeper with an appliance for running into the corners of rooms would supersede the sweepers now in use. [195]

Section 18. Money in the Saving of Life and Property.

640. SAFETY SHAFTS.—A device for separating the shafts from the body of the carriage in the case of a runaway, and thus insure the safety of the occupants.

641. POCKETBOOK GUARD.—Nearly all ladies carry the pocketbook in the hand. A device should be invented for fastening it securely to the hand so that it could not be snatched by a thief.

642. CHEAP BURGLAR ALARM.—If you can invent an effective burglar alarm which can be sold at ten cents per window, you will have a monopoly in that article.

643. COLLAPSIBLE FIRE ESCAPE.—One which may be folded or rolled and kept beneath the window-sill, and which, when occasion requires, may be extended by throwing the unattached end to the street.

644. AIR TESTER.—We have a barometer to test the vapor and a thermometer to test the heat. Who will make a contrivance that will test the quantity of pure oxygen in our rooms, and also detect the presence of disease germs? Vast possibilities of wealth and fame open in this direction.

645. LIFE BOAT LAUNCHER.—The two ends of the boat should be attached to the arm of a crane, one chain of which swings the boat clear of the ship, while another releases it from its fastenings. To the inventor this will be Fortunatus' boat.

646. SAW-TOOTH CRUTCH.—Provide a crutch with[196] teeth on the under side so that it can be used on ice or sleety pavements without slipping.

647. ELEVATOR SAFETY-CLUTCH.—Such a clutch has recently been invented, but it acts too suddenly; what is needed is one which in time of accident will bring the elevator to a stop slowly.

648. GUN-GUARD.—A rubber guard for guns which will prevent their accidental discharge.

649. POCKET DISINFECTOR.—One has often to go into unhealthy neighborhoods and places where disease germs lurk. A small flat can, filled with some disinfectant which could be conveniently squirted, would be not only a killer of offending odors, but also a saver of life.

650. AUTOMATIC FIRE ALARM.—Procure some substance easily melted by heat; which, when melted, releases a spring which operates an alarm bell.

651. KEY FASTENER.—A little thought properly applied will invent a device whereby a key in a door will be proof against a burglar's nippers, it being impossible to turn the key until the device is removed.

652. LIGHTNING ARRESTER.—Why has there been no improvement in the ancient, unsightly, and expensive lightning rod? This is the more remarkable since electricity is so much better understood now than formerly. Invent a cheap means of arresting the deadly fluid, and of turning it into a harmless channel.

653. A WINDOW CLEANER.—One which will do the work as well as human hands, and at the same time[197] do away with the peril of life and limb while cleaning the outside of high windows.

654. SAFETY REIN.—A third rein attached loosely to the others, but capable of being drawn tight under the horse's chin, thus throwing his head back and stopping him when disposed to run.

655. THE ROPE-GRIP.—A grip which will take a firm hold of a rope of any size and not abrade the hand as in the ordinary method of descending by a rope.

656. SCISSORS GUARD.—An attachment to the scissors which closes over the parts when not in use, and thus prevents accidents to or by children by their unskilful use.

657. THE DOUBLE POCKET.—A pocket in two parts, the lower part easily opened by the owner, but of sufficient difficulty to baffle pickpockets.

658. FIRE EXTINGUISHER.—Now we will give you the secret of a fire extinguisher that will do more with the same amount of chemicals used than any patented fire extinguisher in the world. A small demijohn is filled with a substance that looks like water, but sells for the price of brandy. Half a dozen of these demijohns scattered about a building will

protect it from conflagration, for it contains a liquid which is the most inimical to fire that is known. A gallon of it thrown on the flames will subdue any ordinary fire, and yet —here is the secret—it is nothing but aqua-ammonia.

Section 19. Money in the Laboratory.

659. FLY-KILLER.—There is needed some powerful chemical that will destroy flies the moment they enter[198] the house, and yet be harmless to man. He will become richer than Crœsus who shall give us the much needed boon.

660. ARTIFICIAL EGG.—The art of chemistry is now so far advanced that a clever student of the science ought to compound an egg which will be so cheap and such a clever imitation of nature, as to enable him to make money by his skill.

661. SEDIMENT-LIQUEFIER.—Find a chemical substance that will liquefy the residual substances in barrels. There would be an enormous demand for a composition that would do the work effectively.

662. FIRE KINDLER.—A material which will kindle both wood and coal without addition of paper, shavings, or any other article.

663. EGG PRESERVER.—No process has yet been found for preserving eggs for months and keeping them as fresh as newly-laid ones. Here is the chance for the practical chemist.

664. MOSQUITO ANNIHILATOR.—The greatest pest is the mosquito. If some chemical could be found which could be squirted liberally upon the marshes, which are the breeding place of the mosquito, and thus annihilate the pest, a long suffering public would shower its benefactor with gold.

665. ARTIFICIAL FUEL.—There is needed a fuel that can be produced as cheap as wood for use in the spring and fall, when the weather is too mild for the use of the furnace.[199]

666. THE FLAMLESS TORCH.—There are hogsheads full of money for the man who will invent an igniter which will cause combustible matter to burn, but will not itself flame— a device which can ignite a lamp instantly by a thrust down the chimney, or light the gas without the usual hunt for a match.

667. CHEMICAL ERASER.—Some chemical should be produced which will effectively erase the marks of a pen and leave the paper the same as before.

Section 20. Money in Tools.

668. THE INSTANTANEOUS WRENCH.—A monkey wrench, the jaws of which may be adjusted instantly, instead of by the screwing process now in vogue.

669. THE DOUBLE CHANNELED SCREW HEAD.—A screw in which the head has two channels instead of one, crossing each other at right angles.

670. THE DOUBLE POWER SCREW DRIVER.—The last invention requires another, a screw driver, also double at the end, by means of which twice the power may be acquired in the insertion of screws.

671. THE MULTIPLE BLADE PARER.—A knife with several blades so arranged as to cut the skin of the fruit on all sides at once, and with a gauge to fit it to any size of fruit.

672. KNIFE GUARD.—A knife with a guard for peeling fruit, preventing the fruit from being pared too deep.

673. THE ALL-TOOL.—A pocket device on the principle of a many-bladed knife, except that instead of [200] blades the things which open from the handle, besides the single blade, are a saw, gimlet, file, cork-screw, screw driver and other useful tools.

674. A NAIL CARRYING HAMMER.—A device for holding nails to a hammer. Carpenters would work twice as fast.

Section 21. Money in the Cars.

675. A SPEED INDICATOR.—A contrivance for determining the speed of street railway cars. The speed is governed by law, but there is no practical means for determining how great it is. The laws of all our cities will insure the success of such an invention.

676. AUTOMATIC CAR-COUPLER.—A device is needed whereby the simple impact of one car upon another will cause a coupling-pin to be inserted in place. If you can contrive a system by which cars can be coupled by the same mechanism now employed for air-brakes, every one of the million or more cars on our railways will be equipped with it.

677. THE FENDER CAR-BRAKE.—A fender so constructed that when it strikes an obstacle a brake is released which binds the wheels. Hundreds of lives would be saved every year. Companies which now pay heavy sums for loss of life and limb would buy such an invention on most liberal terms.

678. FOLDING CAR-STEP.—To avoid the difficulty of alighting from a car or of climbing into one when a car is not at a platform, invent a step which folds up when not in use.

679. CAR SIGNAL.—A device for signaling would-be [201] passengers when the car is full. The law will soon require such a device, and then there will be a rush of inventors to reap the reward. "The early bird catches the worm."

680. AUTOMATIC WATER TANK.—Here is a valuable suggestion to railway engineers and mechanics. It is believed that it is entirely feasible to construct a railway water tank that shall work automatically. It is to be done by utilizing the waste steam of the engine. It is a new application of the old principle of the forcing of water into and out of a steam-tight chamber by the alternate admission thereto and condensation therein of live steam. The condensation produces a vacuum, and the pressure of the external atmosphere

forces water into the tank. It is only necessary to locate the tank within suction distance of its water supply, and there is the saving of wages, fuel and repairs. It has been recently stated that the cost of pumping at the railway stations of the United States last year amounted to $7,000,000, or an average of $700 per station. Who will put these millions in his pocket by devising an automatic water-tank?

Section 22. Money in Making People Honest.

681. THE HOUSEKEEPER'S SAFETY PUNCH.—We want a device which will do away with the need of trusting to the honesty of the ice-man, grocer, baker, and others who supply our daily wants.

682. THE UNALTERABLE CHECK.—Invent a small, flat leather case with lock and key, into which the check or checks will securely fit. Only the signer of the check and the officer of the bank have the key. The latter, after paying the check, holds the case for the depositor.[202] This would make it impossible for the check to be raised, or, if lost, for a dishonest finder to have it cashed, as he would be unable to give either the name or the amount. The cases should be made very cheap so that a depositor could possess a number at a trivial cost.

683. EGG TESTER.—One which will test eggs by a new method and grade them according to the length of time they have been laid, such as three days' eggs, three weeks' eggs, packed eggs, etc.

684. UMBRELLA LOCK.—A small attachment to an umbrella which will serve as a lock when in place, and will do away with the intolerable nuisance of stolen umbrellas.

685. THE GUARANTEED BOX.—There is sore need of a patented box guaranteed to hold exactly one quart. Not only do present measures differ, but the custom of dealers is not uniform with regard to a heaping or an even measure.

Section 23. Money in Traveler's Articles.

686. THE ADJUSTABLE TRUNK.—Some kinds of traveling bags can be adjusted to suit the degree of baggage a traveler needs. Some similar arrangement should be supplied for trunks. A half-filled trunk is more apt to be broken than a full one.

687. THE HOLLOW CANE.—One which will contain many small articles for the use of travelers.

688. THE ELASTIC TRUNK STRAP.—Avoid the hard work of strapping trunks as well as the unsightly straps[203] by inventing an ornamental band which will do by elasticity what is now done by the buckle.

689. THE SLIDE BAG.—An extension handbag in which when required the ends may be slid out so as to treble the space, and when empty may be slid back, making it very small.

690. THE OUTFIT TRUNK.—There should be a trunk with various divisions for the reception of articles, like the drawers of a bureau or the compartments of a writing desk, in which everything can be properly placed.

Section 24. Money in Toilet Articles.

691. CURLING IRON ATTACHMENT.—A wire frame attached to a lamp. The top part, which is fixed on the lamp chimney, should have a depression for holding a curling iron. May be sold to every lady for ten cents.

692. THE HINGE BLACKING BOX.—Invent a blacking box with a hinge top, and thus avoid the difficulty of opening it in the old way, and also the nuisance of soiled hands.

693. THE MIRROR HAIR BRUSH.—A combined toilet article for travelers, the handle of the brush being enlarged so as to hold the comb, which is released by a spring, and the end of the brush containing a small mirror.

694. THE SOAP SHAVING BRUSH.—A shaving brush with a tin casing containing soap. Turning the brush makes a lather all ready for application to the face. Very convenient for travelers.[204]

Section 25. Money in Amusements.

695. THE DUCKING STOOL.—A game for seaside resorts. Bathers would like a large pool or tank where, by a system of planks fastened to a central post, two bathers could go alternately up and down, one being in the water while the other was in the air, an arrangement like the see-saw which children are so fond of. It should have sufficient capacity to accommodate a number of bathers at once, and should be as near as possible to the sea, so as to be available by persons in bathing suits, who have already had a salt bath.

696. THE DOUBLE MOTION SWING.—A swing or scup, in which the swinger can raise himself up and down at the same time he is being carried backward and forward.

697. THE FOLDING SKATE.—The man who will invent a skate which can be folded and put in the pocket will not only confer a boon upon millions of skaters, but will also put a snug fortune in his own pocket.

698. BICYCLE BOAT.—A boat in which the pedal movement, as used in the bicycle, is employed for driving power, and the boat is propelled in the water somewhat after the manner that the bicycle goes upon the land.

Section 26. Money in War.

699. THE SLOW EXPLOSIVE.—A shell that will penetrate the armor of a vessel before exploding and not, as now, at the instant of contact. A military officer in France says that a fortune awaits the man who shall invent such a shell. [205]

700. THE TRANSPARENT CARTRIDGE.—A mica cartridge would have the advantage of being transparent, permitting the slightest chemical change to be detected, and the danger of premature explosion avoided. Mica has the peculiar property of withstanding intense heat.

701. SHIP'S BOTTOM CLEANER.—Here is an invention that would be cheap at any price; one that would clean the bottom of seagoing vessels without the necessity of docking. Even if it cost as much as docking, it would still be a great invention of immense utility, because it would save the time of a long voyage. It is believed that the road to this invention lies in the direction of electricity, whose industrial applications are so rapidly multiplying. There is more fame and fortune in this than in the much-lauded revolving turret.

702. SELF-LOADING PISTOL.—There is room for improvement in small arms. A pistol ought to be invented which will fire eight or ten shots in rapid succession, the discharge continuing simply by the holding back of the trigger. In many kinds of fireworks the balls are sent off in succession in this way, while the piece is held in the hand. Apply the same or a similar principle to the pistol, and your reward will be that of a Mauser or a Maxim.

Section 27. Money in Minerals.

703. GALVANIZED IRON.—If you can discover a process for galvanizing iron which will save one-tenth of a cent in its present cost, you will, figuratively speaking, sink a shaft into an endless mine of gold, for the amount of galvanized iron now in use is enormous, and the range of its usefulness is constantly increasing.

704. METAL EXTRACTOR.—A solution which will [206] precipitate gold or silver from the ore, and thus save immense sums now expended in the crushing of the ore. Such an invention would revolutionize the mining industry, and make the inventor enormously rich. Mr. Edison says: "I am convinced there is not a single abandoned gold claim in the world, where gold has ever been discovered, from which the precious ore cannot be extracted in quantities to pay a big margin of profit over the cost of operation."

705. GOLD PAINT.—Henry Bessemer invented gold paint, which remains a secret to this day. At first he made one thousand per cent. To-day it yields three hundred per cent. Here is a chance for the man of brains, as the monopoly lies in a secret and not in a patent.

706. STORAGE OF POWER.—No man with brains need go to the Klondike. Diggings that pay infinitely better will be found in your own little workshop. Vast fortunes await those who can think out some means of utilizing the natural forces, such as tides, winds, wave power, and sunshine. These forces can be and soon will be stored compactly, so as to respond promptly to sudden drafts of power. The future of the entire world's work lies along these lines, and there will be inventions and enterprises that in importance will dwarf the discovery of steam power and revolutionize the world's commerce.

707. PICTORIAL TELEGRAPHY.—One of the greatest fortunes ever made by inventors will be realized by him who succeeds in making a perfect picture by means of[207] the electric wire. Already inventors are at work trying "to send pictures by telegraph," and some have nearly succeeded; but the first in this hot race will go to the head of millionaire inventors.

708. SOLIDIFIED PETROLEUM.—Here is a fuel which, if possible—and it seems entirely so—will turn the world upside down. It is said that petroleum can be compressed into a solid, and that three cubic feet will represent the bulk of a ton of coal, and will last combustible as long as fifty tons. Think of the immense saving to our merchantmen, steamboat, and war vessels. Instead of five thousand or six thousand tons of coal, they will have only a few petroleum sticks. No invention of early or modern times contains such possibilities of economy in commerce, of revolution in means of transportation, and of limitless fortune to the lucky discoverer, as this one that promises or threatens to displace coal, as yet the greatest factor in the world's progress. Here is a prize alluring enough to call out the keenest and most devoted powers of the scientific inventor.

709. NON-INFLAMMABLE WOOD.—The vast benefit of a non-inflammable wood has long been realized. As long ago as 1625, a patent for such a process was taken out in England, but the old inventors labored under the disadvantage of being ignorant of the chemical and physical qualities of wood. But the time is now ripe for a successful invention of that kind. The difficulty is to get rid of the combustible gases in the wood without at the same time destroying the cells. This difficulty could probably be overcome by placing the wood in a vacuum, admitting steam, and thus, vaporizing the moisture of the wood, drawing off the product of the vapor. Then, if the wood should be saturated with[208] certain salts, it would doubtless be found that the combustible gases would be destroyed, and the carbonization of the wood under high heat prevented. If the process should be successful, the demand for the wood would be enormous, as it would be immediately required for all vessels, and indeed, for all buildings. The possibilities of wealth from such an invention almost surpass the limit of the imagination.

710. SUCTION PIPE.—There are many delicate operations in manufacture which are now performed at great expense by hand, but which could be done better and cheaper by a

gentle air pressure. The inventor of a device of this kind for spreading and shaping the tobacco leaf in cigar manufacture has his patent capitalized for $2,000,000, and it is paying sixty per cent. interest.[209]

CHAPTER   XVI.

MONEY IN THE SOIL.

Relation between Soils and Skulls—The Secrets of Successful Farming—Why go to Alaska when there are Gold Mines at the Home—Jute, a Keyword to Fortune—A Million Dollars in this Suggestion—What Ignorance Costs the American Farmer—A Rival of King Cotton—Doubling One's Money in Fowls—How to get a Big Apple Crop every Year—$6,000 a Year to go to South America—Or, If you want to Go West, Uncle Sam will give you a Slice of Land—Onions the "Open Sesame" to Fortune—Breaking Records with Potatoes—Yankees and Hickory Nuts—How "Plunger" Walton made a Fortune in Two Years—The Great Elmendorf Stock-Farm.

WE often hear it said that there is no money in farming. On the other hand, there are few occupations in which there is so much money, if the work is carried on in the right way. The trouble is that people often think it takes little intellect to be a farmer. The truth is just the reverse. To get returns out of the soil there must be brains in the skull. We know a farmer on Long Island with less than sixty acres of land who has acquired a fortune in fifteen years of close application to the problems of the farm. He has found the secret of knowing how to make Nature give down her milk. Every foot of land is under cultivation, and although he employs often as many as two score of men, he gives every part of the work his personal inspection. Further than this, his three secrets of success, he tells us,[210] are, What, When and Where—What to plant, When to plant, and Where to market.

Do you know it is a fact that $500,000,000 more was received from the sale of crops this year than last? What do you think of that, you Klondikers who suffer hardships in the Alaskan mountains for the sake of a little gold which, after all, you will probably never get? If the gold output of the newly discovered regions of the far North reaches this year $10,000,000—a most liberal estimate, and probably two or three times the actual yield —remember that the soil right here at home, with one-half the labor and none of the risk of life, has yielded fifty times that amount. And this is not the actual yield, but only the surplus over and above what the fields gave the year before. Five hundred millions of gold more than last year dug out of the soil—think of it! In the following examples we only give the byways of farming—that is, what can be done, by the cultivation of a single product, and not what may be accomplished in the regular way. Of course, much more can be made by the raising of several staples, and by a systematic rotation of crops.

711. SUBSTITUTE FOR SILK.—Send to the Department of Agriculture for jute seed. Jute will take dye as a sponge takes water, and it has a gloss which makes it capable of being used in combination with silk so as to defy detection. Remember that when a thing can be made to look like some other thing at one-twentieth the cost, it opens the way for mines of wealth. A word to the wise is sufficient. Jute needs a warm climate, and you must go to the Southern States.

712. WASHINGTON PIPPINS.—They are known as Newtown Pippins, but let us give you a secret. The[211] soil of the State of Washington is so adapted to this apple that you can raise from one-fourth to one-half greater crops than in any other State. Apple raisers, remember this.

713. DORSETS AND DOWNS.—Fancy breeds of sheep! Two hundred million dollars worth of wool from these breeds were imported last year. That was what we paid for a name, and for our ignorance in not knowing that we can raise just as good sheep here. Reader, if you want a share of this $200,000,000, study a good book about sheep farming, purchase a few of these two famous breeds, and put the wool on the market as the genuine Dorset; for so it is. The place counts for not one atom—only the breed.

714. AMERICAN CHEESE.—Here again we are foolishly playing into the hands of foreigners, paying $1,500,000 every year for that which can be produced equally as good and cheap at home. Everybody should know that there is no better spot on the globe for the kind of pasture that makes delicious cheese than Delaware County in the State of New York. We pay these millions to foreigners because we do not produce enough at home; but here, within two or three hours freightage of the metropolis of the Western World, we have the best cheese-producing country on earth.

715. BUSINESS APPLES.—We call them Business Apples because they will mean a good business for you if you are wise enough to undertake their culture. Go to Missouri and try the Ben Davis variety. The soil of that State is the best for that kind of apple. A man there set out two hundred trees, and last year sold $450 worth of Ben Davis apples. At the same rate, one[212] thousand trees, covering about five acres, should bring you $2,500.

716. FORTUNES IN POPPIES.—Here is another new idea. France has caught upon it; why may not the farmer of this country? Five hundred thousand pounds of opium are sold every year in our drug stores, but it has been thought that the drug could only be raised in the East. This is a mistake. The French farmers sold 5,000,000 francs worth last year. It yields a net profit of $25 an acre and requires little culture. It may yet become a rival of King Cotton in our Southern States, but those who are wide-awake enough to be the first in the field will reap the lion's share of this new bidder for our enterprise.

717. THE CAPON FARM.—One hundred per cent. capons! This is the actual experience of a raiser. He operated on forty, sent them to market and realized $39.24. He estimates the cost of keeping at less than fifty cents each. There are few investments in which the

gross proceeds are double the cost. In addition, the raising of capons may be carried on with the ordinary poultry farm.

718. BARRELS OF BALDWINS.—The home of this market favorite is Northern New York and Northern New England. It is a hardy tree. Apple trees commonly bear only every second year, and often cease to bear altogether. The secret of success is to stir the soil and add a little fertilizer. Good Baldwins, commanding from $2.50 to $3.50 per barrel, may be raised every year with the certainty of clockwork, if the owner only exercises proper diligence and care.

719. RARE RODENTS.—Money in rats and mice! In killing them? No, in raising them. At the pet-stock[213] department and appendage of the poultry show in New York recently, rats and mice, white or finely marked, brought all the way from $1 to $12, according to the fineness of the colors. It will be a revelation to most farmers that there is money in creatures which they have hitherto regarded as pests to be put out of the way.

720. MORTGAGE-LIFTER OATS.—So-called because a man developed a particular variety, and with the sales, advertised as fancy seed and bringing more than double the ordinary kind, lifted a crushing mortgage from his farm. You can develop a variety as well as he. Give it a taking name, and advertise freely.

721. RECORD-BREAKING DATES.—A date plantation of five hundred or six hundred acres, and capable of holding thirty thousand trees, can be bought for $500. The fifth year after planting the trees should bear sixty thousand pounds of dates, worth at least $6,000. Pretty good return for $500! Dates are raised chiefly in South America.

722. DOLLAR WHEAT.—Western farmers have contended that if they could command $1 a bushel for wheat they could get rich. This year their hopes have been realized. If it is, as many believe, the beginning of better times for the wheat-raiser, and the cereal can be kept at that price, you have but to follow the advice of Horace Greeley, and "Go West" to become a rich man. The government will give you the land, and industry and economy will do the rest.

723. LEAF TOBACCO.—Where tobacco can be raised, farmers have abandoned nearly every other crop. It needs a rich, warm soil, and some experience in order to insure success; but if you "once learn the trade," you will hardly try to raise anything else. North of Virginia,[214] it must be raised it the "bottom-lands" of the rivers. Price, $8 to $10 per one hundred pounds.

724. TREE NURSERY.—The expense of a tree nursery is almost nothing beyond the first investment. Small trees before transplanting may be set one foot apart, and hence an acre will hold about forty-four thousand. At nine cents apiece—the average price—this means $3,960. Deduct for labor and expressage. The success of the tree merchant depends almost solely on his finding a market.

725. Round Number Onions.—The round number of one thousand bushels to the acre has been done, and can be done under favorable circumstances. In a certain district in Fairfield County, Conn., nearly all the men are well-to-do farmers. Ask them the secret of their success and the one reply will be "onions." Here, surely, even in rocky Connecticut, farming pays. They get from seventy-five cents to $1.25 per bushel. The crop is not always a safe one, dependent upon weather conditions; but, taken one year with another, the farmers do well, and steadily add to their bank account.

726. Potato Profits.—Let us see what can be done with potatoes. In a prize contest recently the average per acre was 465 bushels. The highest was 975 bushels. The price per bushel was from sixty to sixty-six cents. The next profit was on the average $260 per acre and in case of the highest was about $500. Of course this is vastly above what is accomplished by the ordinary farmer, but it shows what can be done with good soil, liberal dressing, prolific variety, and thorough tillage.[215]

727. Golden Geese.—Here is one man's experience: "I bought a gander and three geese. From the geese I received yearly forty eggs each in two litters, or a total of 120. I find that from this number of eggs I can safely count on seventy-five per cent of matured chicks, or ninety goslings. The weight when fatted is 855 pounds, and at twenty cents a pound I receive $171. Cost of keeping is $46. Profits, $125. Of course, the sum varies one year from another, but this is my average for five years." At the same rate the goslings from 100 geese would pay a net profit of $4,125, but if they paid only one-quarter that sum it would still be a profitable investment.

728. California Prunes.—This great state has now 85,000 acres planted with prunes, and produced last year 65,000,000 pounds. The crop has grown from nothing to this enormous amount in the last few years. People do not rush into an enterprise in this way unless they are pretty sure it is a good thing. The "good thing" in this case is that prunes costing one and one half cents per pound to raise sell for six and seven cents, and the prune raisers are all getting rich.

729. A Bee Farm.—Here is another California bonanza. Says a man in the southern part of the State: "Last year I marketed ten tons of extracted honey, and three tons of comb honey, all from 154 colonies. I received on an average ten cents per pound, or a total of $3,600. The space employed was 1,386 feet, or somewhat less than an acre."

730. The Apple Acre.—A man in New England said that after forty years experience, raising all kinds of crops, he found that his apple orchard averaged $55 per acre, which was better than any crop on his other 200 acres of land.[216]

731. The Sugar Beet.—Purchase a farm within a few miles of a sugar beet factory. With proper cultivation you can grow nine tons to the acre, and the factory price should be $4.50 per ton. The thriftiness of the beet makes little trouble with weeds, and hence the expense of raising is not one-fourth that of onions.

732. GILT-EDGED BREEDS.—The sum of $5,100 was recently paid for a Poland-China boar. A litter of pigs of this breed brought $3,500. These sums seem almost incredible, but when people have both the mania and the money they will pay any amount to gratify their taste. There are persons who take as much pride in pigs as others do in horses. The best way to succeed with new breeds is to cultivate a strain for yourself. It requires time, patience and experience, and some outlay in risk, but in the end it pays, especially if one has the gift of knowing how to trumpet his stock.

733. DECEMBER LAYERS.—With a trifling expense you can have eggs at Christmas as well as at Easter. The price is often more than double at the former season. Connect with hot water-pipes and keep your hens warm. A cold hen never lays an egg. A poultry expert says if a flock is well cared for the whole year round, it should pay annually for each hen $1 net. At the same rate a flock of four hundred would bring a net income of $400.

734. FLORIDA CELERY.—In Florida the first growers made from $500 to $1,500 per acre. Competition has reduced the price, but at present rates men with six acres are getting a comfortable support, and those who have the means to cultivate a large farm of this popular vegetable are rapidly growing rich.[217]

735. ONEIDA HOPS.—It takes a good many hops to weigh a pound, but growers in Oneida County, New York, have raised 1,400 pounds per acre, receiving therefor $112. Probably this is somewhat better than the average, but profits in even low-price years are better in that section of the country than for any other crop. Hops are a safe and easy crop.

736. BOSTON BEANS.—They are not raised in Boston—only baked there. They are a hardy crop, and will grow on any properly cultivated soil. One year with another they bring $2.50 per bushel. Beans are the surest of all crops, and if the price were only as certain, you could figure out your income in advance almost as accurately as if employed on a salary.

737. CHRISTMAS TREES.—Buy for a few hundred dollars an abandoned farm too poor for culture, and pack it with small evergreens. Christmas trees command from fifty cents to $5, and you can grow a thousand of them on a single acre. There are fortunes in what is called worthless land if you know how to improve it.

738. THE GUARANTEED EGG.—A great business can be done with a guaranteed egg. Success depends upon the absolute perfection of your egg. Have a stamp made, and stamp every egg with the name of your farm, and offer to replace any one found faulty. Also stamp the date on which they are taken from the nest. In this way you will absolutely protect your product from the frauds of dealers, your eggs will attain a wide reputation, will have an unlimited demand, and you will grow rich. There is a mine of gold in this suggestion.[218]

739. DOUBLE VEGETABLE CULTURE.—Here is an idea of a New Jersey farmer. He has conceived the notion of grafting tomatoes on potatoes vines, or an air crop on a root crop, and thus raising vegetables at both ends. There is nothing impracticable in the notion, and it is doubtless entirely feasible, if only he is liberal enough with his fertilizers. This is an idea for growers who have only a limited space, and where land is high.

740. ENGLISH SHIRES.—Colts from Lord Rothschild's stud farm last year averaged $875. It costs little more to keep a good horse than a poor one. There are great possibilities in the raising of fine-blooded horses. The colt that won the great Futurity race this year could have been easily bought for $700 before the race. Now $20,000 will not purchase him. "Plunger" Walton made $350,000 in two years on the turf. At the Elmendorf stud farm near Lexington, Ky., a short time ago thirty-three yearling colts were sold at prices ranging from $150 to $5,100, the average price being $1,460.87 per head; at the same time twenty yearling fillies brought an average of $676.50 per head, the forty-three yearling colts and fillies being the product of one breeding farm and selling in one day for $47,130 or an average of $1,095.80 per head.

741. FORTUNES IN NUT SHELLS.—Land too poor for meadow or even for pasture may be utilized for nut-growing. The trees require little attention, but will produce bushels of nuts if the soil is properly stirred and fertilized every year. One man in Connecticut raises each year 100 bushels of hickory nuts from ten trees, and sells them at $2 a bushel. The rocky, waste lands of New England can grow millions of these trees. Chestnuts can be grown cheaper than wheat. The[219] standard price is $4 to $8 per bushel, but large chestnuts, early in the season, that is, in September and October, bring from $10 to $15 per bushel. Judge Salt, of Burlington, N. J., says he has a chestnut tree in the middle of a wheat field that pays more than the wheat. The average is about $19 per tree, and twenty trees have ample room in an acre. This makes $300 per acre with but little cost for cultivation. Here is something of importance about the pecan. The chief pomologist at Washington, D. C., says: "The cultivation of nuts will soon be one of the greatest and most profitable industries in the United States, and there is no use in denying the fact that the Texas soft shell pecan is the favorite nut of the world." The average yield of these nuts in North Carolina is $300 to $500 per acre. Some pecan trees in New Jersey are producing annually five to six bushels of delicious, thin-shelled nuts.
[220]

CHAPTER   XVII.

MONEY IN LITERATURE.

Profits of the Pen—Ten Cents a Word—A Millionaire Novelist—$3,000 for a Short Story—How Hall Caine Won a Fortune—A Pilgrimage of Publishers—"One Thousand Times Across the Atlantic"—$5,000 for a Song —Suggestions to Writers—What It Pays to Write.

LITERATURE requires the least capital of any enterprise with the possibilities of rich reward and wide renown. A pen, a bottle of ink, a ream of paper, and—*brains*. These are all. There is no occupation so discouraging to the one who lacks the last-named quality and few so alluring to those who possess it. Authors are supposed to write for fame, but fame and fortune are twin sisters which are seldom separated. Hack writers are indeed hard worked and poorly paid, but in the higher walks of literature rewards are generous. In London, the rates to first-class writers are $100 per 1,000 words. In one case $135 was paid, and in another $175 demanded. Amelia Barr, the famous novelist, receives $20,000 a year from the sale of her books. There is a great deal of subterranean literature unknown to the critics and the magazine writers, but which, nevertheless, pays handsomely. One Richebourg, of Paris, has 4,000,000 readers, and often receives $12,000 for the serial rights alone, yet he is unknown to the magazine public. In this country the "Albatross Novels," by Albert Ross, sold to the extent of a million copies, and[221] the author acquired such a fortune that he was able to engage in charity on a magnificent scale, yet the author is unknown to fame.

Among the instances of the pecuniary rewards for single works are "Les Miserables," by Victor Hugo, which brought $80,000 and "Trilby," which netted the author the princely sum of $400,000. "Quo Vadis," by Sienkiewicz, sells all over the world, but its author had already made half a million dollars with his pen before he wrote that popular book.

It is not our purpose in this chapter to treat of books requiring transcendent genius to create, but rather to suggest titles of works which may be composed by less gifted authors, books, which if written with fair ability cannot fail to be of interest and profit.

742. THE POPULAR NOVEL.—This is the best paying form of literature. The pen that can touch the popular heart may not be a gold one, but it will bring gold into the pockets of him who wields it. Amelie Rives received $6,000 for "According to St. John." Lord Lytton received $7,500 for some of his novels. Of the "Heavenly Twins," 50,000 copies were sold in 1894; of the "Bonny Brier Bush," 30,000 in five months; and of the "Manxman" 50,000 in four months. Of Mrs. Henry Wood's "East Lynne," 400,000 have been sold, and her thirty-four books have reached altogether over 1,000,000 copies. In France, there are sold every year of Feuilleton's works, 50,000; of Daudet's, 80,000, and of Zola's, 90,000. Hall Caine received outright a check for $50,000 for "The Christian." He had struck the popular chord with the "Deemster." There was almost a pilgrimage of

publishers to the Isle of Man to make engagements for the pen of the new writer when that book was launched upon the market.[222]

743. THE SHORT STORY.—The short story is very popular in this country, and has attained a perfection reached nowhere else in the world. The rules of success in this department are briefly these: First, to be strikingly original; second, to write simply and naturally; and third, to condense into the smallest compass. Be brief. This is the age of electricity. Many a story of 10,000 words has been rejected when if it had contained half that number it would have been accepted. Publishers pay liberal rates for short, good stories. The New York *Herald* recently paid Mollie E. Seawell $3,000 for a short story. Within a very short time a magazine has offered a price of $1,000 for the best short story; another has made the same offer; and a third one of $500. Among the publications that pay the authors the highest rates are *Harper's Magazine*, the *Century, McClure's*, the *Youth's Companion*, and the *Ladies' Home Journal*. There are several others that pay nearly as much.

744. THE VILLAGE REPORTER.—Write up some event that occurs in your neighborhood. Any leading newspaper will pay for it if well written. It must be spicy, but not ornate. Put in strong, nervous adjectives; color well. Take care not to make it libelous. If you succeed you can try again, and if you show aptness at the work you will doubtless secure a position as a reporter.

745. THE TRUTH CONDENSER.—Facts for the million! Do you know that a cyclopedia of the most useful information can be written in a single volume? The "Britannica" has twenty-five volumes. The "International" fifteen. Here is needed the faculty of condensation. Use facts only, and you will be surprised[223] to find how many articles consist only of words. Make use of the great cyclopedias, the newspaper almanacs, government reports, and all books in which knowledge is condensed. Pack the book full of the things the millions want to know.

746. TOWN HISTORY.—Write a short history of your native town or of some other town. Publish the portraits, and residences or places of business, of the leading townsmen. Mention in the book everybody in the town whom you can. Even for the most humble can be found a place in a work of genealogy. The wealthy will give you large sums for the illustrations, and the vanity of the poor will cause them to buy a book in which their name appears. Cost of issue of book, $1,000. One thousand subscribers at $2 apiece, $2,000. One hundred of the wealthier class who will pay you $10 apiece for their portraits, $1,000. Profits, $2,000. If you are satisfied with the result, go on to the next town, and so on *ad infinitum*.

747. THE SHOPPERS' GUIDE.—A small book could be issued in paper covers for twenty-five cents, giving an explanation of every kind of goods, the difference, and the best kinds and brands. Not one person in twenty is posted on these things, and must take the clerk's

word. It should show what firms make a specialty in any line or department, and on what days they make a discount. Merchants would no doubt pay you at advertising rates for such a notice of their places of business. The book should include dry-goods and fancy stores as well as grocers and meat markets. Such a book should sell by the million.

748. A BIRTHDAY BOOK.—We have the "Shakespeare[224] Birthday Book," the "Tennyson Birthday Book," the "Emerson Birthday Book," and many others. Add one more, the "Richter." The writings of Jean Paul abound in felicitous and eloquent passages, just suited for such a work.

749. A CHURCH-WORKERS' BOOK.—A man had a half-written book on church-work, dividing it into twenty branches with one thousand working plans to be given by the most successful ministers and other Christian workers in the land; but owing to a pressure of other duties he was unable to complete it. This lead is still unworked.

750. HOUSEHOLD ECONOMICS.—A book can be written by one who understands the subject which it would pay every housekeeper to buy. The kitchen alone should supply at least one hundred examples of waste. The care of servants would employ another important part of the book. Every room would afford a chapter. Such a book, telling the inexperienced housekeeper what to buy and how to economize would save money for many a beginner.

751. THE PLAIN MAN'S MEAL.—A book with this title should have a ready sale. All cook books are for persons who can keep a butler, or at least one or two servants. The recipes are expensive. Write one by means of which an economical housewife can get a meal for four at an expense of fifty cents. A regular *menu* for each meal for every day of the year would be appreciated. Plain food and simple cooking at cheap cost. The book should not be over 300 pages, and should not sell for more than one dollar.[225]

752. PRESENT CENTURY CELEBRITIES.—Nothing in history is harder to find out than the lives of persons in the last generation. History tells us the remote past, contemporary literature tells us about the present, but there is no book that tells us about the recent past. The men who were prominent in statesmanship, commerce and literature, two or three decades ago are not heard of now. A new generation has come upon the stage and knows them not. This is a want felt by every one who takes the slightest interest in times and men. Get out a book with a short chapter devoted to each of the prominent men who have lived in the last half of the nineteenth century. If this work seems too voluminous, then let it comprise only the leading men in our country since the Civil War. If well written it should command a great sale.

753. READERS' GUIDE BOOK.—A guide book for good reading which can be sold for $1 is a desideratum. Enumerate a few of the best books of all the great departments of literature with a short critique upon each. The list of the books as well as the critiques can be condensed from any of the ponderous reference lists in our great libraries.

754. AMERICAN ELOQUENCE.—There should be a book published which would preserve the different types of American eloquence. If it could be made a kind of text-book on oratory, it would have an immense sale. Tens of thousands of young men are fitting themselves to be lawyers, preachers, elocutionists, and public speakers in various capacities. They want a book which will give them the rules and models of effective speech. A book written with so much care as to make it a kind of standard of eloquence and oratory would[226] pay well for the painstaking task. Our standard schoolbooks have proved mints of money to their authors.

755. RACERS' RECORD BOOK.—A book which should be a reliable record of the fastest times made in horse races, bicycle meets, and sporting matches, ought to have a ready sale. It should consist of condensed tables of all the records of all the great races, interspaced with blank leaves for the jotting down of new records. There are at least a million men interested in racing, and at a very moderate estimate one-quarter (250,000) ought to buy your book, which, we will say, sells for twenty-five cents.

756. YOUR OWN PHYSICIAN.—We want a book on health, written from the latest point of view of hygiene and physiology. Get a symposium of physicians to write on such topics as dress, diet, exercise, sleep, medicine, baths, etc. Most physicians would regard the advertising benefits of these articles as sufficient remuneration, while at the same time their names would help to sell the work, but if necessary pay them for their services. Entitle the work, "Your Own Physician," and sell it on subscription, the canvasser showing how much cheaper it is to keep well at $2—the price of the book—than to get well at $200—the charge of a physician for services in a long spell of illness.

757. THE BOY'S ASTRONOMY.—A small book about the sun, moon and stars, made attractive for beginners. It should teem with illustrations, and the youthful reader should be fascinated as he follows the sun and moon in their courses, learns how eclipses occur, and understands about meteors, comets, and nebulæ.[227] There should also be directions for finding the principal stars on any night of the year. Such a book should command a ready sale, for he who writes for boys and girls has the largest market.

758. RECREATIONS IN CHEMISTRY.—A bishop of the Methodist Episcopal Church once wrote a book entitled "Recreations in Astronomy," which has had a very large sale. But there is just as much room for "Recreations in Chemistry," if written with as much imagination and skill. It should contain such fascinating chapters as "Chemistry of a Candle," "The Dynamics of a Dewdrop," "The Evolution of an Oak." The chief points in the authorship should be accuracy and a charming style.

759. THE CURIOSITY BOOK.—A book packed with the curious things in every department of human research. People like to read about the rare and the curious. A hundred chapters, short, spicy, and containing each a few wonderful things in a special field of learning,

would be very popular with both young and old. As a gift book it would be unexcelled. There is money in it.

760. THE CHILD'S BIBLE.—A Bible which shall contain the numerous stories so connected in narrative form as to make a continuous history from beginning to end. It should be very simple, and in no way do violence to the sacred record. If properly written, this book could be sold by canvassers in almost every home, and should bring much gain to the author.

761. GUIDE TO TRADES.—A complete guide to all the important professions, occupations, callings and [228] trades. This work should show the opportunities in each trade, the comparative chances of success, the remuneration, and a few simple rules for guidance. It should bristle with facts, and should also give one or two examples in the form of stories—short autobiographies still better—of men who have been successful in each department of work. The advantage of this book is that it has no competitor, covering an entirely new field in authorship.

762. THE PLEASURE BOOK.—Here is a unique idea for a book. Let there be three hundred or more sections, one for every week day in the year, and let each section contain a different form of amusement. Books on games, riddles, sports, etc., can be drawn upon for supplies. As you must provide enjoyment for all kinds of weather, it will be well to have a short alternative for rainy days in each section. The amusement should be of the greatest possible variety, from the fox-hunt in the fields to the thimble-hunt in the parlor. As a large number of people have leisure only at night, perhaps a work entitled, "Three Hundred Happy Evenings" would be better than the suggestion above, though it would necessarily have to leave out most outdoor sports. Holidays should have a more elaborate programme.

763. THE SOLDIER'S BOOK.—There are 750,000 survivors of our Civil War. It would be too much to publish in one book even the briefest account of each. The work should be published in several parts, a volume to a State. In a State like New York, three lines only could be given to the record of a private, but even for the briefest mention of himself and his comrades nearly all the old soldiers would buy the book. In smaller States more space could be given to each man's record. Considerable [229] capital would be required in the collecting of facts and records, but the publication of such a work would certainly pay, if accurately written and thoroughly canvassed. We have estimated the cost of collecting the information at twenty-five cents for each soldier. It would be much less in great cities where a large number of men could be seen in one day. Cost for 100,000 soldiers, $25,000. Such is the vanity caused by seeing one's name in print that the book would sell at least to every second soldier. Fifty thousand copies at $2.50, $125,000. Deduct one-fourth for cost and getting out the book, $31,250. Discount for canvassers at

one-third the price of the book, $41,666. Total cost, $72,916. Profits, $51,084 for 50,000 copies.

764. BOOK OF STYLE.—A man well versed in books could write a small volume on literary style which could be sold to advantage for $1 per copy. The number of literary men is constantly increasing. More than 10,000 young men and women are graduated every year from our colleges. At a very low estimate, 25,000 would want a work of this kind.

765. SCIENCE OF COMMON THINGS.—A book of great interest to everybody could be compiled from the vast body of matter contained in the last quarter of a century in such periodicals as the *Popular Science Monthly*, the *Scientific American*, etc. It should contain a number of chapters about the heating and ventilating of dwellings, about clothing and food, about road making and house building, and many other things, and be written in such a fascinating style as to make the work attractive, even to persons who ordinarily take no interest in such discussions. The success of such a book depends entirely upon its style. It is possible to write one containing a fortune for the author.[230]

766. POPULAR SONGS.—If you are a musical composer there is another rich field which invites you. Many a man in the making of bars and clefs has braided strands of gold. Daniel Emmett wrote "Dixie," and it ran like wild fire all over the country. Stephen Foster made a fortune with "Old Folks at Home," Charles K. Harris wrote "After the Ball." Its sales were over a million copies, and it made him an independently rich man. H. W. Petrie wrote "I Don't Want to Play in Your Yard." Its success was phenomenal, and is likely to prove a bonanza to the author; 50,000 copies were sold before they were fairly dry from the press. Edward B. Marks, a young writer of New York, wrote "The Little Lost Child," which netted him $15,000. Sir Arthur Sullivan received $50,000 for his famous song, "The Lost Chord." Mr. Balfe got $40,000 for "I Dreamt that I Dwelt in Marble Halls."

767. FOREIGN TRANSLATIONS.—Another very wide field is that of the translation of foreign works. There are vast numbers of foreign works upon which there are no copyrights in this country, and others upon which the copyrights have expired. This is a profitable field and comparatively unworked. Even of such transcendant works as those of George Sand and Balzac only a few have been translated. Publishers pay for translations about the same as royalties on original works. Dryden received $6,000 for his translation of Virgil, and Pope received $40,000 for his rendering of the "Iliad."

768. CHILDREN'S STORIES.—There are bags of money in children's stories. Every child at a certain age wants to read or be read to, and there are seven million of this age in the United States. The stories should be[231] short, bright, simple and original, and the book should contain a number of illustrations. Whoever pleases the children pleases the world. "Alice in Wonderland" brought a fortune to its author, and every year Christmas stories for the children bring much money into the pockets of the writers.

769. CONDENSED STORIES.—All the popular and standard fiction of the world could be condensed into a dozen volumes by a master hand. It has never yet been attempted. Some omnivorous reader and ambitious writer may yet try it. He must get the heart of the story—the plot—without regard to side issues, by-plays, or ornamentation. See in how few words you can tell one of the Waverley novels without omitting any of the main features. Then publish the entire series in one volume. It is a new idea, and ought to take.

770. THE MANNER BOOK.—How to Act, How to Behave, How to Eat, How to Talk, How to Write Letters, How to Propose—in short, the correct way to get on in life. A book consisting of pert, witty chapters upon good manners ought to make a fast-selling work. Many have been written, but none as yet quite meet the demand.

771. THE GEORGE REPUBLIC.—Something entirely new. Do you know that in the village of Freeville, Tompkins County, New York, there is a republic composed of many hundred persons ruled entirely by boys, and these the worst of boys, taken mostly from the slums of our cities, a class which could not be governed in the ordinary way? It is hardly too much to say that it is the most suggestive experiment in self-government in all history, and it awaits the pen of a practiced{232} writer. The movement is doubtless to be permanent and popular, and the first one to pen it in graphic style will doubtless gather a good harvest.

772. ONE THOUSAND TIMES ACROSS THE ATLANTIC.—Here is a capital idea! Many sea captains have crossed the ocean as many times as that. Get an Atlantic veteran to tell you some of the most thrilling stories of his forty years' sailing. He may not be much of a writer, but you can put the matter into attractive form. For a small compensation, or perhaps for the love of the thing, he would tell you many exciting tales of the sea. The title is taking.

773. THE MAN HUNTER.—Few writings are more fascinating than detective stories, and no one has more interesting matter to relate than one of the sleuths of the law. Think of "Sherlock Holmes," whom Conan Doyle created, and who has made piles of money for his author.

774. STORY OF A RAGPICKER.—It is a new idea. Did a ragpicker ever write before? But he must have had many interesting experiences. Transfer the stories from his tongue to your pen. Paste these uncouth patches into a literary crazy-quilt as an experienced writer knows how to do, and you will have a book whose title will advertise it, and whose unique contents will make it sell.

775. STORY OF A DIVER.—Under the ocean! Jules Verne's "Twenty Thousand Leagues Under the Sea" actualized! No one can have more thrilling experiences than a diver. Catch the homely words from his lips, gild them with a lively imagination, color them with{233} an expert pen, and you have a book whose sales will astonish you.

776. STORY OF A CONVICT.—Here is another new idea. The under side of life is seldom if ever told. Who knows what the convict thinks, feels, and suffers? Let a narrative be written from a convict's point of view. Let him tell how he committed the crime, how he was induced to do it, how he felt when he was doing it, his motives and hopes, the account of his arrest, what his lawyer said to him, his trial, condemnation, and sentence. Then his long imprisonment. A convict who is a good talker could easily give you material which you could skillfully work up into an attractive book, as novel as it would be interesting. Much of the success of "Les Miserables" was due to the vivid portrayal of the sufferings of Jean Valjean.

777. THE STOWAWAY.—Another unique idea! Stowaways are constantly crossing the ocean. Get his story. Tell pathetically his motives for crossing the water, and the account of his privations on shipboard. Here is matter for another Robinson Crusoe.

778. WHEEL AND WORLD.—"Across the Continent on a Bicycle!" "Around the World on a Wheel!" These are attractive titles. All wheelmen—there are 300,000 in New York alone —would read it. If you have not made the journey yourself, get some one who has, for a small sum, to tell you the story.

779. STORY OF A FIREMAN.—A fireman dwells in the midst of alarms. A veteran fireman has been to thousands of fires. Let him tell you twenty or thirty of them in his own way, the thrilling adventures, the[234] hairbreadth escapes, the heroic rescues, and the magnificent and appalling scenes. Every fireman would buy the book, and, if well written, all the fireman's friends, which means about everybody.

780. IN A BALLOON.—Here is a most attractive field which has never been occupied. Edgar Poe's "Journey to the Moon" is celebrated, but it is only a phantasy, while we may have an equally interesting reality—not indeed of a journey to the moon, but through the clouds. If the narrative could be combined with a romance, this might be made the book of the day, which, of course, means many thousands of dollars in the pockets of the author.

781. STORY OF AN ENGINEER.—Another man whose life is worth relating is that of an old engineer. Fill the book with an account of his wonderful runs and his thrilling adventures on frontier roads. Of course, there must be horrible accidents, daring "hold-ups," bold train robberies, stalling in snowbanks, fleeing from prairie fires, and racing with engines of rival roads.

782. STORY OF A MURDERER.—Let the criminal give his version of the affair. Not every murderer has a story, or is willing to tell it; but out of hundreds of convicts you should be able to weave a tale as lurid as Blackbeard among the pirates or Bluebeard among the fairies. If it be a recent and celebrated case which has cut a large figure in the newspapers, so much the better.

783. STORY OF A TRAMP.—New interest is being taken in this erratic and omnipresent individual. And[235] the time is ripe for a facile pen to portray his vagaries and his wanderings. The "Story of a Tramp" affords an almost unparalleled scope for an author, and there is no phase of civilization which may not be drawn upon to make the story interesting.

784. STORY OF A LUNATIC.—A very thrilling story, somewhat perhaps after the manner of C. Brockden Brown's "Weiland," could be worked up from the ravings of a lunatic. There are a vast number of persons who have wild, harrowing tales. In fact, the audience for such stories is larger than the number of readers of the finer quality of literature. A writer in a recent newspaper says: "The masses do not read the magazines, but they do read sensational literature in the form of dime novels and weekly story papers, and this flashy fiction earns far more money for its writers than is made by more ambitious authors and more pretentious publications."

785. STORY OF A CRIMINAL LAWYER.—A retired criminal lawyer might make money by the narrative of his most extraordinary cases. If he does not care to write the narrative himself he might in odd moments give it to you. With the pen of a Doyle you might reap that author's immense royalties.

786. STORY OF THE KLONDIKE.—Many stories of adventure and hardship will doubtless be written about the new land of gold, but the harvest will be reaped by the keen pen of him first in the field. If Alaska has been unkind to you, you may revenge yourself by digging gold from her bowels with the pen.

787. THE EXPOSITION OF FRAUDS.—A very interesting[236] book might be written with this title. Take a few national scandals, like the "Panama Fiasco," "The South Sea Bubble," "The Grant-Ward Swindle," "The Tichborne Claimant." These subjects when handled with a skillful pen are very interesting to business men.

788. SERMONS OF MODERN PREACHERS.—We have volumes of collected and selected sermons, but no volume which contains various specimens of the preaching of the present day. Have one sermon each from the very newest of pulpit celebrities, such as S. Parkes Cadman, Hugh Price Hughes, Wilbur Chapman, together with one each from such well-known preachers as Phillips Brooks, T. DeWitt Talmage, and Sam Jones. There are over 100,000 ordained clergymen in the United States, and at least one-half of them would want this book.

789. THE WONDER BOOK.—A book describing briefly and graphically a few of the great wonders of the world, such as London the greatest city, Niagara the greatest cataract, Monte Carlo the greatest gambling place, while other chapters would be headed, "The Greatest Picture Gallery," "The Longest Railroad," "The Tallest Pyramid," "The Deepest Well," etc. The book would have a vast sale among young people, and would be popular among all classes.

790. HEALTH RESORTS.—Their number is legion. Select a few of the principal in all parts of the country, and write charmingly of their peculiar merits. Especially impress upon your public the specific diseases for which they are beneficial. The 500,000 invalids of the country would want the book.[237]

791. THE ALL-CURE BOOK.—A book which treats thoroughly the newest systems of cure, such as the Magnetic, Water Cure, Massage, Barefoot, Christian Science, etc., giving a history of the same, and an account of the alleged cures.

792. SUCCESS.—A book for young men. Get twenty business men in different lines to tell you each in a few pages how he was successful. It would be very popular if you could secure as authors such men as John Wanamaker, George Gould (for his deceased father, Jay Gould), James Gordon Bennett, Murat Halstead, etc.

793. HOW TO SEE NEW YORK.—Not a guide book, but one far more beneficial to strangers who want to see the great metropolis. It should contain at least three sets of directions for persons preparing to visit the city for the first time. These methods and order of sightseeing should be radically different, giving the intending visitor the choice of the three. The million or more people who come every year to New York for the first time would want the book, and half of them would doubtless buy it if freely advertised and sold for not more than fifty cents.

794. MAP MAKING.—There is money in the making of town, county and state maps. For this you need the services of a good surveyor. Go to a map publisher and get his estimates of cost; he can inform you where to get a surveyor, and give you much other valuable advice. As a rule, maps sell in proportion to the smallness of the territory portrayed, people being chiefly interested in their immediate neighborhood. It is with towns as with boarders—there is not much money in one or two, but he who has the capital to work twenty[238] towns at a time will do well. Jay Gould got his first start in this way.

795. STORY OF THE POLE.—A score or more of great captains have tried to reach the pole, and many of them have told their story in captivating books, but we want a book in which each man's story shall be condensed into a single chapter of fifty pages each. The thousands of people who like comparisons and admire hardy adventures would like a book of this kind.

796. THE MAKING OF A MIGHTY BUSINESS.—We have spoken of the men who made the business, but this book deals with the business itself. What a great book could be made of a few chapters each, one devoted to such themes as "A Great Railroad," "A Great Sugar House," "A Great Banking House," "A Great Steamship Company," "The New York Post Office," "The United States Patent Office." This book would appeal for interest to all classes, and ought to be very profitable to the author.

797. HEROES OF LABOR.—Now let the laboring man tell his story. A book to consist of chapters written by such labor leaders as T. V. Powderly, Samuel Gompers, Mr. Sovereign, and other Knights of Labor, relating the story of their struggles with capital. Technical matters, such as interviews with directors and tables of wages should be made as brief as possible, while strikes, scenes of violence and suffering, should form the chief matter of the book. Here is a chance for a gifted writer to make a second "Uncle Tom's Cabin," a book whose sale in this country has eclipsed that of any other thing ever published.[239]

798. THE ELITE DIRECTORY.—Some cities like New York have such a book, but other cities have not. Here is a field for the talent of the reportorial variety. It will be a delicate matter to decide who shall be included in the gilded circle and who shall be excluded, but if you are discreet and discriminating, careful to make your book contain the names of only the recognized people of society, these will in nearly all cases buy your book, and will not be afraid of a good round price.

799. POPULAR DRAMAS.—These have made the fortunes of their authors. A playwright often receives $100 per night while the play runs. More frequently the manager pays a sum outright for the rights of the play. The sum of $10,000 was paid recently for the right to dramatize a popular work of fiction, the author having already received a fortune from its sale as a novel. Eugene Scribe, the French dramatist, left at his death the sum of $800,000, mainly his earnings as a playwright.

800. FURNISHING A HOME.—A book on home furnishing, treating the subject from an artistic point of view, would doubtless find a market. Each room should have a separate chapter. The furnishing should be considered from the standpoint of expense, comfort, color and harmony. A book entitled "Inside a Hundred Homes" had a large sale.

801. PRETTY WEDDINGS.—Here is a field entirely unoccupied. Select twenty of the most stylish weddings of modern times, and give a full account of them. They should be, of course, weddings among the bon ton. The book would be a kind of fashionable wedding guide, and would be eagerly bought by every lady who expects[240] to be a bride. The book also might contain hints and rules for weddings among all grades of social life.

802. QUOTATION BOOK.—One not classified in the old way, according to subjects, but in relation to occasion. Quotations for the business mart, the theatre, the church, the political arena, the dinner party, etc. If made to be sold very cheap it would have a good sale; or it might be combined at a higher price with a book on manners. See No. 770.[241]

CHAPTER   XVIII.

MONEY IN NEWSPAPERS.

Fortunes in Printers' Ink—Value of the New York *Herald* Plant—Story of Mr. Pulitzer's Struggles—From a Park Bench to a Newspaper Throne—Alfred Harnsworth, the Greatest Paper Man in the World—Serving the News Hot—Secret of the Springfield *Republican* Success—A Prophet as Well as an Editor—How Reporters Earn Big Salaries—Motto, the Penny Reform—Seven Papers in One—Some New Advertising Schemes—Magazines for the Million.

A NEWSPAPER undertaking is a great financial risk, but at the same time it is one of the richest lodes of success if the proprietor has the capital and the qualities needed. Mr. Whitelaw Reid has amassed a fortune in the New York *Tribune*. James Gordon Bennett, proprietor of the paper originated by the senior of that name, estimates his plant as worth $22,000,000. Mr. Pulitzer, of the New York *World*, was a poor boy who slept on the park benches. He got an idea, a little money, formed new plans, and struck out on an untrod path. He rattled the dry bones of his contemporaries, and he is to-day a millionaire many times over. Dana made his fortune on *The Sun* by his fearless, outspoken editorials, using the plainest Anglo-Saxon. Hearst, of the New York *Journal*, succeeded by his sensationalism. Alfred Harnsworth, an Englishman and a very young man, began the publication of a paper called *Answer* with very small capital. Before the age of thirty he became a millionaire. Now at thirty-two [242] he is the chief proprietor of seven dailies and twenty-two other periodicals, and is the head of the largest publishing firm in the world, with a total weekly output of more than 7,000,000 copies. The author of this work has formulated over 200 plans for newspaper success. He is sure that the majority of these plans are absolutely new and perfectly feasible, but the scope of the work will not permit of the insertion of more than ten. The following ten are selected with the firm belief that if they are followed up with ordinary zeal and skill the paper cannot fail to have a very large circulation.

News and Editorial Department.

803. THE NEWS IN ONE MINUTE.—We live in electric times; men must have their news served hot. We want to swallow the day's doings while we cross the ferry. Have an index on first page containing every item of news, and showing in what columns it can be found. Then, one can get the summary in a minute, while if he likes he can spend hours in the details.

804. NUTSHELL NEWS.—You may be sure that the paper which can give the news the quickest and neatest is going to the front. Some people care more for quantity than quality. A vast variety of news from all parts of the country, and each item condensed into a few lines, makes more impression on many people than a page devoted to a single

tragedy. The Springfield *Republican* owes its success to its remarkable number of small items.

805. THE BULLETIN FORECAST.—Most daily papers give out a bulletin. Thousands stand on the street and read the free bulletin, but do not buy the paper. Have [243] a forecast bulletin to read, "To-morrow's News." Then a speculation or prediction of what it will probably be. Put it in a sensational and interesting way. Thus: "The *Bugle* will tell you all about it to-morrow. Buy the *Bugle*." In the paper, conclude each important item of news with the editor's forecast of how the matter will turn out, thus giving it the interest of a continued story. Editors often treat a news item in an editorial, but a vast proportion of the readers never look at that page. Put the cream of the editorial, and especially several pointed questions, after the news item, with the information that the paper will try to solve the problem to-morrow.

806. BOTTOM FACTS.—Readers want facts, not reporters' fancies nor embellishments. It is well known that in many papers reporters are allowed to invent when they have no facts in the case, and as they are paid by the piece it is for their interest to make as much of an item as they can. Hence, our news is adulterated, distorted, and often falsified. We know some reporters who have invented columns of so-called "Facts;" others who have made sensational, highly-colored stories out of the most insignificant occurrences; and still others who have invented fake reports of sermons, lectures, and other public utterances, when they had not time to obtain the originals. Have it clearly understood in large headlines as a part of the policy of the paper that no reporter will be allowed to invent or exaggerate, that he will be instantly discharged if it can be shown that he has in any way distorted the cold facts. In this way tens of thousands who are now disgusted with what is dished up for them as news but know not where to turn for better service, will be drawn to your paper, and you will establish the [244] reputation for absolute truthfulness of statement and bald exactness of form.

807. THE PEOPLE'S PAPER.—Let it be understood that your sheet is distinctively a people's paper, and is not the organ of any party, class, or corporation. Announce that you will publish letters from anybody, regardless of grammar, sentiment, or position, with the only limitation of decency and personality. Advocate persistently cheap and honest public service. Let one of your mottoes be: "A penny a letter and a penny a mile," that is, the conviction that a letter ought to be sent anywhere in the United States for a penny, and that a man ought to be able to travel all over the country at the rate of a penny a mile. Have such mottoes as: "All the People Well Off," "Equal Rights for Everybody," "No Nepotism, no Partiality, no 'Pulls.'"

808. THE BIG SEVEN.—We have heard of the "Big Four" in railroading. Let your paper be seven sheets rolled into one, having one comprehensive name. Let the seven sheets each have a distinctive and peculiar title as if of a separate paper, and let each be devoted to a

particular field. The *Art Mirror* will contain the pictures; the *News Bureau* will contain the crispiest news; the *Sword and Pen* will contain the most pungent editorials; the *World Joker* or the New York *Clown* will contain the comical things. Then there should be a "stock paper," a "sporting paper," etc. Let it be known that when a man buys *The Earth* for three cents, or for a penny, as the case may be, he really gets seven papers.

Advertising Department.

809. Free Wants.—In establishing a paying paper[245] you lose nothing by what you give away. You can well afford to give away space that costs you nothing. Before your circulation is large enough to attract advertisers, you must devise some other means of attracting them. Advertise that on a certain day you will insert everybody's wants free. This will introduce your paper to a large number of persons, who will not only buy the copy in which their want appears, but will in many cases be ready to pay a little when they next need the services of your sheet.

810. Bargain Bureau.—Have a bargain bureau on the first page or in some other prominent place, and let it be understood that you will each day in this bureau call attention to the bargains especially advertised for that day, and to any new or special feature contained in the advertising columns. You will thus please and draw advertisers, and at the same time attract readers who want to know what, where, and when to buy.

811. Reserve Space.—Have a large blank square or rectangle with the announcement that "This space is reserved for —— ——." After two or three days people will begin to wonder who will fill the great blank. It becomes by far the most prominent and valuable advertising space in the paper, and should command a good round sum. Make a profitable bargain for a month or year for the filling of the space. If withdrawn, announce, "This space will now be filled by —— ——." The first advertiser's rival will pretty surely want it, a result which No. 1 will hardly permit if he can help it, and so between competitors in business your blank will always be filled and you can raise your price if competition becomes sharp.[246]

812. The Page Contract.—When your advertising patronage becomes large and you find it necessary to employ assistants, you will find it to your advantage to let the advertising out in contracts to your subordinates. Instead of paying your helpers a salary, you tell them that they can have a page for $50 or $500 (according to the size of the page and the number of the circulation). They then secure the advertisements themselves and make what they can. *They* and not *you* take the risk. Many assistants would not be willing to do that, but others would prefer the opportunity to work for themselves in this way.[247]

CHAPTER XIX.

MONEY IN CLOTH.

Capital in Cloth—How Uncle Sam Helps Linen-Makers—The Mistake of Stocking Manufacturers—5,000,000 Sales if the Maker will get the Right Thing—Better than Starch?—A Chance to Become a Millionaire—Another Eli Whitney Wanted—Go South and Get Rich—Secrets About Silk Manufacture—Startling Suggestions About a New Process of Making Wool.

IN the materials for making cloth and in the improvement of garments there is an unlimited field for development and fortune. Here are a few of the roads in which capital may profitably move:

813. LINEN MILLS.—The schedule of the new flax tariff was framed especially to protect linen manufacturers by cheapening the imports of the raw material so that they can compete with foreign rivals. Money put into linen mills ought to reap a bountiful harvest during the next few years.

814. TRIPLE KNEE STOCKING.—Why do not stocking makers give additional strength to the parts which are the first to wear out? Five million boys and girls in this country are wearing their knees through their stockings and yet makers go on in the assumption that the quicker the wear the better the trade. It remains for some sagacious manufacturer to put a double or triple thickness on the knee, get a reputation for his stocking, and command the market.

815. THE UNFRAYABLE COLLAR BAND.—Shirts, perfectly sound elsewhere, go into the rag-bin because the[248] collar band is frayed. The man who will give us a substitute for starch, which does all the mischief, will earn both gratitude and greenbacks.

816. THE RAMIE PLANT.—A few years ago the ramie plant was introduced into this country from China. It was reported to yield three crops a year, a total of 1,500 pounds to the acre, and that the fiber would produce a cloth equal to cotton or even silk. Great things were anticipated, but the hopes of the raisers were defeated by the lack of a process for separating it into fine filaments. The slow hand press of China makes it too expensive. Here is a chance for some brainy man to do for the ramie plant what Eli Whitney did for the cotton, reaping even a larger fortune than he because of the present greater demand for cloth.

817. COTTON MILLS IN THE SOUTH.—About 9,000,000 persons in the United States and England depend for their livelihood on the cotton trade. Until recently New England had a monopoly of the cotton manufacture in the United States, but of late it has been ascertained that, owing to the cheaper cost of iron and fuel, the business can be carried on more advantageously in the South. The coal and iron in the mountains and the proximity to the raw product will cause New England soon to be distanced in this

important enterprise. For those who seek cotton manufacture for a livelihood or for a competence, and especially for those who are beginning the business, the northern parts of Georgia and Alabama present unrivaled opportunities for the carrying on of that industry; and to such we would say, paraphrasing Horace Greeley's advice to the young, "Go South, young man." {249}

818. ARTIFICIAL SILK.—The man who can invent or discover a substance which has the glossy luster and wear of silk so as to counterfeit the real article can name his own price. Four processes have recently been patented, but the results are a fiber too coarse, too stiff, too weak, or too expensive. The Chardonnet process makes a quality at a cost of $1.23 a pound, and it sells at $2.70 a pound, a very good profit if only it was enough like real silk to command the market. Put on your thinking-caps, cloth manufacturers, and obtain the rich prize which is already almost within your grasp.

819. MINERAL WOOL.—Here is something new. Experiments have proved that rocks, or at least certain kinds of them, can be made into wool. The wool is made from sandstone, and from the waste slag of furnaces. "Mineral wool" is already being used for packing and fireproofing; but the inexhaustible field for the industry in the millions of tons of serviceable rocks, and the unforeseen possibilities in the use of the "new wool," make the subject a startling one and well worth the consideration of money-makers.

820. LEATHER SUBSTITUTE.—The high price of leather and its fluctuation in price have caused many substitutes to be devised, but thus far they have been inferior in quality, and will not stand the test of rough usage and exposure to heat. Imitation leather has always been made of two pieces of cloth pasted together, which are bound to separate or blister. Here is a secret worth a fortune. A single thickness of either drill or duck, with a heavy surface coating, will stand every test that leather can endure, and is every way as good, and can be produced at one-third the cost. {250}

CHAPTER   XX.

MONEY IN FERTILIZERS.

Wanted, a New Fertilizer—How "Golden" Forests Drop Gold—Why the Fields Near Berlin are so Productive— How We Lose $5,000,000 a Year—The Peat Treasures of New Jersey—Fortunes in Phosphates—Millions of Fish on Land as well as in the Sea—$1,000,000 for Him Who will Pick It Up.

WE are yet in the infancy of this important product. The desideratum is a fertilizer that will do the best work in the least bulk. The 4,565,000 farmers and vegetable growers of the United States will make independently rich the man who can produce a good fertilizer at small cost of transportation. The field of chemistry is particularly rich in suggestions; experiments in this line are constantly going on, and there is reason to hope that an agricultural Edison will soon arise. Meanwhile, there is money in the following fertilizers:

821. GARBAGE.—Every truck load of garbage is worth at least a dollar for manuring purposes, and yet thousands of these loads are dumped every day into the water. Instead of the city paying a round sum for the removal of garbage, it ought to receive a bonus from a contractor who knows how to turn it to account.

822. LEAVES.—Rotted leaves form the rich base from which nearly all our forests, and indeed nearly all the vegetation of the earth, springs. The number of loads of leaves that fall from the trees in the autumn are entirely [251] incalculable. The keeper of a country livery stable could add one half to his compost heap, and thus double his sale of fertilizers.

823. URBAN SEWAGE.—The best of all fertilizers is allowed to float out to sea and is lost. The Germans are wiser. They utilize all these waste products, and the surprising fertility of the soil near Berlin is the result of this wise employment of nature's richest fertilizer. There are fortunes for those who will study the foreign system and apply it to the large cities of this country.

824. ASHES.—We lose at least $5,000,000 annually in the waste of ashes. In the cultivation of gardens and city lots, where the expense of transportation is small, there is a field for the profitable use of this fertilizer. It could be combined with some product rich in phosphates, as, for example, bone dust, and then put up in barrels for sale. An Ash Fertilizer Company would pay.

825. PHOSPHATES.—The phosphate rocks of North Carolina, South Carolina, and Georgia contain fortunes for the men who will develop those industries. The quantity is practically unlimited, and the price of phosphate is $18 a ton. Cheap freights will make these rocks mines of wealth.

826. COTTONSEED MEAL.—This sells for $20 to $25 a ton, and being a waste product the cost is light. Its sale could be made more general among the farmers if they knew its value.

827. CITY STABLES.—Much of the product of city stables is carried to the country in barges and sold, but [252] more is wasted; especially is this the case with single and small stables in the suburbs, where the accumulation is light, and the law does not require its removal. But a systematic collection of these products would pay any one who should undertake it on a large scale.

828. PEAT.—New Jersey has more than 1,000 square miles of peat lands, for the most part undeveloped. The peat is from three to six feet in depth. When phosphates are selling for

$18 a ton, there ought to be a market for peat at $5, which would still leave a good margin of profit, if, as seems entirely reasonable, the labor and freightage could be covered for $3.

829. MENHADEN.—The farmers of the eastern end of Long Island have found this an excellent fertilizer. The fish are strewn whole upon the land. More than 1,000,000 of the tiny creatures, or upward of 100 tons, have been caught by one vessel in a single day. The industry is chiefly confined to the vicinity of Gardiner's Island, but it might be made profitable along other parts of the coast.

830. FISH SCRAP.—The chemists' valuation is $41 a ton, but it ordinarily sells for $35 to $38. It is admirably adapted for plant food. One of the largest producers of dry ground fish claims that the farmer gets more for his money in this than in any other fertilizer.

831. SOOT.—For some crops soot is one of the most powerful of all fertilizers, and yet it is allowed to go to waste. The total amount of soot produced in London twenty years ago was 1,100,810 bushels, and is probably about the same for New York to-day. The average[253] price was five cents a bushel, and the total worth $109,165. Probably in this country—at least until its worth is discovered—it could in most cases be obtained free by any one who will take the trouble to pick up this $100,000.[254]

CHAPTER   XXI.

MONEY IN ADVERTISING.

More Money in Ink—Millions Paid for it Every Day—New Devices to Catch the Eye—Exposure of Advertising Tricks—Cupid on the Counter—What "Bargain Day" and "Below Cost" Really Mean—How an Advertising Agent Made a Fortune in a Day—"Delivering" 5,000 Customers—A Line that Every body is Sure to Read—A Great Advertising Success—Playing With Mystery—A Sure Way to Draw a Crowd—Novel Ways of Advertising in Paris—Almost a Street Fight.

Do you realize what an important part advertising plays in trade? The men who succeed are those who let the public know what they have and at what price. The great newspapers contain every day vast mines of advertising matter. There are many merchants who pay over $100,000 a year in letting the public know the cheapness and value of their goods, and one enterprising company, the proprietors of a celebrated baking powder, expend $1,000,000 a year in advertising their product. These merchants are constantly seeking the best means to get their wares before the public eye; also manufacturers, builders, real estate agents, railroad companies, and in fact all persons doing business on a large scale, are seeking to let men know how and what they do. Owners of proprietary medicines have been known to expend $10,000 in a single advertisement in order to secure the attention of ailing people. All these persons will pay you well for any ingenious suggestions whereby they can increase their patronage. The following are some of the methods suggested:{255}

832. MONEY AND THE MUSE.—Select some liberal advertiser and note what he has to sell or what he has to do, and embody his peculiar merit in a poem. The poem should be short, spicy and humorous, and not be more than eight or ten lines in length. Let it hit off some of the fads of the day. If it be headed by some catch-word of the hour, so much the better. An ingenious person who can write a verse or two of this kind will find a ready market for his muse.

833. CENTS IN NONSENSE.—If you have artistic talent instead of poetic, you can do still better with a drawing. Let the cut be as original and humorous as some of the cartoons in our daily papers.

834. WORD PUZZLE.—A puzzle to some minds will be still more effective. Many will be disinclined to use their brains to work it out, but those who do will remember it, and that after all is the merit of an advertisement. A puzzle which may be patented and sold to the advertiser promises much greater profit. See the "Chinese-Get-Off-the-Earth Puzzle." A puzzle of this kind is commonly sold exclusively to one firm, and ought to bring quite a sum of money to the inventor.

835. TRACKS TO WEALTH.—The inventor who can produce a scheme to cause the customer to become his unconscious advertiser has found the very highroad to success. Such a scheme might be a word in raised letters on the heel of a shoe. Thousands, especially in country towns where there are no sidewalks, would constantly be leaving impressions in the mud, and people would be astonished to find advertisements stamped on the very earth.

836. THE STORY ADVERTISEMENT.—Write a short{256} story which ends in an advertisement. This is one of the best methods to gain the reader's eye. Everybody likes a story, and will read it if it be short. The narrative should lead up gradually and naturally to the advertisement. This requires some ingenuity and skill in writing.

837. THE FICTITIOUS BANK BILL.—A piece of paper which at first sight looks like a ten-dollar bill, but turns out to be a clever advertisement, would be picked up and read by everybody.

838. THE POCKETBOOK FIND.—A clever imitation of a pocketbook would be picked up by every pedestrian, and when it is opened with the expectation of money, one finds instead an advertisement of Pluck & Company.

839. EVERYBODY'S EAGLE.—A gold (?) eagle with the name of a firm in the place of the usual inscription, will be readily pounced upon, when the lucky finder will learn that "all is not gold that glitters," but will also learn where and what he can buy to advantage.

The firm's name, of course, is not stamped until the sale of the golden bird is effected. Millions of such eagles could be sold.

840. THE WITTY DIALOGUE.—Few things in literature are more attractive than a witty dialogue in which the questions and answers are very short and the denouement is a surprise. If the last word is the magical one of a certain kind of business, such as "Ozone," "Electrophone," "——'s Baking Powder," "——'s Stove Polish," etc., the maker or merchant will be sure to appreciate it and pay for it.[257]

841. THE STEREOSCOPE BULLETIN.—It pays to give a large sum to the proprietor of a paper who makes a practice of flashing election returns on screens. There is commonly a long wait between the reports, and the vast crowds will meanwhile have nothing to do but study your advertisement flashed between the successive returns.

842. THE ARC REFLECTOR.—Have a reflector with an electric light arranged to throw a bright, round light, like the dial of a clock, on the depot platforms, the pavements of crowded streets, or other places where many people congregate. On the background of this strong light let your magic word appear. This is an expensive but very effective way of advertising.

843. THE LAST SCENE.—Tens of thousands of persons every night are looking upon scenes depicted by the stereoscope. After the "Good Night," which generally closes the entertainment, immediately, and before the lights are turned on, have your advertisement flashed upon the sheet. As the programme is concluded, the manager would doubtless for a small sum grant a privilege which would be worth many dollars, as no one in the audience can fail to see the display.

844. THE RED-LETTER BAT.—For a consideration, the manager of a baseball team would probably let you furnish the players with an excellent bat stamped with your design in large red letters. Your advertisement would flash with every stroke of the bat, and even if many in the crowd were too far away to read the letters, their curiosity would incite them to inquire, and curiosity is the very emotion advertisers seek to arouse. The idea might perhaps be extended to the ball, which is the center of struggle in football matches.[258]

845. THE RESTAURANT FAN.—Waiting men will read anything to kill time, but a fan with your enterprise stamped upon it will attract attention, whether one is inclined to read or not. By the hundred thousand these could be produced extremely cheap, and should be presented free to the restaurant keeper. They might also be used in theaters and music halls.

846. THE CIGAR WRAPPER.—It is estimated that 3,000,000 cigars are purchased in New York and vicinity alone every day. For a small sum, say five cents a box, you could doubtless prevail upon most dealers to permit you to wrap each cigar in a piece of paper;

especially if the latter were pretty and very attractive, as in the latter case it might even help his sales. The wrapper might contain an alluring picture, but, of course, it contains your advertisement. A small additional sum must be paid a boy for the work of wrapping. As an advertisement, the method would be exceedingly effective, and the idea is certainly a novel one.

847. THE GROWING WORD.—In a reserved space of a daily paper begin with a single glaring letter. Over the letter announce, "Watch this space to-morrow." The next day another letter is added, and curiosity is excited. If you can get a name for your advertisement similar to the name of a man in the public eye, the success of the scheme is assured. For example, the first letter is G. Is it Grover Cleveland or Garfield? Two letters are given—GA. Is it Garfield or Gage? The third day GAR appears. Is it Garfield or Garland? But in the end it proves to be neither; it is GARLOCK, the name of your invention or brand of goods. Ingenuity can play endlessly upon words in this way,{259} and the curiosity aroused makes it one of the best forms of advertisement.

848. THE POLITE STRANGER.—This is a French idea. In Paris a lady is astonished to see a handsome, faultlessly dressed man, generally an elderly person, step directly in front of her, make an extremely polite bow, turn and walk away, when instantly the mystery is solved. On his back appears an advertisement.

849. THE FUNNY QUARTETTE.—This also is from Paris, with adaptations. Four odd people— a little, shabbily dressed old woman, a splendidly attired and pompous gentleman, a country youth in blouse and overalls, and a man in the garb of a priest, make up the queerest quartette imaginable. They at once attract attention, but when they begin to sing a crowd gathers instantly. At the conclusion of the song, one says in a loud tone, "Where?" All reply, "At ——." "When?" "To-night."

850. THE STREET BRAWL.—This is on the same line and even more exciting. Readers of "Sherlock Holmes" remember the detective's ruse to gain entrance to a forbidden house. In the same way, let two men engage in a wordy quarrel. Nothing draws a crowd more quickly than the prospect of a fight. Of course, on a city street the quarrel must not come to actual blows, and the participants must keep an eye open for policemen, but the climax should be the advertisement in the mouth of one or both of the disputants, and the crowd should be dispersed with a hearty laugh.

851. THE BOX-KITE.—The box-kite presents almost unrivaled opportunities for advertising, and the wonder is that it has not been utilized for that purpose. By a{260} clock-work arrangement and at regular intervals, while the eyes of all are turned skyward, the box releases a host of white leaves, which, floating to the earth, are caught by the crowd. Every leaf contains your advertisement. This method would be especially effective at ball games, horse races, and before election bulletins, while the crowds are waiting for returns or exciting events.{261}

CHAPTER   XXII.

MONEY IN THE POWERS OF NATURE.

Vast Forces yet Unknown—The Human Form a Key to unlock Nature's Caskets of Gold—The Storage of Air—The Waste of Steam—The March of Electricity—How One Company saved $50 a Day—Sunbeams for Sale—Winds and Waves awaiting Man's Sail and Wheel—How a Western Man Invented a Sand Mill—Enormous Power of Sea Waves—A New Use for the Artesian Well—Eureka! The Right Kind of a Storage Battery—Opportunities for Enterprise and Wealth.

THE finding and unlocking of the forces of nature have been sources of some of the world's largest fortunes. Steam and electricity are to-day among the earth's greatest contributors to wealth. It is not, however, the simple discovery of a new force, but its ingenious application, that brings financial reward, and there may be a hundred, or even a thousand ways of applying a new power. These powers are perhaps all known at the present time, but many of them are little utilized, and some have never been harnessed. It is probable that we have as yet only begun to unlock the secrets of nature.

852. COMPRESSED AIR.—There are vast possibilities in the use of this power. In a few years lightning expresses will fly over the land, swift vessels will skim the deep, monster passenger eagles will soar in the air, and tons of mail matter will be blown through tubes from sea to sea, all driven by this powerful motor, compressed air. These things only wait for money and brains.[262]

853. STEAM.—In the application of steam about ninety per cent. of power is lost. This is an enormous waste. Here is room for a second Watt. In the race for primacy as a power, steam need take no second place if only its unutilized forces be turned to account by some inventor. Here is a field worthy of the noblest powers of man.

854. ELECTRICITY.—At present electricity sends our telegraph messages, projects our voices through the telephone, propels our street cars, lights our streets and dwellings, and in some States executes our criminals. But it is altogether likely that this as yet comparatively unknown power will be extended into a hundred untried fields. Here is a single example of the economy in its use: The Baldwin Locomotive Company discovered that they were losing eighty per cent. of steam power in shafts and belts. They installed electric motors and reduced the bill for power immensely. Hundreds of large establishments waste from one-fourth to three-fourth of steam in the same way. If electricity can save from $14 to $50 per day, as in the case just quoted, it is surely well worth a trial.

855. CALORIC.—The time will come when the billions of cubic feet of sunlight that fall upon our earth will be utilized and will doubtless be the cheapest and most efficient of all the motor forces. If you can only focus this widely distributed energy, you can obtain any amount of heat and consequently power. It has been proved that you can boil two

pints of water with the heat of the sun falling upon one and one-half square yards of surface. One square yard of sunshine represents one horse power. The problem, therefore, is to concentrate. This will be done some day by the use of[263] immense convex mirrors. Already experiments are being tried, and the first promoters of this scheme will have the power of the world at their feet and its wealth in their hands.

856. WATER POWER.—The time will also come when the thousands of cataracts and rapids that now waste their energies will all be harnessed and set to work. It is estimated that the water power of Niagara is as great as would be the steam power produced by 226,000,000 tons of coal a year. This one cataract has power enough to make a thousand millionaires, and there are hundreds of smaller waterfalls running to waste.

857. WINDMILLS.—Steam is costly and water is not always available, but the wind is everywhere, and costs little or nothing. It has the disadvantage of inconstancy and uncertainty, but it is invaluable for storing up force for future use. The windmill is susceptible of great improvements, and waits for another Morse or Watt.

858. A SAND MILL.—One ingenious man out West has equipped his windmill with an endless belt provided with buckets, like a grain elevator. These dip into a box of dry sand and discharge it upon a large wheel like an overshot water-wheel, which it turns as water would. The sand is discharged again into the box and thus is used over again endlessly. We think the man has not patented his invention; he has missed a fortune which somebody else will pick up.

859. SEA POWER.—Next to the power of the sun is the power of the ocean. An experiment with a dynanometer has shown that the pressure exerted by the sea waves during a storm often exceeds 7,600 pounds[264] per square foot. Multiply this by 1,393,920,000,000,000 feet, which the surface of the ocean presents, and we gather some little notion of the inconceivable power that is running to waste. When will come the inventor who will harness the sea and set it to lighting our cities and carrying men and mail-bags? There is said to be millions upon millions of gold strewn on the ocean's bed as the result of wrecks, but there is vastly more gold for the daring inventor in the waves that forever pound upon the beach.

860. ARTESIAN WELL.—The artesian well plant is coming into prominence. Formerly the well was only employed as a means of getting water to drink; it is only recently that it has occurred to people that here is an immense and unused water motor. Water power from running streams is only available here and there, but with the advent of the artesian well there is no spot on earth that may not have as much cheap power as it needs, the cost being almost nothing when once the power is obtained. Here is another opportunity for enterprise and fortune.

861. LIQUID AIR.—This is a new discovery, and one very rich in promise. Here is doubtless the long-sought-for method of the storage battery. It has been found that the

same force of liquid air as applied in the electric storage battery scores from one-tenth to one-twentieth more than the electric fluid is able to do. Here we have a power whose application will result in such unknown quantities of usefulness and wealth as to defy the power of figures and even the imagination itself. [265]

CHAPTER   XXIII.

MONEY IN BUILDING MATERIALS.

Boundless Wealth in Brick, Wood and Stone—Farmers Who have Untouched and Unknown Mines—A Man With 2,000,000 Acres—How a Farmer Astonished a Lawyer—A New Way to Measure Land—Men Who Don't Know They are Rich—Are You One?—More Money in the Builder's Stone than in the Philosopher's Stone—Secrets of Brick Making—The Exploits of "Lucky" Baldwin—A Man Who Lives in a Glass House—The Floor of the Future—Time is Money, but the Shorter the Time the More the Money.

IT is certain that nearly all the structures now upon the earth will have to be rebuilt during the next half century. When we consider the immense cost and vast number of these buildings, aggregating thousand of millions of dollars, the demand for building materials surpasses all computation and imagination. During the next few decades untold myriads of persons will get rich, either in this discovery of new fields for these materials, exploiting the old ones, or in the invention of new building matter.

"How large is your farm?" inquired a lawyer of a verdant farmer whom he meant to guy. The man of the law winked at his companion as much as to say, "See what sport I will have with the old fool!" "Well," said the haymaker, "I reckon I have about 2,000,000 acres." "Two million acres!" gasped the attorney, gazing round; "pray, where is it?" "Down yere," replied the farmer, pointing his long, skinny fingers at the ground. "I have got a hundred acres on [266] top, and I reckon I own about down to the middle of the y'arth." The man of the soil spake wiser than he knew. He was rich, but not exactly in the way he imagined, for a granite quarry of the finest kind was found on his land, which caused him to realize a large sum.

862. STONE QUARRY.—Says a recent publication: "A man who has a quarry of good building stone, easily accessible, is richer than if he owned a gold mine." But there are immense numbers of such quarries unworked and even unsuspected. It is not too much to say that there are at least a thousand farmers bemoaning unproductive land which contains beneath the surface that which can make them richer than anything they can possibly grow from the soil.

863. ARTIFICIAL STONE.—Many kinds of artificial stone are now employed, such as Ransom's concrete, Portland stone, etc. They are made by a mixture of cement, sand and

gravel, and are molded into blocks. The value depends upon the kind of cement. No really good lime for this purpose has yet been found in the United States. The man who can discover a calcareous deposit capable of making a good, silicious or argillaceous hydraulic lime will have the market for manufactured stone practically in his hands.

864. BAKED BRICK.—Late improvements in baking brick have reduced the time required to bake 100,000 bricks from fourteen to four days, and the amount of fuel from forty cords of wood to sixteen. The following suggestions by a brick-burner will show the path of fortune to those who can reduce the time still further. Mix a little charcoal in the clay. Double the length of the brick. If by either of these ways you can make the {267} bricks a trifle cheaper, while retaining their qualities, you have acquired a fortune. "Lucky" Baldwin, a man afterward famous for his mining and real estate speculations, made his first large money in brick-burning. "I had no experience whatever then," he said, "but I studied up the subject, thoroughly mastered the details, and cleared $1,500 in a month."

865. GLASS BRICK.—Another new idea! Why not make a brick of glass, partially hollow, so that, filled with rarefied air, it can be a non-conductor of heat? Such a brick would be a great improvement on the present method of constructing conservatories, greenhouses and the walls of winter gardens. The plan is being tried in Europe, but there is no patent on the introduction, and nothing to stop an American from introducing a new kind of hothouse. The adage about the "man in a glass house" may be realized yet.

866. RUBBER FLOORS.—Why do we go on in the old way, employing rough-sounding and creaking flooring, when there is a material which meets every want for a desirable floor? India rubber tiles prevent slipping, emit no sound under the foot, and have the additional element of an agreeable elasticity. It is a positive pleasure to walk on an India rubber floor. It is, of course, more expensive than wood, but the time is surely coming when every elegant dwelling, all expensive halls and public buildings, as well as the saloon decks of our first-class steamships, will have these improved floors. A man, ambitious to be rich and possessing a few thousands of capital, could hardly do a better thing than to manufacture rubber interlocking tiles, advertising them extensively and exhibiting models to builders. {268}

CHAPTER   **XXIV.**

MONEY IN AMUSEMENTS.

Money in Fun—Salary of a "Star"—A Fortune in "A Parlor Match"—A Pianist Who Got $2,500 a Night—How to Get a Start on the Stage—A New Field for the Amusement Artist—Humor and Hard Cash in Shadowgraphs

PEOPLE who cater to public amusements are so many, their entertainments so diverse and their talents so unequal, that no general statement can be made about the remuneration for this kind of work. There are "stars" at the top who receive from $200 to $1,000 per night, and there are "mediocres," or worse, at the bottom who barely eke out a living at $7 a week. No one should enter this field unless his talent is equal to his ambition. Here are a few of the prizes taken before the footlights:

867. THE FARCE COMEDY.—Evans and Hoey purchased a comedy entitled "A Parlor Match." Mr. Evans says: "We played it over 3,000 times, and at a rough estimate I think we must have cleared from $300,000 to $400,000."

868. INSTRUMENTAL CONCERTS.—The possibilities of dollars in instrumental music are seemingly unlimited. Celebrated pianists have received almost fabulous sums. Rubinstein's six months' tour in America is said to have netted a profit of $60,000, and a second engagement[269] was made for him at the rate of $2,500 per night.

869. STAGE STARS.—The stage, like every other profession, is crowded at the bottom, but has room at the top. Beginners seldom get more than $15 per week and commonly they receive much less. Leading people in road companies get $50 per week. Stars receive from $100 to $500 per night. Madame Celeste made $50,000 in this country. Edwin Forrest never received less than $200 per night. Edwin Booth sometimes played for $500 per night.

870. POPULAR LECTURERS.—These are richly rewarded for their hour or two of entertainment of an audience. John B. Gough's price was $200 per night. Henry Ward Beecher, Wendell Phillips, and Bayard Taylor averaged the same figures. The receipts for Professor Tyndall's thirty-five lectures in this country were $23,100; and Max O'Rell earned $5,290 by his lectures during a single week in Johannesburg, South Africa. Says a magazine note: "Money-making's most promising field is that of a popular lecturer."

871. HAND SHADOWS.—Here is something new: Some amusement artists in England have conceived the idea of entertaining audiences with hand shadows. A candle, an oil lamp, or an arc light is used, and the beam of light passes through a small circular opening upon a sheet of ticket-writer's holland. Sometimes a pipe or a piece of cardboard is used to heighten the effect, but for the most part the artist employs his hands only. With diligent practice the most comical effects, such as "Dressing for a Party," "The Dog Fight," etc., can be produced. Mr. Devant, the originator of the shadowgraph, convulses his audiences and[270] reaps large profits for himself. America, where the humorous is quickly and keenly appreciated, offers a large field for this new kind of entertainment.

872. MUSEUM AND CIRCUS.—The vocation of the popular showman is a highly paying one. It appeals to two of the most powerful motives of human nature—the desire to be

amused and amazed. P. T. Barnum made and lost two or three fortunes; Bailey, the successor of Barnum, and Dan Rice have also conducted highly successful shows. Dime museums in large cities often pay vast sums for curiosities and monstrosities, and still conduct a very profitable business.

873. GYMNASTS.—Athletes need to begin early in life in order to acquire suppleness of muscle. There is no profession that demands a severer training or regimen. A vast number of performers are constantly traveling through the country. Engagements with companies are made on exhibition of skill. Managers are always on the alert for something new. Some equestrians receive as high as $500 a week for self and horses; clowns often receive $100; rope walkers, $50.

874. OPERA SINGERS.—Voice, gesture, grace, and beauty are the four qualities of success in the opera artist. Those who succeed receive princely sums for their services. Mario got $400 a night in Philadelphia. Tamberlik every time he sung a high note demanded $500. Piccolomini cost her manager over $5,000 a month. Madame Perer received $14,000 for the season. Genius and hard work are nowhere better paid than in the opera.

875. MIMIC BATTLES.—Pain's fireworks at Manhattan Beach, reproducing the "Capture of Manila" and [271] "The Fall of Santiago," have been immensely popular, sometimes drawing crowds numbering 10,000. A thousand dollars' worth of fireworks and *papier maché* are burned in a single night during the season, but enormous as are the expenses we are informed that the proprietor seldom makes less than $500 a night. There is no patent on these exhibitions, and they may be repeated or imitated anywhere. A man who dares "burn money" in this way, or a stock company where the individual risk would be comparatively small, exhibiting these fireworks in all our great cities, would certainly reap handsome gains. Especially at this time, while the fervor of patriotism and the glow of enthusiasm over our recent victories are still at white heat, the enterprise could not fail to be paying. We would almost guarantee that a company which could set up as brilliant an exhibition as Pain's in fifty leading cities would realize twenty-five per cent. on the investment.

876. THEATRICAL ENTERPRISES.—Running a theater is risky business; it has its ups and downs, and the downs are as swift as the ups. Oscar Hammerstein, who has just lost all by an unsuccessful venture, says that once during the short period of four weeks he made $60,000. Daly, Frohman, Lester Wallack, and many others, have grown rich in the theatrical business.

877. DANCERS.—Members of the vaudeville are not so well paid as in many other arts for amusing the public, but special dancing "artists" sometimes receive almost fabulous sums. Famous dancers have received as high as $10,000 in the course of a season. Freda Maloff, the Turkish dancer, has just returned from the Klondike, where in the course of a

few months she has made $62,000 in her profession, the miners literally showering her with nuggets.[272]

878. MOVING PICTURES.—This latest and most popular form of amusement is coining money for the owners of the cinematograph, biograph, vitascope, or by whatever other name the instrument is called which causes the scenes portrayed on canvas to be instinct with moving life. The charge for an evening's service is commonly $50.

879. BAND PLAYERS.—Band players get from $1,000 to $5,000 a year, according to proficiency. Sousa, the leader of the celebrated band by his name, received $6,000 a year. There are always openings for good band players.

880. IMPERSONATORS.—Dickens will probably always be the great resort for this class of entertainers. Of seven leading impersonators now on the platform, four portray his characters almost exclusively. It is a fine field for the elocutionist who has talents for mimicry. The average charge is $25 per night.

881. ANCIENT BURLESQUES.—There are at least three forms of this amusement which are having great success. They are "The Village Choir," "The Old Folks' Concert," and "Aunt Polly Bassett's Singing School." The last named has often cleared $100 in a single evening.

882. RECITERS.—Reciters and readers, from Dickens to Hall Caine, have always been popular. The highest paid are well-known authors, who read from their own writings. Charles Dickens seldom received less than $200 an evening. But the majority are glad to get engagements at from $10 to $25 a night.

883. BELL RINGERS.—The discovery that many objects in nature could be made to give forth musical[273] sounds has vastly widened the field of entertainment. Rocks, steam pipes, tumblers, and dinner bells have been drafted into service, the last named with notable success. In one company four young ladies have charmed the public ear with the melody of a score of hand bells. They have reaped rich harvests all over the country.

884. MAGICIANS.—This field has been somewhat overworked of late years, but the phenomenal success of such men as Blitz, the ventriloquist, and Hermann, the prestidigitator, show the possibilities in this line. Both these men bewitched the public for a whole generation, and made great fortunes.

885. STORY TELLERS.—This is a late revival of a form of amusement as old as the times of Homer. Those succeed best who are authors as well as elocutionists, making their own story and telling it fresh from the heart. We predict that this kind of entertainment is going to have a great run, and persons who have talent in this line will do well to furbish up their weapons.

886. CARTOONISTS.—Cartoonists and crayonists receive high figures for their work, as this kind of talent is rare. The chief of this class of artists received from $50 to $150 per

night. Since his death, no worthy successor has been found, but there are many young fingers that are clever with chalk, and there is room for more. It is a very inviting field for persons who have the right gifts. [274]

CHAPTER   XXV.

MONEY IN ROD AND GUN.

> How to Combine Profit and Pleasure—Some Truths About Trout—Stories of the Wild North—Fortunes in Furs —Nearly Five Million Skins a year—Cost of Birds for Ladies' Hats—$25 a Day and Your Own Game Keeper —An Elephant Hunt in Africa.

HAPPY is the man who can combine pleasure and profit. Most men use the rod and gun for sport, but there are a number of persons who follow the business "professionally." Especially in the great forests of the north are found thousands of men to whom the skins of wild beasts may be said to be meat and drink. Some of them even attain a competence and retire on their savings from the sale of furs. This is less surprising when we remember that people in the great northern wilderness spend little beyond what is needful for the bare necessaries of life.

887. FAT QUAILS.—The quail has been called the game bird of America, because it is found almost everywhere. Some of the best shooting is found in North Carolina and Maryland, where a hunter of average skill can bag fifty birds a day. Price, $1.75 per dozen, or $7 for his day's sport. Hunters must consult the game laws, which differ in various States of the Union.

888. TROPICAL BIRDS.—It is estimated that the number of birds it is necessary to slaughter annually for the decoration of ladies' hats amounts to the enormous number [275] of 9,250,000. These are mostly tropical birds, and are shot in the forests of Brazil, Central America and Mexico. Some are natives of our Southern States, especially of Florida. On account of the great difference in the worth of the feathers, no estimate of the value can be given, but it is said that a skilled hunter of these bright wings can easily bag $10 worth of the birds in a day.

889. IVORY.—Elephant hunting in Africa is very profitable for those who have the courage and taste for the work. Seventy-five thousand elephants are slain yearly to supply the world's knife-handles, billiard balls, and piano keys. There are a number of persons engaged in the killing of elephants for the sake of the sport, but most hunters do so for the profit. Ivory is worth about $1 a pound, and the tusks of a male elephant weigh about fifty pounds. The average of one elephant a day is considered a good day's work,

although five or six have been taken under the most favorable circumstances. The safest plan is by means of a pitfall, as then the enraged beast is unable to attack his aggressor. The elephant hunting business is worth about $5,000,000 a year.

890. THE TROUT POND.—In New England there are hundreds of fish dealers who own ponds which they have stocked with trout, and which they sell for $1 apiece; and this price they often receive even when the buyer as sportsman catches them himself. The profits of fish raising lie in the fact that fish are prolific to an extent vastly greater than any other creatures used for human food, the female sometimes laying as many as 150,000 eggs. There are owners of trout preserves who receive as high as $25 a day from sporting clubs for the exclusive use of their ponds. [276]

891. FABULOUS PRICES FOR FURS.—Hunting and trapping in British America and in the North Woods of the United States have always been very profitable. Here is a list of the number of furs taken, with a few of the prices obtained: A good sable skin brings from $20 to $150, according to quality; 15,000 are caught yearly. Almost as valuable is the fur of the pine marten; 200,000 skins taken annually. Another high-priced skin is that of the mink; 250,000 are taken every year. The ermine is another choice fur, of which 400,000 are taken yearly. A beautiful material for robes, ladies' sets, trimmings, etc., is the fur of the Canada lynx, of which 50,000 are taken yearly. The fur of the otter is much esteemed for caps, collars, and gloves; 40,000 taken yearly. Almost the same number of beavers are captured every year; the fur is used for caps and mufflers. Three million muskrat skins are in demand every year. Of all kinds of foxes some 200,000 find their way into our markets or are exported to Europe. The skin of the silver fox of Labrador has been sold in London for $500. The raccoon furnishes us yearly with 500,000 skins, and the badger with 50,000. We have as a summary 4,745,000 skins marketed every year, affording employment for thousands of hunters and trappers. [277]

CHAPTER   XXVI.

MONEY IN THE FOREST.

Unappreciated and Unappropriated Wealth in Trees—$5,000,000 Burned in Florida Forests—Reckless Waste of Timber—An Opportunity to Make a Fortune in Paper Cane—Chances in Cedar—Small Spools Help to Wind Great Fortunes—How Some People Throw Away $50,000 a Year.

THERE is doubtless more money in the forests that clothe the mountains than in the metals that are buried beneath their granite and limestone backs. Much of this wealth has been squandered through lack of knowledge of its worth and because of meager facilities for its utilization. In the State of Florida alone more than $5,000,000 worth of timber has been ruthlessly burned in order to clear the ground for orange plantations. Forest wealth in the future will probably be obtained in the following ways:

892. WISCONSIN PINES.—The merchantable timber in the forests of the Wolverine State, according to Government estimate, reaches the enormous amount of 41,000,000,000 feet. There are many fortunes yet to be carved out of the endless pines of this State.

893. NORTH CAROLINA TAR.—Eight million dollars is the sum earned annually by the people of North Carolina from the making of tar. The pine forests that yield tar are not costly, but a large amount of acreage is required.[278]

894. VERMONT MAPLE SUGAR.—The people of Vermont last year earned more than $12,000,000 by making maple sugar. It is one of the surest sources of revenue. The work is light, pleasant and romantic.

895. ALABAMA CHESTNUTS.—Thousands of acres of chestnut timber are wasted in Alabama because its worth is not known. The timber is felled for the tanbark, but the Commissioner of Forests estimates that in a single region $50,000 could be made annually by cutting this waste wood into railroad ties.

896. IDAHO CEDAR.—The finest body of red cedar on the continent exists in the State of Idaho. Red cedar is one of the most valuable of woods. Endless tracts can be purchased now for $10 an acre. It is probable that in ten or fifteen years, with better railroad facilities, the standing wood alone without the land cannot be purchased for $100 per acre.

897. MAINE BIRCH WOOD.—Nearly all the wood used in making spools for thread in this country and in Great Britain is supplied by the Maine forests. So great is the demand, and so profitable the work of felling the trees that the birch wood of this State is being rapidly consumed. A good, though long-time investment can be found in the setting out of birch trees on the waste lands of New England. A thousand acres of land, not worth $10 an acre at present, may be stocked with birch trees, which can be sold in from twenty-five to thirty years for $40 per acre. Profits, less taxes, $30,000.

898. SOUTHERN CANES.—One of the most important factors of modern civilization is paper. The United States consumes yearly about $75,000,000 worth of[279] paper. From rags, which once afforded all the material for paper making, but which are now entirely insufficient, manufacturers are experimenting with all kinds of vegetable growth in search of the best paper pulp. Paper is now being made of the fiber of trees. In the Southern States there is a kind of coarse cane which affords an inexhaustible supply, with a peculiar adaptation for the purposes of paper making. Here is a hint for the benefit of the one first to seize it. A buyer who should purchase a thousand acres, or even ten thousand acres, of paper cane would soon find a profitable market.[280]

CHAPTER   XXVII.

MONEY IN THE SEA.

The Magician who Makes Gold Swim—$30,000,000 in a Shoal of Cod—200 per cent. Profits in Salmon—How French Sardines are Made in Maine—Vast Money in Bivalves—John Bull, Brother Jonathan, and the Seal Fisheries—Chasing a Greenland Whale—Old Salts who Have Made their "Pile"—Why Salt Fish is Worth More than Fresh—The Greatest Reservoir of Wealth—A Leaf from a Business Ledger.

GOLD floats in the air, swims in the sea, springs up out of the earth, and lies deep hid in the mountain bed. How can gold swim? In the form of millions upon millions of tiny creatures whose destruction brings gold into the pockets of their captors. Literally, the ocean is the biggest field of revenue on the planet. It is a reservoir of wealth which all the ages are not likely to exhaust. Further, the ocean, unlike the land, has not been and cannot be partitioned out among individual owners. Any man can enter upon any body of water not actually occupied by another, and appropriate all that he finds there. The following are among the most profitable of the fisheries:

899. OREGON SALMON.—The female salmon lays a thousand eggs for every pound of her weight. For salmon profits go to Oregon. Immense factories, making enormous profits, are already in the field, but there is room for more.

900. MASSACHUSETTS COD.—Professor Huxley estimates[281] the number of cod in a single shoal at 120,000,000. What do you think of that, you who pay twenty-five cents for a small codfish? A shoal of fish worth $30,000,000! Go to Newfoundland if you want to catch cod.

901. FRENCH SARDINES.—So-called French sardines are put up in Maine. They have a foreign label, and command twice the price they would if it were known that they are a native product. The deception, however, is only in the name, for they are in no way inferior to the foreign brand. As an example of the enormous profits, we have it for a fact that herrings worth when fresh not more than $50,000, were put up as sardines in cans holding one pound each, and in that style they brought $770,000. This is the secret of the way some people get rich.

902. SEA OTTERS.—These are not so plentiful as formerly, but the increased price of the skins partly makes up for the less number of furs. A few years ago a schooner sailed from Boston to the Northern Pacific in quest of these slippery sea tenants, and in the course of three trips netted $75,000.

903. ARCTIC WHALES.—Rivals of whale oil have reduced the price of that lubricant, but there are yet many vessels engaged in the enterprise. When we consider that the whaling industry has contributed $680,000,000 to the wealth of England, Holland, and the United States, we can see what enormous profits have been reaped by those engaged in the

business. From Sandy Hook to Cape Cod, all along the coast, there are retired sea captains who have "feathered their nest" with the sales of whale-blubber. [282]

904. BEHRING SEALS.—Go aboard a sealing vessel. The business is very profitable. Above 1,000,000 seals of all kinds are taken yearly, a single vessel sometimes catching as many as 5,000. As these seals are taken by vessels owned and manned by legalized companies, the profits are not so subject to fluctuation as in what is called individual luck. To be a member of a sealing company you must have some capital, but the business is so profitable that it pays at least twenty-five per cent. John Bull and Brother Jonathan have had many disputes about the right to catch these seals. They are undoubtedly United States property, but England bases its rights in old treaties. However, if the catch is not restricted, the indiscriminating slaughter will soon diminish the number so that there will not be enough seals worth fighting about.

905. SEA GOLD.—Though this product of the sea has no fins, it falls more appropriately under the heading of this chapter than any other. The South Sea Bubble has had a parallel in the recent excitement over golden sea waves. A clergyman, a Connecticut Yankee by the name of Jernigan, together with his brother, after many experiments, announced that they had discovered a process for extracting gold from the sea. A stock company was formed, a large capital raised, and a mill erected. But the bubble exploded with loss to all except the reverend projector of the enterprise, who is said to have made $100,000 out of the scheme. At least, a loose leaf from his ledger, which he left behind in his flight, indicates that about that sum was inveigled from the pockets of the deluded members of the "company." However, some of them still have faith in the enterprise. It has been known to chemists for a long time [283] that gold is contained in sea water. The only question is whether it is in sufficient quantities to pay for the cost of its extraction. It may yet be found that what is at present regarded as a gigantic swindle contains the seeds of a profitable industry. [284]

CHAPTER   XXVIII.

MONEY IN WASTE MATERIAL.

The American People Waste More Fortunes than Other Nations Make—The Shoreditch Experiment in England—The Tonner System of Germany—Millions in Ashes—Coal Fortunes Waiting to be Picked Up—Astonishing Possibilities in Irrigation—Tons of Tin Thrown Away Every Day—$5,000,000 Lost in Sulphur Every Year—A Fortune Waiting a Stovepipe Inventor—Enormous Waste of Gold and Silver.

THE American nation is a wasteful one. Every year by neglect, poor economy and extravagance, material is lost which if saved would be enough to make many people rich. There are fortunes in ashes, garbage, sewage, and cinder piles. Why explore new fields when the old is yet unworked? Here are a few ways in which capital can be expended with a certainty of quick and large profits:

906. WASTE OF SEWAGE.—The wasteful methods of civilization cause the destruction of by far the most valuable of all our fertilizers, which passes out of our sewers into the sea, and is lost. It is estimated that the amount in New York City alone is worth over $5,000,000 yearly. In Germany, what is known as the Tonner system saves this richest of fertilizers; and the time is ripe for some one in this country to save this enormous waste and make himself many times a millionaire in the Book of Wealth.

907. WASTE OF COAL ASHES.—Two hundred million[285] tons of coal are consumed annually in this country. About one-half of this amount goes to ashes. It is safe to say that, after all the cinders and slag have been sifted out, there are still 100,000,000 truck loads which are worse than wasted, as they threaten to hinder the free navigation of our harbor. Coal ashes have a value as a fertilizer. Even at the cheap price of twenty-five cents a load, we have an aggregate of $25,000,000 lost by this careless waste. The time will come when some enterprising firms, with means for collecting and distributing this refuse, will make fortunes by its sale to farmers and gardeners.

908. WASTE OF GARBAGE.—Shoreditch, population, 124,000, a borough of London, by a new system for the disposal of garbage, called the Dust Destructor, saved in one year $11,000, or enough to defray the expense of its electric lights. What formerly cost eighty cents a ton for barging, is now done by the new system for thirty cents. In New York City (not the Greater New York) the number of truck loads last year was 1,582,287, and it is estimated that a similar system, in place of the one which now costs the city ninety-four cents per load, would save $712,132, equivalent to the interest at six per cent. on a capital of $11,868,675, or more than sufficient to light the whole of Manhattan Island.

909. WASTE OF SULPHUR.—Attention has recently been called to the enormous waste of sulphur which is going on in the copper furnaces of Western mining towns. It is said that the annual waste is 128,000 tons. The price of sulphur is $32 a ton. Where is the man who will stop the pouring out of this vast quantity of poisonous vapor upon the atmosphere, save the enormous[286] waste of valuable material, and make for himself a gigantic fortune? The lists are open.

910. WASTE OF TIN.—Thousands of tons of tin cans are daily thrown in the rubbish heap. It is believed that by treatment of sulphate the tin may be recovered and again utilized. It is a question whether the same amount of money now invested in tin mines, if put to this novel use, would not be the better paying investment. It is estimated that there are two cents' worth of tin in an average-sized can. Cans could be collected at a cost of fifty cents per hundred, or $5,000 per million. If we estimate the chemical process of

recovering the tin at as much more, the total cost would be $10,000 per million cans. Worth of the tin recovered at two cents per can, $20,000. Profits, 100 per cent.

911. WASTE OF HEAT.—In our present systems of heating, from one-fourth to one-third of the heat passes up the chimney and is lost. Could not some method be perfected by which this could be saved? It would be a great boon to the poor, who need to save every pound of coal, if this could be done. We suggest as one plan a stovepipe radiator—two pipes, open at top and bottom, traversing the vertical leg of the smoke-flue, by means of which the air of the room shall be taken in at one end and sent out at the other. There are at least 100,000 apartments heated by steam. A system which will add one-fourth to the heat of these rooms will be a material blessing. There should be millions in the invention.

912. WASTE OF LAND.—Judge Emory, at a recent irrigation convention, stated that the arid and semi-arid lands of the United States are one-half as large as all [287] our domain, except Alaska. It is estimated that good homes, fit for 75,000,000 to 150,000,000 people, could be made by irrigation. This system is yet in its infancy. In a few years hundreds of millions of dollars will be invested in making our desert lands "blossom as the rose," but like all other enterprises, first on the field will be the first in fortune.

913. WASTE OF GOLD, SILVER AND IRON.—The present clumsy methods of extracting the ore of metals must soon be superseded by a more economical system. To say that there are $100,000,000 worth of gold and silver in the refuse piled up around the mines would be much beneath the actual figures. The loss in iron and other metals, owing to the same cause, is utterly incalculable. The recent discoveries in magnetism point to the solution of the problem and the utilization of the waste. It is not impossible that the electro-magnet contains more gold for its fortunate inventors than all the mines of the earth will yield to operators during a single year. [288]

CHAPTER   XXIX.

MISCELLANEOUS WAYS OF MAKING MONEY.

Odd Ways of Making Money—Millions for Cents—How to Live Without Paying Rent—X-Rays and X-Bills—Fortunes in Old Iron—Newspapers, Like Wine, Increase in Price With Age—High Price for a Wig—900 per cent. Profit in Old Books—What the "Old Furniture Man" Makes—The Five-cent Millionaire—Profits of Peddlers—Why Pawnbrokers Get Rich.

THE ways of making money are as multifarious as the diversity of human industry. Some men earn a fortune, some discover it, some win it, and some marry it. Every year new schemes are developed for the earning of one's bread. Many of them are unpromising and even startling, and yet all the great industries that to-day pour wealth into the pockets of the capitalists were once derided as the folly of unpractical dreamers. There is not one of the thousand or more methods of making a living in which there is not the possibility of a fortune. The following methods are sufficiently out of the beaten track to be novel to most people, while some of them are absolutely new and untried:

914. THE NATIONAL ADVERTISING COMPANY.—Form a company of live, energetic, intelligent young men. Ascertain the extent of circulation of some of our literary magazines. For every subscriber and buyer there are at least three readers; some estimate [289] five. Bunch together the circulation of some of the leading periodicals, and when you are sure of a million readers, begin operations. Divide the country up into sections, with a central headquarters, and let one of a pair of your young men work each. One member of the firm remains to control the office. The magazines should be those whose circulation covers the entire country, and the advertisements you seek to gain should not be of a local but of a general character. Then you can work your field, promising that for so many cents per thousand or dollars per million, you will place the advertisements before the eyes of that number of people. Have circulars headed "Millions for Cents." The power of numbers has a charm for most people, and few advertisers will be able to resist your array of figures.

915. FREE RENT.—Get your rent free on the same plan that some men get a building lot free. Take a large house, which, we will say, costs you $75 per month. Such a house should have at least twelve rooms, six of which should be bedrooms. These rooms should be readily sublet for $3 a week, which, allowing for the fractions over the even weeks in a month, exactly pays your rent. By means of folding-beds you can readily convert some of the remaining six into sleeping rooms. If your family is small, a parlor can be so used.

916. X-RAYS AND X-BILLS.—The fluoroscope is a new thing. It is a great thing to see the bones of one's hands, or keys imbedded in two inches of solid wood. You can invent many other ways of making the novelty interesting. People pay to see what is novel. With proper advertising, a really good fluoroscope exhibition should net at least $10 a night. [290]

917. GOLDEN SAILS.—Cleopatra's barge may not have had golden sails, but if you live along shore, especially near a summer resort, you can turn your sails into gold, and make the wind waft you money by taking parties for an outing on the water. You should get $10 for a party of six; $15 for a party of ten, etc. The requisites are a good boat, made attractive by awning and colored cushions, fishing tackle, bait, etc., and a pleasant, obliging disposition.

918. GAME PRESERVE.—If you live far inland, you can buy at cheap rates a wild mountain or a large tract of wilderness. Around this construct a high fence and stock your purchase

with game. All this will require capital, but you will find ample returns for your investment in the rates which you will charge city sportsmen for a day's sport. These hunters care little for the money if they can have a good day's sport. After your game preserve becomes well known, through liberal advertising, $25 a day on your investment during the season should be a very modest expectation.

919. THE JUNK SHOP.—One of the things most in demand to-day is iron. This is the iron age. It is displacing brick for building and wood for ships. And yet how much goes to waste! Stoves, pots, kettles, rails, machinery, wagon springs, car wheels, pillars, girders, and a multitude of other forms of this valuable metal go to waste. The junk shop is a mine. Manufacturers will pay you fifty cents per 100 pounds. The fact is not generally known, but many junk dealers have become rich.

920. OLD NEWSPAPERS.—Newspapers should not be sold to the ragman until they have been scissored, and [291] perhaps not then. In New York there is a man who makes a business of preserving newspapers. You can get almost any copy of any paper for a number of years back. Copies forty years old bring as high as $20 apiece. A copy twenty years old will bring $4 or $5. Copies more than one year old and less than five sell from fifty cents to one dollar. If salable, every day increases the value of your stock.

921. THE BOOK STALL.—Where come the books on the street stalls that sell for such marvelously low prices? From the cellars (would-be sellers) of publication houses. These are the books that will not sell at rates profitable to the publishers, and are bought up by the thousand at small rates. Many of them come from the libraries of persons deceased, and from the bookcases of men tired of carting them around in this moving age. Sold at fifteen, twenty or twenty-five cents apiece, there is a large profit in these books, for they are often bought at $10 per thousand—that is, a penny apiece. Profits at ten cents, 900 per cent. Bought at $50 per thousand, you have still 400 per cent. Pretty fair profits indeed! Let us no longer despise the old dealer in second-hand books.

922. OLD FURNITURE.—Furniture made of the best material brings large prices. Only slightly marred, chairs and other kinds of household furniture often made of costly woods, are stored away as useless in the attic. These could frequently be purchased at very low prices, the owners being glad to get rid of them as an incumbrance. Yet a little money would make them as good as new. Five dollars expended on a chair that originally cost $50 and was repurchased in a dilapidated state for $10; it was sold by the adroit second-hand [292] dealer for $25; and the purchaser considered it an excellent bargain. The dealer's profit was $10. Time consumed in repair, one day and a half. The man earned $6.66-1/3 per day. Some in the same line have done much better. With competent helpers and with industry in hunting up old furniture, these figures should be trebled and quadrupled.

923. PUBLIC CONVENIENCE ROOM.—Establish it on some prominent thoroughfare. It need not be very large. Suppose the rent to be $25 per month. Let it be understood that for five cents you will furnish materials for correspondence (pen, ink and paper), a writing desk, brushes band lacking for shoes (not the services of a bootblack), a whisk broom, a mirror, the use of a daily paper, a city directory, a large map of the city, information on points of interest concerning the things worth seeing, directions how to reach any part of the city, sofas and easy chairs for resting, and the use of a toilet room. All for five cents! You should have at least 200 patrons a day; receipts, $10. Besides, you could sell stationery, confectionery, cigars, magazines, and many other small articles in common use. The place could advantageously be established in connection with a restaurant. Do you know that some of the largest fortunes have been made from just such five-cent charges. A millionaire street-railroad magnate, being asked recently what his business was, replied: "Oh! just a five-cent business—that's all."

924. GENERAL ADVICE.—Here is something entirely new: Thousands of people want information, but do not know where to get it. Some write to the newspapers, some ask friends. It would be of great advantage if such persons could consult people who have more[293] time to look into their affairs than a newspaper editor, and who are more disinterested than friends. Let it be known that you will give tips on horse races, inside information about stock, points about the purchase of real estate, advice about law matters, suggestions about the investment of money, or any other information that may be required. Have on hand a stock of dictionaries, gazetteers, directories, encyclopedias, and world books of general information. You may charge ten cents for a simple consultation of five minutes. You can give a great deal of information in five minutes, if your questioner knows how to ask and you how to answer. Fifteen cents for ten minutes, twenty-five cents for twenty minutes, thirty-five cents for an half hour, and half a dollar for an hour. This business might be combined with the Public Convenience Room in the last number.

925. LANGUAGE CLASSES.—Here is one on a new plan. A French teacher has hit upon the idea of combining work and play in a novel manner. The classes form a club, which meets as in progressive euchre. The game is played after the old style of authors. Upon blank white cards are written the words to be used in sentences at the table. One table has cards containing the names of clothing, another of furniture, and so on. The players remain a certain length of time at each table, and then pass to the next, each player visiting every table during the session of the club. Afterward light refreshments are served by the teacher, and the subjects announced for the next meeting. The idea is a taking one, and capable of great elaboration. An up-to-date teacher ought to have immense success with this plan.

926. BUSINESS OPPORTUNITIES.—The business opportunities[294] advertised in a single New York paper average 25 a day, 200 on Sunday, or about 17,500 a year. One man claims

that $10,000 can be realized in two weeks by the opportune venture of $1,000 in real estate. Another offers stock in a $10,000 mine which he is sure will shortly be worth $100,000. A third offers $5,000 for the use of $3,000 one year in mining operations. A fourth wants a backer for a new power, in which $5,000,000 will be easily realized. Most of these "opportunities" are doubtless illusive, while many are bare-faced frauds; yet among the myriads there may be some genuine chances for money-making. A shrewd man might find a bonanza in this mine of opportunities.

927. MINE OWNERS.—Mr. Demullers, of Jefferson County, N. Y., a few years ago went to El Paso, Mexico, as a workman. To-day he owns the most valuable turquoise mine in the world, and is known as the "Turquoise King." One recent shipment netted him $10,000. Another man in South America is known as the "Nitrate King," and is said to be the richest man on the Western Continent. He also was once a poor man.

928. CATTLE RAISERS.—Six years ago Grant Gillet was a station agent in a small town in Kansas, working for a bare living. He made an engagement as cattle feeder, and from that position worked himself up into wealth by buying and selling cattle. He actually made half a million dollars in four years, and was known as the Millionaire Cowboy. Another man this last year bought Texas cattle for $432,000, and sold them for $540,000, making $108,000 in four months. This simply shows what opportunities there are for shrewd men in the cattle business.[295]

929. STUMP SPEAKERS.—Men of oratorical ability have an opportunity during two or three months of every year to earn considerable money in political campaigns. Both of the great parties employ the best talent, the pay depending partly upon one's convincing logic, but mainly upon the celebrity of the speaker. The lowest compensation is $5 a night, but noted speakers have received $100, and even more, for one short speech.

930. ARTISTIC HOME BUILDERS.—These are not speculators, but men who have built homes for their own occupancy, yet have been induced to sell by the high prices offered. We know of no less than three persons in this present year who have made $3,000 to $5,000 each in this way.

931. CEMETERY OWNERS.—Cemetery lots have proved good paying property to those who know how to manage it. Land which costs from $1,000 to $5,000 an acre is divided up into parcels one rod or one-half rod square, and sold for from $100 to $500 a plot. Mr. Th. E. Tinsley became a millionaire through graveyard operations in Texas.

932. GLASS BALL SHOOTERS.—The names of Carver and Bogardus have become continental by reason of their skill in hitting glass balls shot out of a trap. There is hardly any kind of sport more exciting, and there is always a large class who will patronize a rifle contest. These men pocketed fortunes by the exhibition of their skill.

933. ENTERTAINMENT BUREAUS.—A Lecture Bureau in Brooklyn has the names of over 500 persons, embracing[296] all kinds of talent, booked to interest and amuse its patrons. The manager, by having several engagements on every night of the week, and charging five per cent. of profits, is growing rich. There is room for a bureau of this kind in every large city.

934. ICE-CREAM MANUFACTURERS.—Ten million quarts of ice-cream are annually sold in New York, 65,000 quarts a day being the average consumption in warm weather. "It is nothing," says a prominent maker, "for a great establishment to dispose of 35,000 quarts in one day." An idea of the money in the business may be formed from the fact that the value of the annual output is about $3,500,000, of which fully one-third is profit.

935. GOLD HUNTERS.—F. E. Simmons, of Montana, went to the Klondike less than a year ago. He suffered every hardship and nearly lost his life on the journey, but he returned with half a million dollars. There are a few prizes there, as in all mining districts, but the majority of gold hunters do not succeed. Yet Mr. J. Partridge, a mining expert, who has thoroughly examined the region, says the wealth of the Klondike is inexhaustible, and he predicts that $30,000,000 will be taken out next year.

936. ASPHALT COMPANIES.—Here is an example of the enormous profits made by these companies. In one city the mayor, suspecting the charges were exorbitant, forced them to a lower scale, when the company actually agreed to do for $1.50 per yard what they had hitherto received $2.25 for laying. This last was a living profit, but the profits over and above a fair compensation[297] were seventy-five cents per square yard. This is the way contractors for the government get rich.

937. HORSE JOCKEYS.—Small men weighing not over 100 pounds have an opportunity to earn money by riding horses on the race track. As the race often depends upon the judgment, skill, and balance of the rider, the owner wants the qualities of a man in the body of a boy. Jockeys receive on different tracks from $10 to $25 for their day's work, but riders of winners often receive presents of $10 and even more. Tod Sloan, a rider for the Dwyers, it is said, received $1,000 for a trip to the English Derby.

938. WIG MAKING.—In a large city where there are several theaters, you can do a good business in wigmaking. The trade is easily learned, and the goods will command prices varying from the mustache of fifty cents to the court wig for which you should receive $7 or $8. A location near a large theater is desirable. Actors are very fastidious about their make-up, and willing to pay good prices. It is said that Edwin Forrest once paid $300 for a striking wig.

939. BOOK REPAIRING.—Almost everybody has books that are out of order, and yet, strange to say, we have never heard of any one making a business of repairing books. For your outfit you need several sheets of paper of different sizes and thickness, a few strips of leather, some stout pieces of cloth, a bottle of glue, a penknife, and a pair of scissors.

These can be carried in a small hand bag. Practice on your own and your friends' books before striking out.

940. THE HOUSEHOLD PACK.—Select twenty-five{298} articles most needed in a household. They should be compact, so as to go in a small box or bag. They should be such things as soap, starch, shoe blacking, shoe polish, stove blacking, cement, mucilage, matches, bluing, yeast cakes, baking powders, etc. These are articles in constant demand and consumption. They can be sold from door to door, mostly among people of limited means, and if sold cheap there is profit, because they are articles which every one wants, and many sales, even if the profits are small, mean large results. There are many peddlers who are foreigners, and having made a competence, go back to their own country to enjoy it.

941. PAWNBROKERS' PROFITS.—The pawnbrokers' business has been largely given up to the Jews, but there is no good reason why it should be. Pawnbrokers make immense profits. The amount of the loan is not above one-third the value of the article. The goods are frequently not redeemed. Then there are the pawnbrokers' sales, at which the articles command at least one-half their value. The pawnbroker gets ten per cent. or more on money loaned, and if the goods are sold he gets the difference between one-third and one-half values; that is, if an article be worth $100, the loan is $33.33-1/3. The amount realized at the sale is $50. Pawnbrokers' profits, $16.66-2/3. This is the reason most pawnbrokers get rich.{299}

MONEY IN SPECULATION.

True Stories that are Stranger than Fiction—Fortune's Great Army—The Rise of Jay Gould—The Meteoric Career of James Fisk—Ferdinand Ward, the Napoleon of Finance—How Vanderbilt Made a Million in a Day—A Man who was Devoured by both Bulls and Bears—Some Rules for Timid Investors—John C. Eno, the Free-Lance Operator—The Wonderful Success of James R. Keene—How Daniel Drew Spelled "Door"—The Great Leiter Wheat Deal.

THIS is a dangerous sea, strewn with wrecks, but the fascination in the thought of making a fortune in a single day ever has and ever will cast its spell upon the human mind. Some men will take great risks in the hope of glittering gains. We give a few of the most promising forms of speculation, with examples of those who have been successful with the dice of fortune.

172

Jay Gould was employed as a map-maker at a salary of $30 per month. He trudged over whole counties in New York State as a surveyor. A lucky hit brought him into Wall Street, where he made over $70,000,000 in forty years.

James Fisk came down from Vermont a penniless boy, but getting into the company of Wall Street men he soon amassed an immense fortune.

Ferdinand Ward, called the Napoleon of Finance, had an unequaled gift for shrewd speculation, and might have excelled all contemporaries had he chosen[300] to stick by honest methods. He made a fortune before he was arrested for "crooked ways."

Cornelius Vanderbilt at twenty earned a living by rowing a boat between Staten Island and New York. At sixty he was proprietor of a fleet of sixty-six steamboats and owner of several railroads. He made his money in stocks. In the fluctuations of the Erie, on one occasion he made a million dollars between rise and set of sun.

John C. Eno was called the free-lance operator. He was one of the boldest manipulators of stocks, and acquired an immense fortune.

Perhaps the most striking success was that of James R. Keene, who made $9,000,000 in three years.

Others who have won their fortunes in Wall Street are Russell Sage, William Belden, George I. Seney, Henry Villard, William H. Vanderbilt, William R. Travis, C. P. Huntington, and Daniel Drew.

Of the last named it may be mentioned—to show how little a college education has to do with success in business—that he was very illiterate, possessing only a scanty knowledge of grammar, and even of spelling. It is related that on one occasion he told his cashier that he would set the safe lock on the word "door." When the cashier wanted to open the safe, he tried "door" in vain. Knowing his employer's queer methods of spelling he tried varieties on "door," such as "dore," "doar," etc., but all in vain. At last he was obliged to go to the hotel and awake his employer, who had gone to bed. "Uncle Dan'l" was quite crusty at being awakened, and told his cashier again that he had set the safe on the word "door." "But how do you spell 'door'?" inquired the cashier. "Why," said "Uncle Dan'l" tartly, "any fool can spell 'door.' You'd better get out of the business if you[301] can't spell, and I've a mind to discharge you on the spot. How do I spell 'door?' Why, 'd-o-a-r-e,' of course!" The next day, however, on reflection the old man relented, and concluded not to discharge his trusted employee for so trivial a blunder.

A rule for speculators is: "Don't invest on professional advice." Your advisers have "an ax to grind." A man once ordered a broker to buy 1,000 shares of Erie when the price was 94; it immediately dropped, and he ordered it sold when it was 92-1/2. In half an hour he returned and ordered it bought again. It had then gone up to 95. After consulting again with "friends," he again ordered it sold. The market then was down to 90. He came back the fifth time and said: "I consulted one man who told me to buy; then another who told me to sell. I understand that one is called a bull and the other a bear. I don't know much about these names, but I do know that I have been a jackass."

A much safer plan is to follow the lead of shrewd speculators. In Wall Street you should reverse the advice given to the disciples concerning the Pharisees. Christ said, "Do as they say, but not as they do." But with speculators the direction should be, "Do as they do, but not as they say."

The chief form of speculation is in stocks. These stocks may be railroads, mines, wheat, corn, cotton, wool, tobacco, oil, gas, coal, and, in fact, almost any industry where capital has constantly vacillating values. We have room to mention only a very few:

942. City Bonds.—These are generally among the best securities for investment. The element of speculation comes in when they are bought below par in the belief of an early rise. A sharp Yankee bought $100,000 of defaulted bonds of the city of Houston, Texas, forced a settlement at par, and doubled his money.[302]

943. Colonial Trade.—We have the very best authority for the information that the trade in our newly acquired territory, the Philippine Islands, will be worth one billion dollars annually under American development. Here is an immense opportunity for every form of profitable speculation. Cuba, Porto Rico, and Hawaii, also, are inviting fields, and there is no doubt that the next decade will witness the making of many fortunes in those islands, and the foundations of hundreds of others. Now is the time to begin, as those earliest in the field will have the first chance to buy up depreciated stocks and lagging industries.

944. The American Tobacco Company.—One of the most vacillating stocks lately has been that of the American Tobacco Company. In January of the current year—1898—Mr. J. R. Keene purchased 80,000 shares at $90. September 26th, fearing the market was about to decline, he began to sell, and in two days had completely unloaded at figures ranging at $145 to $139. He cleared about $1,500,000 in the two days.

945. Collapsed Railroads.—For a capitalist there are few more promising fields than the buying up of collapsed or run down railroads. Mr. George I. Seney accumulated a large fortune by purchasing at a little more than nominal figures bankrupt or embarrassed roads, and by thorough equipment, and by connection with more prosperous roads, soon put them in a paying condition. If you can get one end of a small road into a large city, or if you can arrange to make it the feeder instead of the rival of a large road, it will be almost certain to yield abundant returns.

946. Wheat Margins.—Fortunes are daily made[303] and lost in wheat. Everybody has heard of the great Leiter deal. Joseph Leiter often made $100,000 in a single day. In ten months he rendered things lively in every great center of the world, and in this period of

less than a year he actually made $4,500,000. True, he lost it again, but the fact that one could corner such a fortune in so short a time shows what may be accomplished with courage and capital. The safest rule for small and timid operators is to follow in the wake of these bold speculators, but not too far. It may be laid down almost with the certainty of a logical premise, that, when a man of vast resources and thoroughly familiar with the field enters the market, he is bound to win at first, but bound to lose if he presses things too far, because the tremendous stress produces at last reactionary conditions which no manipulator and no combination of speculators are able to face. It does not matter so much whether you are a bull or a bear, if you can perform the difficult feat of holding yourself in. [304]

CHAPTER   XXXI.

WHERE TO INVEST MONEY.

What Shall I Do with My Money?—Enormous Profits in Trust Companies—The Most Costly Bell in the World—The Bell Telephone—Edward Bellamy's Vision—The Best Paying Stocks—$11 per Day in a Lodging House—How a Young Man Made $10,000—How to Start with Nothing and Be Worth $100,000 when You are 40 Years Old.

THE first question is, How to get money? The second, How to invest it? The general distrust of money concerns is seen in the enormous deposits in the savings banks—a disposal of savings which yields the smallest returns—and also in the readiness, not to say rush, to take government bonds when only three per cent. or even less is offered. We give a few of the best paying investments, but the list is by no means exhaustive. The first four are in a section (Brooklyn Borough) of a single city, but there is no reason to doubt that other cities, and other sections of the same city, can make an equally good showing. Indeed, many Western concerns pay much higher dividends.

947. ILLUMINATING COMPANIES.—Of the ten illuminating companies of Brooklyn, not one last year paid a less dividend than five per cent., and one paid ten per cent.

948. TRUST COMPANIES.—Of the eight trust companies in the same borough, only one paid less than eight [305] per cent., and that paid six. The highest paid sixteen per cent.

949. BANKS.—Of the twenty-three banks of Brooklyn, State and National, one paid its stockholders sixteen per cent.; one fourteen; two, twelve; one, ten; and four, eight; only one paid less than five per cent.

950. INSURANCE COMPANIES.—Of the four local insurance companies, one paid its stockholders twenty per cent., and the others twelve, ten and five.

951. TIN PLATE COMPANY.—All the tin manufacturers of the country are about to be associated in one great company, to be known as the American Tin Plate Company. The stockholders expect to double their profits.

952. POTTERY COMBINATION.—Under the laws of New Jersey, the pottery trust has just been organized with a capital of $20,000,000. The price of the stock is rapidly advancing.

953. CONSOLIDATED ICE.—An ice company, to be called the Consolidated Ice, will soon control all the trade of New York City. Prices are to go up, and profits, instead of a meager four or five per cent., as at present, will, it is expected, be eight or ten per cent.

954. FLOUR TRUST.—British and American stockholders have combined to form one of the biggest trusts in the world. The capital of the new company will be about $150,000,000, and the output 95,000 barrels of flour daily. Should the profits be only twenty-five cents a barrel, the net earnings will be nearly $25,000 a day; [306] but it is expected that with the increased price, the profits will be at least double that figure.

955. FURNITURE COMBINE.—This is a new trust which is soon to be floated, and which proposes to control the manufacture of all the school furniture in the United States. The capital is to be $17,000,000. Some idea of the enormous profits awaiting the stockholders may be formed when it is stated that the present output is more than $15,000,000. The combination means decreased expenses in operation, higher prices for customers, and, of course, greater incomes for stockholders.

956. TELEPHONE MONOPOLY.—One of the greatest monopolies of the country is that of the Bell Telephone. The company has increased its capital stock in eighteen years from $110,000 to $30,000,000. In that time it has earned $42,903,680. It pays dividends of eighteen per cent., and could pay more, if allowed to do so by its charter. The surplus is used to increase the capital stock, so that in addition to its enormous dividends, every little while it presents its stockholders with new blocks of this exceedingly profitable stock. The present price of shares is about $280.

957. A GREAT ELECTRICAL COMPANY.—Another of Bellamy's dreams is to be realized. New York capitalists, with millions of dollars at their command, have united in a great scheme to supply electrical energy to run the elevated and surface railroads and the factories of the metropolis. They propose to do away with steam entirely, except for heating purposes. They will control more than 1,000 square miles of the watersheds of the Catskills, and the mountain streams will be harnessed to furnish electricity for New York. The company [307] claim to have the names of such well known persons as Thomas C. Platt, Silas B. Dutcher, and Edward Lauterbach as interested persons in the scheme, and it is said that the undertaking will be on a much grander scale than the similar one at Niagara, to which the Vanderbilts, the Webbs, and other famous manipulators of finance have furnished backing. If this scheme should materialize, it will undoubtedly be one of the best paying investments.

958. INDUSTRIAL STOCKS.—Here is a partial list of the best paying stocks. Of course, where the interest is large, the price of the stocks is correspondingly high. The investor, before paying the high prices asked, should use his best judgment in considering whether the present rates are likely to be maintained. The highest dividends on industrial stocks last year were as follows: Adams' Express, 8; Consolidated Gas (New York), 8; Peter Lorillard (tobacco), 8; American Tobacco, 9; Diamond Match, 10; American Sugar Refining Company, 12; American Bell Telephone, 18; Standard Oil, 33; Welsbach Light, 80.

959. RAILROADS DIVIDENDS.—Stock in such railroads as the Pennsylvania, Lake Shore, Michigan Central, New York Central, New York and New Haven, are safe and profitable investments, if you can get them. The last-named road has paid ten per cent. for many years, though recently the figures have dropped to eight. The railroad stocks paying the highest dividends last year were as follows: New York, New Haven and Hartford, 8 per cent.; Great Southern (Alabama), 9; Manchester and Lawrence, 10; Norwich and Worcester, 10; Boston and Providence, 10; Connecticut River, 10; Georgia, 11; Northern (New Hampshire), 11; [308] Philadelphia, Germantown and Northern, 12; Pennsylvania Coal, 16.

960. LODGING HOUSE.—A man leased an abandoned hotel, containing 100 small rooms, and fitted them up with single beds. He charged a uniform price of twenty-five cents a night. The location was down town in New York, the congested district where congregate travelers, tradesmen, workingmen, and the vast class of floaters. His rooms were nearly always full. Income per day, $25. Daily expenses: Night clerk, $2; two chambermaids ($15 each per month), $1. Rent, $5; lights, $1; laundry, $3; sundries, $1. Total expenses per day, $13. Net profit, $12 per day. He says, "I am sure I could double these profits if I could double my accommodations."

961. REAL ESTATE.—A young man twenty-one years of age, and possessing $500, bought a tract of land in the outskirts of a suburban city for $1,500. The tract contained twenty acres, and he paid $500 down and gave a mortgage for the remainder. He had the property surveyed and divided into lots, eight to the acre. The tract was located on the bend of a river, and he called it "Riverside Park." Lots were advertised for sale at $100 each. The first year he cleared off the mortgage by the sale of lots. He had remaining 145 lots. In five years he sold all these lots at an average price of $85. Total amount received for lots, $13,825. Price of land, $1,500. Taxes, $625. Surveying, grading, etc., $762. Advertising and other methods of booming the property, $1,272. Total cost and expenses, $3,534. Net profit, $10,291. By repeating this process on a larger scale in another city, this young man, who started at sixteen years of age with nothing, and by [309] hard work and economy had save $500 at twenty-one, found himself at the age of forty with $100,000. The secrets of his success were four: Shrewdness in foreseeing where property would be likely to advance; energy in quickly changing the property

from a farm into building lots; taste in making them attractive, and giving the place a pretty name; and, most important of all, the knowing how to create a market. We have known this process repeated by others with almost equally marked success. In all our large cities there are land companies developing suburban property and making money rapidly.{310}

CHAPTER   XXXII.

MONEY IN SPARE TIME.

Fortunes in Spare Moments—Millions Missed for Want of Economy of Time—Stories of Famous Men.

Lost! somewhere between sunrise and sunset, two golden hours, each set with sixty diamond minutes. No reward is offered, for they are gone forever.

962. Five Minutes a Day before a box of paints or a bunch of finely shaded ribbons will make you expert in colors, a position of great importance and large salary in many stores.

963. Ten Minutes a Day practicing stenography after you have learned the system from a good text-book, will fit you in a year's time to take any place where the services of a short-hand writer are required.

964. Fifteen Minutes a Day cutting out of newspapers data in regard to persons of note and classifying the same, will give you in a few years an accumulation of material which you can dispose of to advantage to reporters and publishers on sudden demand of such matter—as the occasion of the death of the men in the public eye.

965. Twenty Minutes a Day drumming on a writing machine should give you an expertness with the keys that will insure steady and profitable employment.{311}

966. Twenty-five Minutes a Day will enable you to master any language in a year, then tutorships, professorships, and translations of foreign works at good prices, await your energy.

967. Thirty Minutes a Day running rapidly over figures will make you an expert accountant, if not even a lightning calculator, for whose services business men are willing to pay liberally. Time is money.

968. Thirty-five Minutes a Day writing up some incident of news will give you a facility of the pen in the course of one or two years, so that you can command a good salary as a reporter. Success in this department depends upon a writer's imagination and skill.

969. FORTY MINUTES A DAY over reading selections will make you an elocutionist. Readers and reciters receive all the way from $10 to $100 for an evening's work.

970. FORTY-FIVE MINUTES A DAY will give you a knowledge of bookkeeping in all its branches. Let the spare time be spent in acquiring a plain, round business hand. Then master a book on the subject. After that you should offer your services free to a friend for three-quarters of an hour every day. Bookkeepers command from $1,000 to $3,000 salary.

971. FIFTY MINUTES A DAY divided into periods of twenty-five minutes each, should make you a good singer, even if you have only a mediocre voice. One quarter's work under a good teacher should give you the rudiments of the art, together with foundation practice, and from this you can go on by yourself. You can always get a friend who will correct your faults *gratis*,[312] and it is the elimination of faults, with steady practice, that brings success. Singers in churches command all the way from $100 to $5,000 a year. And the work is done chiefly on Sundays, when it does not conflict with other employments.

972. FIFTY-FIVE MINUTES A DAY with a book containing teacher's examination questions, will give you such a command of the branches taught in our public schools as to insure you a position on the educational staff. You should master not one book only, but all you can procure which have a list of questions asked at examinations. Teachers get from $500 to $5,000, according to ability.

973. SIXTY MINUTES A DAY imitating the styles of our best story-tellers will give you, as it did Stevenson, an easy command of all styles, and an ability to write stories netting thousands of dollars.

974. SEVENTY-FIVE MINUTES A DAY will make you in the course of four or five years an engraver or painter in all the fields of the increasing application of those arts. Prices for this kind of work are so varied that no figures can be given, but they are always high, and some persons have made fortunes with pen and brush.

975. EIGHTY MINUTES A DAY placing letters in pigeon holes and in learning such other knowledge as any handler of the mails will willingly impart to you, will give you such deft fingers and such quick brains that it should not be difficult for you to secure a well-paid position in a large postoffice.

976. NINETY MINUTES A DAY will enable you to master the intricate and almost infinite details of the[313] insurance business in all its branches. Knowledge of the business and ability to persuade men are the two requisites of highest success in this occupation. There are insurance agents receiving as high as $10,000 a year, and presidents of companies $25,000, and even more. There is no reason why you should not reach the top. The horses, Plod and Pluck, will draw you there.

977. ONE HUNDRED MINUTES A DAY will initiate you thoroughly into the banking or brokerage business. Read all books on the subject, classify your knowledge, repeat it over and over in your spare moments, ask some friend in the business about any point you do not understand. After three years of hard study, offer your spare time free to a banker or broker, informing him of what you have done. You will have to begin at the bottom, but the salaries grow fat as you rise, and are enormously rich at the top.

978. ONE HUNDRED AND TEN MINUTES A DAY will give you for each year of your study a knowledge of a separate branch of the Civil Service. Five years will give you five branches. Appointments are now nearly all made by competitive examination. Salaries in some departments rise as high as $10,000.

979. ONE HUNDRED AND TWENTY MINUTES A DAY should enable you to master any musical instrument under the sun. You will require a teacher for a part of the time, but the most important thing is steady, persistent practice. The field for good music is constantly widening, the demands for good musicians are steadily increasing, and the remuneration is correspondingly advancing. Money is literally pouring into the lap of persons who can captivate the human ear. [314]

CHAPTER   XXXIII.

MONEY IN ODDS AND ENDS.

How a Family Saved $100 on a Salary of $700.

ECONOMY is quite as large a factor as industry in the gaining of a fortune. With people living on small incomes, it is often the one element that determines whether they "make both ends meet," or run in debt and ultimately fail. The following example shows how one family, whose income was only $700 a year, actually saved $100. Mr. ——, of ——, found himself getting behind in money matters, and determined to practice rigid economy. He found a great many leakages in the household. Perhaps some one who reads this will find the same or similar leaks, and learn why he is not prospering:

980. WASTE.—Scraps of meat thrown away, making loss of dinners worth, $12.50; puddings thrown away, $6; waste of coal in not sifting, $5; one-half barrel of apples from not sorting, $1.50; wash tub fell to pieces because left dry, $1; one-fourth loaf of bread every day thrown away (90 loaves at 10 cents per loaf), $9; ten dozen preserves, one-fourth lost at twenty-five cents per can, $7.50; twenty barrels of ashes, five cents per barrel, $1; waste of bones which could be used for soup, $1.50; waste of heat at the damper, one-tenth in a ton of coal, ten tons per year, $5; waste of gas in not turning

down lights when not needed, $12; canned salmon,[315] one-fourth spoiled because can was left open, twenty-five cans, $1; cheese (one-half used, the rest thrown away because hard), twenty-five pounds, $2; potatoes, for want of sprouting, one barrel, $1; clothing, for lack of attention, $15; milk, 375 quarts at eight cents per quart, one-fifth allowed to spoil, $6; umbrellas which could be mended, $1; shoes thrown away when they could be used by having heels fixed, $3; kitchen slops, $1; waste of vegetables, $5; wear of carpet for lack of rugs in places most used, $3; Total waste, $100.[316]

CHAPTER   XXXIV.

STRANGE WAYS OF MAKING MONEY.

A Thousand Ways to Make a Living—The Humbug of Great Names—The Mania for Old and Rare Things—The "Relic" Manufacture—The "Imitation Enterprise"—The "Box Office" Clique—The "Cure" Fad—The "Fake" News Agency—The Museum "Freak"—The "Treasure" Excitements—The "Literary" Bureau—The "Watered" Stock.

THERE are ways of making money that lie so far out of the ordinary channels as to warrant this chapter. Some of them are only strange because they are new, as the telephone and the wood pulp were strange a generation ago. Others, being decidedly odd in themselves, will doubtless always be pursued only by a few, and considered by the many to be curious ways of making a living.

Success is easy when once you succeed. This is the case with goods which have achieved a name. Frequently the founder of the name is bankrupt, retired or dead; but the goods continue to be manufactured and sold under the original trade-mark. Countless thousands of dollars are paid every year for shoes, hats, hardware, groceries, and innumerable other articles, at rates above the average price when the goods are not a farthing better. The deluded buyers are simply paying for a name.

Others have a mania for the collection of all kinds of bric-à-brac—old coins and rare books are seized and hoarded as eagerly as if made of gold. This mania is[317] harmless in itself, and gives its possessors no doubt much pleasure, but they are made the prey of Shylocks who carry on a regular trade of manufacturing "old" articles.

So also with the "relic" craze. There are actually manufactories where relics are made. Conscienceless persons take advantage of the curiosity and piety of travelers to palm off all sorts of "relics" upon them at preposterous prices.

Then there are the limitless imitations that are on the market. Some of them, such as patent medicines, brands of groceries, oleomargarine, etc., are imitations pure and simple; others are adulterations with more or less of the genuine. So vast and profitable are these methods of deception that the government has been compelled to interfere to protect its citizens from fraud.

The box-office clique is only a less pernicious, but equally barefaced, means of getting money. When a Bernhardt or an Irving is to perform, an announcement is made that the box-office will be open at 9 o'clock on a certain morning, as early as 10, or even 6, on the previous evening you will see a solitary man wend his way to the theater and silently square his back against the door. In time he is followed by another, and yet another, so that by midnight perhaps a dozen or twenty of these grim-faced men are lined against the wall. Not one of them has the slightest idea of seeing the play. It is simply their way of earning a living. For the next morning they will sell their places in line to the highest bidders.

Of the "cure" faddists there number is legion. We do not mean the makers of patent medicines, of which we have treated elsewhere, but the men who profess to believe they have some unique and original way of ridding mankind of evil. Thus we have the gold cure,[318] the barefoot cure, the mind cure, the faith cure, the cold water cure, and the hot water cure—in fact the whole great family of 'pathies. Many of these curists no doubt are sincere, but whether so or not, they have reaped large sums of money.

Equally industrious is the "fake" news agency. There are agencies that manufacture news to order. Papers, they reason, must have news. If there is any subject concerning which the public is eager to read, and for any reason the reporters cannot give the facts, the "fake" news agency is a welcome resort. These bogus news agents are paid a certain amount a "stick" for their false news.

Museum "freaks" too, are manufactured to order, and sometimes are made beforehand in anticipation of a market.

"Treasure" enthusiasts are not quite as common now as formerly, and yet the hot Klondike fever is but a "Kid's Buried Treasure" under another name, and on a mammoth scale. Of the 100 who attempt to get to Dawson City, seventy-five will reach the place, fifty will earn a bare living under all manner of hardships; twenty-five will make about the same as if they had stayed at home; ten will bring back a $100 worth of dust; three will do tolerably well, and one will get rich.

The "literary bureau" is a more ingenious means to make a living. A set of bright young men advertise that for a "consideration" they will send a sermon, lecture, address, or after-dinner speech, to any person who may suddenly find himself called upon when unprepared.

Of the "watered" stock and other incorporated swindles, almost every investor has purchased his experience at a dear rate. This is a method of increasing[319] one's capital stock in a company without the contribution of any new funds, and it is one of the most common of frauds.

These are but a few of the many curious and ingenious ways by which people attempt to make a living. In many cases, especially the last-named, there is no doubt that the promoters of these enterprises often do get rich at the expense of the public.

Other strange ways of making a living are the catching of butterflies or canary birds at a penny apiece, and the sifting of ashes and collecting of cinders. In London sand is sold on the street for scouring and as gravel for birds. Then there is "the curiosity shop." In Genoa, there are marriage brokers who have a list of names of marriageable girls, divided into different classes, with an account of the fortunes, personal attraction, etc., of each. They charge two to three per cent. commission on a contract. In Munich there are female bill posters, and in Paris there are women who make a living by letting out chairs on the street. Also, in the same city, men are hired to cry the rate of exchange. Then there are the men who gather old clothes, and the street sweepers. There are 6,000 rag gatherers in Paris. Then there are the refuse cleaners, and the glass-eye makers, the latter furnishing you with a crystal eyeball at rates from $10 to $20 when the physicians and oculists charge $60 or $70 for similar services. Then there are postage stamp gatherers and chair menders. In fact the ways of making a living are legion. We formulate a few of the best of this class:

981. Experts.—There are many kinds—accountant, color, handwriting, etc. Any one who confines his life-work to a very small and special field can command a large price for his services. Experts often receive $10 a day.[320]

982. Detectives.—Besides the men in the employ of the United States and local authorities, there are many who work in private agencies. The pay depends upon the nature of the work and the wealth of the employers. In celebrated cases where suspected parties had to be shadowed for months, a detective has received as much as $5,000.

983. Traveling Poets.—Since the days of Wesley, the traveling preacher has been a familiar figure, but who since the time of Homer has seen a traveling poet? yet one called on the author the other day. His patrons are chiefly obscure people who pay from $1 to $10 to have their history, home, achievements, or virtues lauded in verse. It is hardly necessary to say that the poems are not published, but kept as household treasures for coming grandchildren.

984. Old Coins.—Some have found a profitable source of revenue in the hunting and hoarding of old coins. One numismatist recently sold a dollar coin of 1804 for $5,000.

985. Purveyor of Personals.—A Russian named Romeitre started this enterprise in a small way. Now we have press-clipping bureaus so large as to employ seventy persons each. In some of these places from 5,000 to 7,000 papers are read every day, and the weekly

clippings amount to more than 100,000. There are now press-clipping bureaus in nearly all of our large cities.

986. GOLD ON SEA BOTTOM.—Another class of men make money out of other men's misfortunes; that is, by stripping wrecks of their valuables. Others secure the services of divers and search the bottom of₍₃₂₁₎ the ocean, where vessels containing treasures are supposed to have gone down. A few years ago a company from England went with divers to a place near Bermuda, where a vessel had been sunk a long time before, and secured from the wreck the sum of $1,500,000.

987. RARE BOOKS.—The art of book collecting has been pursued with profit by some persons. It requires no capital, if one simply confines his efforts to book-stalls, though, if pursued on a large scale, money is required for advertising and correspondence. Mr. Charles B. Foote, of New York City, is a veteran bibliophile, and has made a specialty of first editions. Recently he made three auction sales of his stores, and realized more than $20,000, and his home is full of treasures.

988. OLD ITALIAN VIOLINS.—They sell at prices ranging from $500 to $5,000, when you can buy them at all, which is seldom, for they are mostly in the hands of wealthy collectors. Now we will let you into a great secret. It is not the kind of wood or the form of the instrument alone which produces the rare quality of sound, but it lies also in the kind of varnish used. By experimenting with varnish, you can produce a "Stradivarius," which will sell for almost any amount you choose to ask.

989. MAGIC SILK.—It seems like the trick of the magician to speak of turning cotton into silk, but it can actually be done, or at least cotton can be made to resemble silk, so that discrimination between the two fabrics is impossible. About fifty years ago, one Mercer, a French chemist, showed that cotton when subjected to the action of concentrated acid or alkalies, contracts and₍₃₂₂₎ has a greater affinity for dyes, but it has only just been discovered that "mercerization" gives also a brilliant luster to the cotton. The cotton is stretched violently during the operation, and when an energetic rubbing is added to the tension the tissue receives a permanent luster. It thus replaces silk at a fraction of its cost, and offers a splendid chance for financial enterprise.

990. THE GOLD CURE.—If the gold cure for which so much is claimed can really take away the appetite for liquor, there is an immense field for its exercise and room for the making of many fortunes in the cure of America's drunkards. In the United States alone an exceedingly moderate estimate makes the number of this unfortunate class 1,600,000. At the very modest calculation that only one-tenth of these can be induced to try the cure, and if each case nets the proprietor of the institution only $25—and the estimate should probably be doubled and even trebled—there are $15,000,000 in it for the public benefactors who can thus curb the evil of dram-drinking.

991. THE TELEPHONE NEWSPAPER.—Here is an idea for newspaper men: In Budapest, Hungary, there is a telephone newspaper, the first and only one in the world. The main office is in telephone communication with the Reichstadt (corresponding to our Congress), and it often happens that important speeches are known to the public while the speaker is still addressing the house; the latest reports from stock exchanges as well as political news are heard before any paper has printed them, a short summary of all important items is given at noon and again in the evening; subscribers are entertained with music and literary articles in the evenings, the latter being often spoken into the telephone[323] by the original authors. The cost is only two cents a day, and the company are said to be making money even at that figure.

992. RACE AND STOCK TIPPERS.—In addition to the regular brokers who supply tips to their customers, there is now a set of professional tippers who profess to have "inside information," and make it a business to give tips to anybody who will pay for them. They receive in some cases a fixed sum from their patrons, and in other cases they take a liberal percentage of the profits.

993. PROMOTERS.—This is a new vocation. The promoter "promotes" anything and everything that will pay. If you want to accomplish anything from the launching of a railroad enterprise to the selling of a penny patent, you pay the "promoter" a certain sum to do the work. He buys influence, lobbies legislators, controls newspapers and hypnotizes the public generally. Not all promoters come as high as Mr. Ernest Tooley, whose own price can be imagined when he claims to have paid $250,000 to English peers for their influence; yet we learn that the American Tin Plate Company gave the promoters of the Trust $10,000,000 in stock for their work.[324]

CHAPTER   XXXV.

HIGHLY PAYING OCCUPATIONS.

Some Golden Plums—What Electrical Experts Get—The Confidential Man—Rapid Rise of an Advertising Agent—Editors in Clover—Railroad Presidents Come High—A $25,000 Engineer—The Paying Berths in Medicine—Some Astonishing Lawyers' Fees—What Vanderbilt Paid a Steamboat Man.

THERE are some positions in which enormous salaries are paid. They are, of course, places where great responsibilities are incurred. Strange as it may seem, however, occupations where thousands of human lives are imperiled are not compensated at so high a rate as those where great finances are at stake. Here are a few of the golden plums:

994. ELECTRICAL EXPERTS.—The use of electricity has so increased in the last few years, and so many new uses have been found for it, that there are to-day nearly fifty different departments of human labor where it is employed, and naturally these have differentiated as many kinds of electricians. A young man in a New York establishment says "I am in receipt of a salary of $4,000 as superintendent of the dynamo building, and recently I had an offer of $7,000 to go with a new company out West."

995. THE CONFIDENTIAL MAN.—Another man in New York began his career in a store at wages of only $7 a week. He is now the firm's confidential man, who [325] decides on all important purchases, and receives a salary of $8,000 a year.

996. THE ADVERTISING AGENT.—The advertising agency is from a financial standpoint the most important department in the make-up of a paper or periodical. On one of our most popular magazines there is to-day a young man hardly over thirty years of age who has advanced through the various grades of work until he is now superintendent of the advertising department, receiving a remuneration of $7,000 a year.

997. GREAT DAILY EDITORS.—Editors of leading departments in our great dailies receive from $2,000 upward. Managing editors and editors-in-chief receive many times that sum. One man in the New York *Sun* office has for his services a salary of $15,000, and besides this does outside literary work to the amount of $5,000 yearly.

998. MEDICAL SPECIALISTS.—There is still "room at the top" of the medical world. The largest harvests are reaped by those who devote themselves to particular parts of the human framework, and at last are able to set up as "consulting physicians." One doctor, whose apartments are crowded daily, informed the author of this work that he was treating eleven hundred and fifty patients. The celebrated Dr. Loomis for some time before his death made $50,000 a year.

999. LEGAL COUNSELORS.—What is true of medicine is equally so of the law. Specialists in such branches as real estate, legacies, insurance, etc., are in receipt of immense revenue. Celebrated bar-pleaders also have grown rich. The names of Rufus and Joseph Choate, [326] of Wm. Evarts and Ben. Butler, are examples of men who have received single fees of $10,000. One young lawyer says: "I began seven years ago and during this period my earnings, with their investments, amount to $200,000." Legal talent is also liberally paid for by the great corporations, all of which employ at a regular salary one or more attorneys.

1,000. CORPORATION PRESIDENTS.—Presidents of banks receive from $5,000 to $50,000; of insurance companies, there are at least three which pay their presidents $50,000; of railroad presidents, one receives $100,000, three receive $50,000, eight receives $20,000, and twelve $10,000.

In other occupations, deep-water divers are paid at the rate of $10 an hour and fractions thereof; circus managers, $5,000 a year; and the buying man of great mercantile firms about the same. Bank cashiers get from $4,000 to $7,000; custom house officers from $3,000 to $7,000; judges of city courts (New York), $6,000; lecturers from $10 to $200 per night; preachers, from $20,000 in John Hall's pulpit to a pitiful $300 in some country town; school principals from $1,500 to $3,000. Among exceptional salaries may be mentioned that of a steamboat manager of the Vanderbilt lines on the Mississippi, who once received $60,000 a year; also the engineer of a large manufactory, who is paid $25,000. "Is not that high?" inquired a visitor at the works. "He is cheap for us," was the reply, illustrating the truth that talent and skill are everywhere and always in demand. The concern could not afford to lose him to rival firms who wanted his services, and so found it cheaper to retain him even at that high figure.[327]

APPENDIX.

We subjoin a table showing the average salary or wages in one hundred of the leading occupations. In most cases the figures have been compiled from government reports, but where no reports could be obtained an estimate has been made by taking the average receipts from certain districts. In the latter instances, of course, the table cannot be considered perfectly reliable; this is especially the case with the professions of the lawyer, the doctor, and the clergyman. Still, as the sections of the country taken may be considered as fairly representative of the whole, the figures will probably be found not far amiss.

Some persons will be surprised to learn the average lawyer and physician receive respectively only $1,210 and $1,053, but they should bear in mind that while the pay in these professions is sometimes as high as $25,000 and even $50,000 a year, a great number of beginners and unsuccessful men are toiling—or not toiling—for a mere pittance. Were it not for the ten per cent. of very successful men in these professions who are making fortunes, the average receipts would be even smaller by two or three hundred dollars than they appear in the table.

Other cases where the figures may not have as much value as could be desired are under the headings which really comprise a group of occupations instead of a single one, as that of the journalist and the electrician;[328] yet others where the general name is that of a genus comprising many species, as that of the engineer; and still others where there is a great difference in the value of the work performed, as in the case of teachers and factory operatives. Again, in business ventures, such as those of storekeepers, bankers,

187

brokers, and others, many have actually lost money, and this reduces immensely the average, while among the so-called working classes, days of idleness, willing or enforced, operate in the same way.

Yet, on the whole, if any one consults the table as a general guide to the pecuniary rewards of the various trades and professions, he will find that they have been placed in their relative financial standing. In the occupations named, employees are generally meant, employers and independent workers being printed in capitals.

AVERAGE PAY IN ONE HUNDRED OCCUPATIONS.

Engravers (wood),	$1,684
SURGEONS,	1,616
THEATRICAL MANAGERS and SHOWMEN,	1,605
BANKERS and BROKERS,	1,601
Electricians,	1,560
SALOON-KEEPERS,	1,475
Designers (textile),	1,383
Decorators (china and stone ware),	1,248
HOTEL-KEEPERS,	1,245
LAWYERS,	1,210
Architects,	1,206
Teachers (all kinds of schools),	1,153
DAIRYMEN,[329]	1,152
MERCHANTS,	1,149
DENTISTS,	1,115
Engineers (all kinds),	1,092
Draughtsmen,	1,090
Furniture-Workers,	1,087
PHYSICIANS,	1,053
Dyers,	1,040
Furriers,	1,036
Engravers (metals),	1,014
Actors,	989
LIVERY-STABLE KEEPERS,	981
Journalists,	979

CLERGYMEN (house-rents not included),   963
MEAT-DEALERS,   951
Painters (house),   936
GROCERS,   935
Gunsmiths,   930
RESTAURANT-KEEPERS,   924
Masons, bricklayers and plasterers,   919
Plumbers,   919
Electrotypers,   911
Hatters,   910
Musicians,   899
Miners,   892
Bookbinders,   884
Goldbeaters,   858
Watchmakers,   832
Door, sash, and blind-makers,   780
Glass-workers,   778
Boot and shoemakers,   773
Blacksmiths,   750
Carpenters,   750
FARMERS (including living),   749
Conductors and motormen,{330}   728
Telegraphers,   720
Cooks,   720
ARTISTS,   713
PHOTOGRAPHERS,   702
Typewriters,   690
Cigarmakers,   676
Coopers,   675
Printers,   660
Millwrights,   650
Harness-makers,   648
Soapmakers,   646
Upholsterers,   642
Quarrymen,   635
Sawyers,   630
Tailors,   626
Locksmiths,   624
Machinists,   624

189

THE END.

THE

Abbey Press

114
FIFTH   **AVENUE**
NEW   **YORK**

======

ANNOUNCEMENTS

======

May be ordered through any bookseller or will be mailed free for the published price....

{334}

{335}

AUTHORS AND ARTISTS

Collins,   Wilkie. Kent,   Charles.

ADVERTISING AGENTS' DIRECTORY, THE.

Arranged alphabetically and in States, including Great Britain and Canada. Nothing of this kind has ever before appeared. All who for any reason wish to know who the advertising agents are and how they may be reached, will find the desired information here. The Directory is brought down strictly to date. Cloth. One Dollar.

AMERICAN ELOQUENCE.

Characteristic Types from Colonial Times to the Present Day. A Text Book of Oratory. By Carlos Martyn.

AMERICAN MEN OF THE TIME.

Being a Dictionary of Biographical Records of Eminent Men of the Day. Revised to date and edited by Charles F. Rideal, Fellow of the Royal Society of Literature.

AMERICAN WOMEN OF THE TIME.

Being a Dictionary of Biographical Records of Eminent Living Women. Revised to date and edited by Charles F. Rideal, Fellow of the Royal Society of Literature. It is the first time a book of reference of this kind has been compiled in the interests of any women in any country. The efforts of the publishers will be directed towards the end of securing a standard work, founded on reliable data, and which will be a suitable addition to any bookshelf.

CHARLES DICKENS' HEROINES AND WOMEN FOLK.

Some Thoughts Concerning Them. A Revised Lecture. By Charles F. Rideal, with drawings of "Dot" and "Edith Dombey," by Florence Pash. Third Edition. Cloth. Twenty-five Cents.

"A delightful little book."—*Institute.*

{337}

CHARLES DICKENS READER AND RECITER, THE.

For the Home, School and Platform. Compiled with an introduction by Charles F. Rideal, Fellow of the Royal Society of Literature. Formerly member of the Council of the Lecturers' Institute of Great Britain. Author of "Wellerisms," "Charles Dickens' Heroines and Women Folk," etc.

CHURCH WORKER'S BOOK.

One Thousand Plans. By as Many Successful Clergymen and Other Christian Workers. By Carlos Martyn.

CONTINENTAL CAVALIER, A.

By Kimball Scribner. Author of "The Honor of a Princess," (twenty-third thousand), "The Love of the Princess Alice," (fifteenth thousand), and "In the Land of the Loon."

The author writes here in his well-known popular style and contributes one more (and not the least) to the eagerly awaited historic novels of Revolutionary times. His characters are resurrections and in them the past lives again. Mr. Kimball Scribner is rapidly becoming one of the most popular of the younger writers of to-day. With four illustrations on copper. Cloth, 12mo. One Dollar.

CURIOUS CASE OF GENERAL DELANEY SMYTHE, THE.

By W. H. Gardner, Lieutenant-Colonel U. S. A. (retired). Not in many years has a more interesting or mysterious story appeared than this. Those who follow the fortunes of General Delaney Smythe will certainly corroborate this statement. The book will have a wide and permanent sale. With four illustrations by Miss Lowenstein. Cloth. One Dollar.

THE SALESLADY. From "Some People We Meet"{339}

CROSS OF HONOR, THE

A Military Dramalette in One Act. By Charles F. Rideal and C. Gordon Winter (Jean de Mezailles). Very daintily printed and bound. One Dollar

DANGER SIGNALS FOR NEW CENTURY MANHOOD.

By Edward A. Tabor. Is a masterly discussion of the dangers that confront the individual as well as the society of to-day in the United States. It is also a beautiful portraiture of the young manhood which should exist in the 20th century. Including photograph and biographical sketch of the author. 12mo, cloth bound, 316 pages. One Dollar.

DEVOUT BLUEBEARD, A.

By Marie Graham. This is a keen, satirical story which hits off foibles and humbugs in religious administration; not in an infidel spirit, but by a friendly hand and from the inside; one is kept guessing who's who. Cloth 12mo. One Dollar.

DRY TOAST.

Some Thoughts upon Some Subjects not generally dealt with. By Charles F. Rideal.

Contents:—A Piece of the Crust; Brains and Black Butter; On the Mending of the Bellows; On Backbone, or rather the Want of It; Some Phases of Modern Honesty; On Giving Advice—and Taking It; Concerning "Hums"; On Flap-doodle—the Thick and the Thin; On Cranks; On Pouring Cold Water; On the Art of Making Oneself Uncomfortable; On Always Doing Something; Some of the Advantages of Being Religious; On Playing One's Cards; On Living it Down; On Friendship; On Fame, etc. Cloth. One Dollar.

{340}

DIRECTORY OF MEDICAL WOMEN, THE.

Being a List of those Ladies who have Qualified in Medicine and Surgery, and who are Officially Registered as such, with Statistical and General Information of Universities, Colleges, Hospitals, etc.

FROM CLOUDS TO SUNSHINE;

or, The Evolution of a Soul, by E. Thomas Kaven. Author of "A Duel of Wits," etc. Cloth, 12mo, 200 pages. One Dollar.

GEMS OF JEWISH ORATORY.

A selection from the finest specimens of Jewish oratory; together with an introduction. By Madison C. Peters. Author of "Justice to the Jew," etc.

GEMS OF JEWISH PROSE.

A selection from the finest authors of Jewish prose; together with an introduction. By Madison C. Peters. Author of "Justice to the Jew."

GEMS OF JEWISH VERSE.

A selection from the finest authors of Jewish poetry; together with an introduction. By Madison C. Peters. Author of "Justice to the Jew," etc.

GREATEST THING IN THE WORLD, THE.

By Henry Drummond.

HAUNTS OF KIPLING.

Fully illustrated. A complete history and description of all the localities described by Rudyard Kipling in his works. By Margherita Arlina Hamm and Charles F. Rideal.

HOUSE OF A TRAITOR, THE.

By Prosper Merimée.

SAM WELLER. From "Wellerisms."{342}

HOW AND WHAT TO WRITE.

A book for authors; with some practical hints on Journalism; together with a chapter on illustrating for the press. By Charles F. Rideal, Fellow of the Royal Society of Literature.

HOW SUCCESS IS WON;

or, the Fight in Life. With Celebrated Illustrations. Drawn from Life by Carlos Martyn. In this book the author has produced a number of stirring illustrations written in a style and manner that command the attention of both the young and old. It is an essential book for everybody.

INTELLECTUAL PEOPLE.

By William Adolphus Clark. Since most readers belong to this class, all such will find their lineaments reflected in these pages "as in a looking-glass." Many surprises await those who gaze herein; whether of mortification or of gratification, we must read to see. Cloth, Fifty Cents. Japanese paper, Twenty-five Cents.

INTERNATIONAL DIRECTORY OF AUTHORS, THE.

With a full list of the titles of their works, dates of publication, etc. Compiled and edited by Charles F. Rideal.

LAST OF THE MUSKETEERS.

A Novel founded on the Romantic Career of General de Gallifet, French Minister of War. By Carlos Martyn.

LITERARY LIFE.

The most popular magazine for authors, publishers, booksellers and every one interested in literature, issued. It is a thoroughly impartial journal, readable from cover to cover, Five cents per copy or fifty cents per annum, mailed free.

LITTLE SCARECROW, THE.

By Maurus Jokai.

{343}

LODGING IN THE NIGHT, A.

By Robert Louis Stevenson. This is the first time that this celebrated story has been produced in a manner worthy of the reputation of its talented author. It will be fully illustrated and issued in a most dainty binding, forming a dainty and unique gift book.

LOVE AND PRIDE.

By R. R. Napoliello. This novel admirably portrays the play and counterplay of master passions. The hero, an Italian, bares his soul to inspection, so that we see and participate in the struggle. A rare psychological study. Cloth, Fifty Cents. Japanese paper, Twenty-five Cents.

LOVE'S RANDOM SHOT.

By Wilkie Collins.

MAGISTRACY, THE.

Being a Directory and Biographical Dictionary of the Justices of the Peace of the United States. Compiled and edited by Charles F. Rideal.

MASTER AND MAN.

By Count Tolstoy.

MORE PEOPLE WE MEET.

By Charles F. Rideal. Illustrated by Mark Zangwill, etc. A limited edition of signed and numbered copies at One Dollar.

NURSES WE MEET.

Some piquant Pictures. By Charles F. Rideal. A limited edition of numbered and signed copies. One Dollar.

OLD SCHOOL DAYS.

By Andrew J. Miller. This book should have a wide reading. It is healthy and breezy with youth and sport. In its pages the experiences of all of us are laughably and vividly recalled. Cloth. One Dollar.

{344}

CAPTAIN D. T. ROOKER. From "People We Meet."{345}

ON THE CHARLESTON.

By Irene Widdemer Hartt. The smell of the sea and the odors of the woods and fields of Guam are in these pages. The tale sways, like the ocean swell, between Jack Tar and the soldiers in the Yanko-Spanko War. Cloth, 12mo. One Dollar.

PAIR OF KNAVES AND A FEW TRUMPS, A.

By M. Douglas Flattery. The literary quality of this fascinating novel would alone call attention to it. When to this are added plots and counterplots, dramatic contests and dénoûments, the book presents a combination of attractions quite unique and irresistible. Mr. Flattery's books are always readable and interesting. Cloth, 12mo, illustrated. One Dollar.

PEOPLE AND PROPERTY.

By Edwin B. Jennings. An animated, logical discussion of the question of corporate rights versus human rights. Lincoln said that "when a dollar comes in conflict with a man he sided with the man." This book is timely, able and interesting. Cloth, Fifty Cents. Japanese paper, Twenty-five Cents.

PEOPLE WE MEET.

By Charles F. Rideal. Fully illustrated by Harry Parkes. Third and Revised Edition. Twenty-five Cents.

"A collection of characteristic sketches drawn with much humor and crisply described."—*Scotsman.*

PICTURES FROM A NEW YORK BOARDING HOUSE.

Fully Illustrated. By Charles F. Rideal. One Dollar.

PULPIT ELOQUENCE.

Characteristic Types, with Brief Prefatory Sketches of Illustrious Preachers. By Carlos Martyn.

POCKET ISLAND.

By Charles Clark Munn. A story of country life in New England. A remarkably attractive book written in a remarkably attractive manner. With frontispiece. Cloth, 12mo, 200 pages. One Dollar.

QUAKER SCOUT, A.

By N. P. Runyan. The contradictory title adopted by Mr. Runyan piques curiosity, which, upon investigation, will be abundantly rewarded. Incidents without number succeed one another in rapid and romantic succession, making the reader hold his breath and pant in sympathy with the recital. Cloth, $1.25.

RIDEAL'S ELOCUTIONIST.

A Book of Readings and Recitations for the Home, School and Platform. Selected and arranged, together with a chapter on Reading and Speaking, by Charles F. Rideal, Fellow of the Royal Society of Literature, and formerly a member of the Council of the Lecturers' Institute of Great Britain.

SERMONIC SILHOUETTES.

Three Hundred Outlines of Sermons by Three Hundred Distinguished Clergymen on Various Themes. With index. By Carlos Martyn.

SLAVEHOLDER'S DAUGHTER, A.

Full of Southern life and character, and readable from cover to cover. By Belle Kearney. With 11 full-page illustrations and frontispiece. Cloth, 12mo, 270 pages. One Dollar.

SOCIAL SINNERS.

A realistic novel of to-day. By Emile A. Palier. Portrays a number of Sinners and a few Saints in the modern social order. Certain passages hold the reader spellbound. There are several heroes and heroines, all true to life after their respective kind. Cloth, 12mo. One Dollar.

TEMPER CURE, THE.

By Stanley Edwards Johnson. In the guise of a novel, the author gives a fanciful account of a cure for bad temper. There are no dull pages in this book. Cloth, Fifty Cents. Japanese paper, Twenty-five Cents.

TEN YEARS IN COSSACK SLAVERY.

By Mary De Mankowski. This is a graphic, thrilling description of the personal experiences of a patriotic Pole, condemned to Siberia for loving his country "not wisely but too well." The book explains the existing hatred of the Russian government and gives the reasons therefore. Cloth. $1.25.

VENGEANCE OF THE MOB, THE.

By Sam A. Hamilton. An exciting story of Florida, in which the characteristics and the effects of "Judge Lynch's" rule are exploited. A thrilling love story runs through the novel, with which the vengeance of the mob comes into collision. Cloth, 12mo. One Dollar.

WELLERISMS

from "Pickwick" and "Master Humphrey's Clock." Selected by Charles F. Rideal and edited with an introduction by Charles Kent, Author of "The Humor and Pathos of Charles Dickens." Fourth Edition. With a new and original drawing, by George Cruikshank, Jr., of Mr. Samuel Weller. Cloth. One Dollar.

This book has met with remarkable success. The original drawing of Sam Weller, by George Cruikshank, Jr. (a nephew of the original Cruikshank), is alone worth the money, for the reason that it shows a mastery of fine work and detail, in pen and ink not possessed by any other artist of the time. It is a unique and acceptable addition to Dickensiana and every lover and admirer of Charles Dickens should possess a copy.

{348}

WHEN AT HOME AND SOCIETY GUIDE.

Giving Days when "At Home" of the Upper Classes. Compiled and edited by Charles F. Rideal. To which is added a chapter on the Etiquette of Calls and Calling. By Lady Constance Howard. Each Season.

WIDOWS WE MEET.

Twelve of Them. Brief, pithy characterizations by Charles F. Rideal. Fully illustrated.

YOUNG GENTLEMEN OF TO-DAY.

Eighteen of Them. By Charles F. Rideal. Fully illustrated.

ZENITH MEMO-PAD, THE.

Designed by Lady Constance Howard and Mr. Charles F. Rideal. Containing Seven-day Tear-off Sheets and Cover, in convenient form either for laying flat on the desk, or suspending from rack, etc., a Complete Calendar for the Year, Postal Information, Chief Events, Lessons for Sundays, Quotations from well-known Authors, and Spaces for Memoranda, Appointments, etc. Indispensable for every one who writes, makes notes, etc. Twenty-five Cents.

"This useful addition to the writing table is nicely got up."—*Princess.*

"Is very well arranged, with suitable quotations and memoranda for every day in the year. It may be kept on the table or suspended against the wall or bookshelf, whichever may be most convenient, and in either position it is handy, and takes up but a small amount of space."—*Queen.*

Lightning Source UK Ltd.
Milton Keynes UK
UKHW032236211119
353992UK00013B/241/P